WHO'S WHO IN EGYPTIAN MYTHOLOGY

Other Books by Anthony S. Mercatante
GOOD AND EVIL: Mythology and Folklore
THE MAGIC GARDEN: The Myths and Folklore
of Flowers, Plants, Trees and Herbs
ZOO OF THE GODS: Animals in Myth, Legend and Fable
THE HARPER BOOK OF CHRISTIAN POETRY (Editor)

ANTHONY S. MERCATANTE

WHO'S WHO IN EGYPTIAN MYTHOLOGY

Foreword by Dr. Robert S. Bianchi, Associate Curator,
Department of Egyptian and Classical Art,
The Brooklyn Museum

ILLUSTRATED BY THE AUTHOR

Clarkson N. Potter, Inc./Publishers NEW YORK
DISTRIBUTED BY CROWN PUBLISHERS, INC.

Published simultaneously in Canada by General Publishing Company Limited
First edition
Printed in the United States of America

Library of Congress Cataloging in Publication Data

Mercatante, Anthony S.
    Who's who in Egyptian mythology.

    Bibliography: p.
    1. Mythology, Egyptian—Dictionaries. I. Title.
BL2428.M47 1978   299'.3'1   78-14477
ISBN 0-517-53445-2
ISBN 0-517-53446-0 pbk.

For Jack Haber
"in deep and abiding friendship"

CONTENTS

FOREWORD

In *Who's Who in Egyptian Mythology* Anthony S. Mercatante has given us a concise, easy-to-use dictionary of ancient Egyptian deities. There has been no comparable work in English for the general reader since the volumes published in the early part of this century, which are often outdated and misinformed. Because, as in any subject of such complexity, there are a variety of opinions on each aspect of Egyptian mythology, as well as different versions of each myth, the present book contains an annotated bibliography as a guide to further investigations.

At a very early time in their history the ancient Egyptians began to create myths as a means of explaining natural phenomena. Because the forces of nature seemed immutable and eternal, they chose familiar and fixed images to represent them in their stories. The images that were most easily adapted came from the animal kingdom. The Egyptians observed that animal behavior was predictable in the wild, and that, moreover, one falcon looked like any other falcon, as one generation of lions seemed very nearly like the next. The immutabilility of the animals' character and form and their association with certain natural forces provided the symbols for the unique mythology of ancient Egypt.

All animals of a species were living reminders of the gods, but the Egyptians confined their reverence to specific animals, who were chosen by the priests of their temple. They did not regard every ibis, falcon, or cat as a god, although they might have worshipped particular animals of these kinds. At the same time, the Egyptians could live quite comfortably with animals from one species representing a number of distinct deities. For instance, we know that in Memphis a bull was worshipped as Apis, while in Armant another bull was celebrated as Buchis, and still another as Mnevis in Heliopolis; each was thought to represent a different nuance of the divine.

In this way, too, the Egyptians were able to accept cosmologies that for us might seem contradictory; these often existed simultaneously throughout the cities of ancient Egypt. The interpretations reflected varying attitudes toward the divine; in each instance, the features and hierarchy of the gods that the adherents felt were important were emphasized. The residents of Memphis thus adopted Ptah, with all his attributes, as their supreme deity who came into being out of himself, untroubled that this role and history were given to Amen, with all his attributes, in other cities.

As time passed, some of these distinctions became less apparent, for an important development in Egyptian religion was its growing tendency toward syncretism. Amen-Ra, the prominent divinity of the religion of the Eighteenth Dynasty, is the most frequently cited example of this merging of characteristics. In the cult of Isis we find still another model of one deity's absorption of the attributes of others. By the time of the Romans, Isis could be invoked by using the names and titles of almost all the Egyptian goddesses. She had become the only goddess of any consequence and was later to be readily adopted as the Mother of God by the early Christians.

The Egyptians were fun-loving people—they liked to drink, to hunt, and to attend banquets where entertainment was provided by dancing girls. Their tomb decorations celebrate the pleasures of life. Although there are the usual scenes of funerals and mourning, most of the narrative art depicts the inhabitant in life: surveying his estates, hunting in the deserts or marshes, fishing, or seated before an offering table receiving a wealth of gifts from an endless procession of family and servants and friends. At the same time, the Egyptians were a moral, ethical people who, living in a society of priests, were constantly aware of the obligations of mankind. Among the autobiographical inscriptions on the tombs are such phrases as: "I gave bread to the hungry, water to the thirsty, clothing to the naked"; "I oppressed not the orphan"; and "I took no advantage of the widow."

Religion played an essential part in the existence of this civilization. Almost every name known to us from inscriptions that have survived belonged to a priest of one of the religious cults. In a culture that was viewed as unique by its people, where life was seen as distinct from the life of any neighboring civilization, to be a priest was to be associated with what was specifically Egyptian. Priests were the link between the immutable and the eternal forces of nature and an earthly society and heritage that was thousands of years old. In their immutability and permanence the gods were a symbol of the Egyptian state.

In *Who's Who in Egyptian Mythology* the reader encounters the values of an ancient civilization and learns how a society thousands of years old approached the divine in an attempt to explain the forces of the physical world.

Dr. Robert S. Bianchi, Associate Curator
Department of Egyptian and Classical Art
The Brooklyn Museum

AUTHOR'S PREFACE

Every year hundreds of thousands of people visit the Egyptian collections of the world's great museums and, in increasing numbers of late, tourists of all nationalities have been exploring the country and monuments of Egypt. They are confronted by a profusion of symbols and representations of deities, of myths and ancient religious practices of such varied richness that many of these visitors are undoubtedly overwhelmed by the complexity of Egyptian beliefs. Who are these mysterious deities, some of them half-human and half-animal, who were worshipped for thousands of years? Who is Osiris? Who is the jackal-headed god who watched over the dead?

In *Who's Who in Egyptian Mythology* I have tried to furnish informative answers to these questions and many others, and to provide an entertaining and comprehensive selection of historic facts and myths and stories. There are entries on all the major deities of ancient Egypt. Along with Osiris, the mummy god, and Anubis, the jackal-headed god who watched over the embalming of the dead, the reader will be introduced to a host of lesser divinities, such as Bes, the dwarf god, who was invoked by common people for good luck, and Taurt, the hippopotamus goddess, who was a patron deity of childbirth.

You will be introduced to the fascinating and little-known myths associated with each deity as well as to the symbols by which each was represented. There are entries not only on gods and goddesses but also on such topics as mummies, the Pyramids, and various other aspects of Egyptian civilization that help shed light on their beliefs. A special feature of the dictionary is the inclusion of complete translations of major Egyptian tales, *The Shipwrecked Sailor, The Doomed Prince, The Taking of Joppa, The Tale of Two Brothers, The Tale of Sinuhe, The Peasant and the Workman, The Treasure of Rhampsinitus, Setna and the Magic Book* and *Tales of the Magicians*. As a further aid to the reader there is A Chronology of Ancient Egyptian Dynasties; an Introduction that examines the basic framework of Egyptian mythology and religion; and an Annotated Bibliography that lists sources used in writing the book, as well as books for further reading.

A dictionary of mythology does not spring full-grown from the head of its author, as Athene did from the head of Zeus. Instead, it depends on the aid of scholars. I wish first to thank Dr. Robert Steven Bianchi, Associate Curator of the Department of Egyptian and Classical Art at The Brooklyn Museum, for his time, intelligence, and patience. His knowledge has been invaluable. Also to be thanked are Juan Montoya, John Spina, Robert Hawthorne Smyth, Richard Stack, Richard Johnson, Allan Knee, Bruce Singer, Susan Ann Protter, Professor Ronald Suter of Fairleigh Dickinson University, and my editor, Nancy Novogrod.

Anthony S. Mercatante

A CHRONOLOGY OF ANCIENT EGYPTIAN DYNASTIES

Egyptian history is divided into Dynasties, which may or may not consist of the members of one royal family. This system was devised by the Egyptian priest Manetho in the third century B.C., and has been used by Egyptologists ever since. Only fragments of Manetho's *History of Egypt* have come down to us through the writings of others.

The dates ascribed to Dynasties often vary among scholars. Please note that in this list some Dynasties overlap, while in others no dates have been assigned.

Dynasty I	B.C.2955–2780
Dynasty II	B.C.2780—2635

Old Kingdom

Dynasty III	B.C.2635–2570
Dynasty IV	B.C.2570–2450
Dynasty V	B.C.2450–2290
Dynasty VI	B.C.2290–2155

First Intermediate Period

Dynasty VII	
Dynasty VIII	B.C.2155–2135
Dynasty IX	B.C.2134–
Dynasty X	B.C. –2040
Dynasty XI	B.C.2134–1991

Middle Kingdom

Dynasty XII	B.C.1991–1785

Second Intermediate Period

Dynasty XIII	B.C.1785–1650
Dynasty XIV	B.C.1715–1650
Dynasty XV	
(Hyksos)	B.C.1650–1544

Dynasty XVI	
(Hyksos)	B.C.1650–1550
Dynasty XVII	B.C.1650–1554

New Kingdom

Dynasty XVIII	B.C.1554–1305
Dynasty XIX	B.C.1305–1196
Dynasty XX	B.C.1196–1080

Third Intermediate Period

Dynasty XXI	B.C.1080–946
Dynasty XXII	B.C.946 –720
Dynasty XXIII	B.C.792 –720
Dynasty XXIV	B.C.740?–712

Late Period

Dynasty XXV	B.C.745–655
Dynasty XXVI	B.C.664–525

First Persian Period

Dynasty XXVII	B.C.525–404

Independent Dynasties

Dynasty XXVIII	B.C.404–399

Dynasty **XXIX**	B.C.399–380	**Roman Conquest**	B.C.30
Dynasty **XXX**	B.C.380–342		

Second Persian Period

Dynasty **XXXI**   B.C.342–332

Alexander the Great Conquest
B.C.332

Ptolemaic Period   B.C. 332–30

Roman Period   B.C. 30–A.D. 395

Byzantine Period   A.D. 395–638

Moslem Conquest   A.D. 641

A NOTE ON
THE SPELLINGS USED

There is no standard way of transcribing ancient Egyptian names into English. In *Who's Who in Egyptian Mythology* I have therefore adopted the most frequently used English forms of Egyptian names, many from the Greek, as they appear in books and museum publications. For example, the god who personified the earth is variously listed as *Geb, Keb, Qeb,* and *Seb*. However, because *Geb* is the form most often encountered, the information for this entry appears under *Geb*. As an additional aid the variant spellings are also listed—in alphabetical order—and will refer the reader back to the main entry under *Geb*.

The book is arranged alphabetically, with compound names considered as one word for this purpose.

INTRODUCTION

"They are religious to excess, far beyond any other race of men . . . " wrote
Herodotus in his *History* (Book 2). The Greek historian had observed
Egyptian religious rites; he had studied the elaborate hymns to their
great sun god, Amen-Ra and, a practice he especially abhorred, their
worship of animal gods. However, he underestimated the scope of Egyptian religious beliefs.

Animal worship was but one limited development, of relatively short
duration, in the rich tradition of ancient Egyptian religion. For most of
their history the people of ancient Egypt revered only the sacred animal,
who was dedicated to the deity of their temple and believed to be that god
incarnate, and considered him as a god. All other animals of the same
species were honored but not worshipped. Zoolatry, or animal worship,
did not originate until the Twenty-sixth Dynasty (B.C. 664–525) and was
common in the Ptolemaic periods (from B.C. 332–30 a number of Egyptian
kings were named Ptolemy), when the distinction between the elected
one and his species was lost to the common people. Both Herodotus and
the Latin satirist Juvenal studied late Egyptian religious practices at
this time, and reached their conclusions about the ignorance of Egyptian
beliefs and their barbaric animal worship, based on this one aspect of the
entire range of their customs and ideas. In his fifteenth satire, *On the
Atrocities of Egypt,* Juvenal lambastes the Egyptians for their zoolatry:

> Volusius, who knows what monsters demented Egypt worships?
> One city adores the crocodile,
> Another worships the ibis that stuffs itself on snakes. . . .
> In another part the cat is worshipped,
> In another a fish, still another honors the dog!
> No one worships Diana, but it is a sacrilege to crunch leeks and onions
>   with the teeth!
> Just think, their gods grow in gardens. . . .

Juvenal hated anything that was not Roman, and this prejudice, and
his Latin bias for humanlike gods such as Diana and Apollo, can in part be
credited for his reactions against Egyptian practices. Then too the in-
coherencies and contradictions of Egyptian mythology and religion undoubtedly offended his sense of order. Juvenal did not find an Egyptian

pantheon of twelve Olympian gods, familiar to him from Greek and Roman mythology, but instead a series of local deities who were claimed as supreme creators, and many separate Egyptian deities, who shared joint identities as composite gods. To add to the confusion, most of the myths of Egypt were preserved orally.

There was no Hesiod, Homer, Virgil, or Ovid to interpret Egyptian mythology. The best-known narration of an Egyptian myth, that of the deified man Osiris, was offered by Plutarch, a Greek writer. There are many references to myths in the Pyramid Texts (inscriptions written on the walls of pyramids) and in the *Book of the Dead* (a handbook for guiding the souls of the dead through the underworld), but the stories were simply alluded to, and the reader of both texts was expected to be familiar with them and to fill in the gaps in the accounts. The problem survives to this day; what has often come down to us, since the oral tradition has been lost, are often only fragments of myths rather than detailed narratives.

The predynastic Egyptians (before B.C. 3400) believed that the sea, earth, air, and sky overflowed with spirits, some of whom were engaged in carrying on the works of nature, and others in helping or hindering man in the course of his existence on earth. All the events of nature were attributed to these spirits. It was thought that the continued friendship of the good spirits could be secured and the hostility of the evil spirits averted by gifts, or, more accurately, bribes.

The earliest representations of these spirits, who had evolved into both good and demonic gods, appeared about the middle of the fourth millennium, before the introduction of hieroglyphs. Each tribe had its own protective deities, who were incarnated as animals, birds, reptiles, or simple fetishes, such as rams, bulls, hippopotamuses, cats, baboons, hawks, crocodiles, and snakes. The animal deities gradually gained human characteristics, while usually retaining some of the animal's features in their new form. The animal then became sacred to the god.

The number of gods who existed during the long history of ancient Egypt is legion—at one time there were more than a thousand—a profusion developing as the early local cults, which were originally separate, were gradually absorbed into the growing unity of the state. While certain gods, such as Osiris, were worshipped all over Egypt, there was no one inclusive pantheon. Egypt was divided into nomes, or districts, each having its own chief god, temple, and college of priests. A mythology developed in one nome regardless of the beliefs of a neighboring nome, even though the same god, who was chief deity of one section, might hold a subordinate position in another. The Egyptian regarded his chief local god as all supreme.

The identities of deities were merged to create composite gods. There were, for instance, combinations of gods, such as Osiris-Ra and Amen-Ra, in whom two distinct natures and sets of attributes were joined. When a dynasty achieved preeminence, the cult of its chief god was spread throughout Egypt, and the local gods were in some way identified with it, or were thought of as manifestations or servants of the chief god.

From the time of the Hyksos (B.C. 1650) there was a marked tendency to merge the natures and names of all the gods with the sun god Ra. However, the most famous of these composite gods, Amen-Ra (whom the Greeks identified with Zeus), never succeeded in dislodging Osiris from his exalted position. The cult of Osiris survived undiminished, notwithstanding the powerful influence that the priests of Ra and the worshippers of Amen and Aten exercised throughout Egypt. This longevity is no doubt due to the cult's promise of resurrection and immortality.

The Egyptian interest in the afterlife was not morbid. Their early writings in tombs and monuments attest to the belief that life on earth was good and should be continued after death. Many of the scenes in the tombs depicted the happiness and joy of pure physical existence, and there was a spell for the dead specifically intended to guarantee that full sexual powers be carried into the next world.

In contrast to most other mythologies, which, like the Greek, characterized the earth as feminine and the sky as masculine, Egyptian belief represented the earth by Geb, a masculine god, and the sky by a feminine deity. According to one of the Pyramid Texts, at the time of the creation of the world, "when men and gods did not yet exist, and there was as yet no death, masses of land and water formed from the original ocean." A number of myths tell of the origin of the sun god, who was believed to die and be reborn each morning.

The creation myths were interpreted by the priests at the centers of worship, such as Hermopolis, Heliopolis, Memphis, and Busiris, and the work of creation was attributed to the greatest local god. Thoth, Ra, Ptah, or Osiris was proclaimed to have created the world. At some places the god was said to have issued from the mouth of the primeval god or Demiurge and all other existence was thought to have been created from his voice; at other shrines, it was taught that men came from the tears or blood of the local god.

The priests devised enneads of nine gods and triads consisting of the god of the district, a goddess, and their son. Because the gods were considered as mortal as man, the son was destined to take his father's place and was created as the exact physical counterpart of the older god. This gave rise to such epithets for the son as "self-begotten" and "the husband of his mother." Although mortal in one sense, the gods were made eternal by the merging of their physical features and personalities across the generations. This may have been a symbolic expression of the idea of immortality. In other instances the family triad was supplanted by a combination of gods, such as the ennead of nine deities, a later attempt at systematic groupings. There were two enneads, "the great ennead" and "the lesser ennead." In both the chief god stood at the head of the other gods who formed his court and assisted him in governing the world.

The chief god of the nome lived in the temple dedicated to him in his animal form or in the form of a symbol; the temple served as a place of worship and sacrifice. On the great festival days the god was borne in procession from the temple. The worshipper approached the enclosing wall of the sacred precincts along sacred ways guarded by rows of sphinxes. He passed through the gateway to enter the temple building. Two obelisks, a statue of the temple's founder, and tall masts decorated with brightly colored streamers stood before the doorway of the temple. The pylon, or doorway, a narrow entrance between two lofty towers, ushered the worshipper into a colonnaded court that was open to the sky and adorned with richly painted sacred pictures. Beyond was the dark sanctuary of the god, flanked by rooms where the vestments and sacramental ornaments were kept. The lay people hardly ever entered; only a few select celebrants were allowed.

The priesthood of the temple was organized around various priestly duties: they tended the sacrifices, explained the oracles, studied the sacred texts, or served as teachers, often becoming officers of the state. The priesthoods were powerful and wealthy.

During the reign of Amenhotep IV (B.C. 1372–1355), more commonly known as Akhenaten or Ikhnaten, the name he chose for himself, the supremacy of the priesthood came under attack. Akhenaten sought to introduce the worship of a single god, Aten, symbolized by the sun disk, and opposed the priests of Amen by building a new capital at Akhet-Aten (the modern Tell el-Amarna), where his followers worshipped Aten. The priests were incensed by his neglect of politics and the fanaticism of his beliefs (he had all pictures of other gods removed from the temples and their names erased). After Akhenaten's death, the new king, Tutankhamen, reintroduced the worship of Amen at Thebes, and the Amarna heresy, as it has come to be called, was wiped out. Akhenaten's name was then deleted from the list of kings.

The religion of ancient Egypt remained diverse and at the same time conservative throughout her long history. In B.C. 30 Egypt became a Roman province, and a dramatic change in her faith soon followed. Egypt evolved into the cradle of Christian monasticism, a new faith which at first existed side by side with the now dwindling old beliefs in Osiris, Isis, and Horus. When the cult of Osiris finally gave way to the new man-god, Jesus Christ, the Egyptians embracing Christianity found that the worship of Osiris and Jesus were compatible if not similar. Isis and her child Horus were identified with the Virgin Mary and the Christ child. In apocryphal literature of the first few centuries following the conversion of Egypt to Christianity, several legends of Isis were transferred to the Virgin Mary, as well as one of the goddess's epithets, Mut Netchet, which became Theotokos, or Mother of God, a very old and common title of Isis.

It was not until the reign of Justinian (A.D. 525–565) that the cult of Isis was abolished. In A.D. 641 when Byzantine control was destroyed by the Arab conquest of Egypt, Islam was brought to the land.

WHO'S WHO IN EGYPTIAN MYTHOLOGY

A

AAAPEF   see Apophis.

AAH   An early moon god who was later associated with Thoth, the great moon god. Aah was often portrayed as a young man with the lock of youth. A variant spelling of his name is Ah.

AAH-DJUHTY   A composite god made up of the moon gods Aah and Thoth.

AAI GODS   Three divine beings in the ninth section, or hour, of Tuat, the underworld. Their function is to help the sun god Ra destroy the archserpent Apophis. They are portrayed driving pikes into the monster.

AAKHUI   see Achet.

AA-NEFER   see Onuphis.

AARU   see Sekhet-Aaru.

AAT-AATET   see Perit.

AAT-KHU   see Perit.

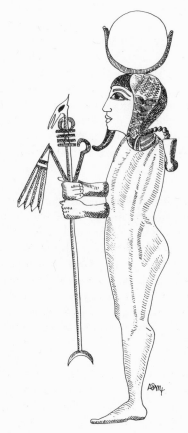

Aah

AAU   A jackal-headed mummy at one end of the corridor in the fifth section of Tuat, the underworld. The

1

other end of the corridor is watched over by Teka–hra.

AB In Egyptian belief, the heart expressed desire, lust, courage, wisdom, feeling, sense, disposition, and intelligence.

The importance of the ab to the Egyptian is reflected in the *Book of the Dead,* in which not fewer than five chapters are devoted to its preservation. In one chapter the deceased prays for a heart, for if he has no heart, he says, "I cannot eat of the cakes of Osiris." And "with the mastery of my heart, I am the master of my arms and legs, and I can do whatsoever my Ka pleaseth, and my soul will not be fettered at the gates of Tuat."

The ab, or heart amulet, was made of many kinds of red stones—red jasper, red glass, red paste, and red wax. It was inscribed in the breast of the mummy in place of the heart which was mummified separately. The upper part of the ab amulet was sometimes in the form of a human head. Egyptian texts show that the ab was supposed to contain the soul of Khepera, the self-created god, and was therefore immortal. A variant spelling is Ib.

ABDU and INET Two fish who were supposed to swim, one on each side of the bow of the boat of the sun god Ra, to drive away from it every evil being in the waters.

AB-ESH-IMY-DUAT A monster crocodile who acts as guardian of the tomb of Osiris in the seventh section, or hour, of Tuat, the underworld. When the sun god Ra passes by the monster, the god utters magical words which disarm the beast. Then Osiris, who is under the ground beneath the crocodile, raises his head to look at Ra. After this, all the followers of Osiris look upon Ra, the sun, thus restoring them to life.

AB-SHE A monster crocodile who eats lost souls in the seventh section of Tuat, the underworld.

ABSTRACT PERSONALITY see Ka.

AB-TA A monster serpent who guards the entrance to the ninth section of Tuat, the underworld.

ABU SIMBEL Site of twin temples carved out of a sandstone cliff on a bend of the Nile in the thirteenth century B.C. for Rameses II and his consort Nefertari. The temples have been removed to a higher elevation on this same cliff to protect them from the waters rising behind the new Aswan dam. The preservation effort was undertaken by UNESCO and the Egyptian government, and financed by funds obtained through an international appeal.

ABYDOS Egyptian city, located between Asyut and Thebes, noted for its shrine to Osiris. It is believed that Isis, the wife of Osiris, buried her husband's head in Abydos after his body had been mutilated by his evil brother Set. Every year the city drew thousands of pilgrims, who came to perform the rites associated with the death and resurrection of Osiris. Abydos contains temples erected by Seti I as well as Rameses II.

ACHET Amulet made of red stone and red glass or paste, representing the sun rising in the eastern horizon. It was to give the wearer the strength and power of the sun god Ra and was symbolic of renewed life after death. A variant spelling is Aakhui.

ADON see Aten.

ADULTERY see Family.

ADZE A metal tipped carpenter's tool, like a hoe, whose handle was of wood, used in the ritual of the "opening of the mouth" that was supposed to bring the statue, mummy, or body back to life.

AESCULAPIUS Greek god of medicine identified by the Greeks with the Egyptian sage Imhotep, who was deified.

AF The dead, or setting sun, portrayed as a ram with his head surmounted by a solar disk. The word means "flesh."

AFA Lesser gods or spirits mentioned in several Egyptian texts.

AF-OSIRIS A form of the god Osiris, meaning "flesh of Osiris."

AF-TEM A god whose name means the "flesh of Tem."

AH see Aah.

AH-HETEP One of the four sovereign chiefs in the fifth section, or hour, of Tuat, the underworld, when the sun god Ra passes in his serpent boat.

AHMES-NEFERTARI Mother of Amenhotep I, the Pharaoh who was deified. She was worshipped with her son.

AÏDA Italian opera by Giuseppe Verdi, with a libretto by Antonio Ghislanzoni, based on a plot by Auguste Mariette, a French Egyptologist. Verdi was commissioned by the Khedive of Egypt to compose an opera for a new theater in Cairo as part of the ceremonies for the opening of the Suez Canal. The opera was first performed in 1871, two years after the Canal was opened.

The opera's plot revolves around Aïda, an Ethiopian princess captured in war and made a slave, and her love for the Egyptian captain Radames. Amneris, the daughter of the king of Egypt, also loves Radames. In the end Radames betrays the Egyptians and is put to death with Aïda.

AIR, GOD OF see Shu.

AKEBIU Four bearded gods, whose name means the "wailers," found in

3

the eleventh section of Tuat, the underworld.

AKENEH A serpent demon mentioned in a magical formula of Unas, a king of the Fifth Dynasty.

AKER A lion god who guarded the gate of the dawn through which the sun god passed each morning.

AKH According to the Pyramid Texts, the Akh, or spirit, of a god lives in heaven and when a man dies, his Akh will eventually go to heaven as well. The Akh was generally thought of as a being of light, comparable to a star. In some texts, however, the Akh was considered demonic. In the *Book of the Dead,* for instance, it is written, "My mouth is strong; and I am equipped against the Akhs. Let them not have dominion over me." Connected with the Akh was the Sekhem, or vital power, but its exact function is not known.

AKHAKHU A word meaning "god-like beings."

AKHEKH Griffinlike animal regarded as a form of the evil god Set. It had the body of an antelope and the head of a bird which was surmounted by three uraei and wings.

AKHEM-SEK A class of celestial beings whose name means "those who never go down," referring to the circumpolar stars that to the Egyptians never "set," that is, they never dropped out of sight below the horizon, and hence were believed to be eternal.

AKHEN A monster serpent who guarded the entrance to the seventh section of Tuat, the underworld, as the sun god Ra passed in his boat. The name means "to split" or "wear out the eyes."

AKHENATEN (B.C. 1372 – 1355) Name chosen by Amenhotep IV when he adopted the worship of Aten, the sun disk. He was the son of Amenhotep III and Queen Tiy. Either during his father's last years or sometime shortly after his father's death, Akhenaten undertook the building of a gigantic temple at Karnak. After he came to the throne Akhenaten left Thebes, the capital, and moved his court to a new city in Middle Egypt, Tell el-Amarna. He vowed never to leave the city limits and devoted himself exclusively to the worship of the Aten. Near the end of his life Akhenaten became estranged from his wife, the beautiful Nefertiti, who removed herself and four of their daughters. He later married his fifth eldest daughter. On his death Akhenaten was succeeded by Smenkara, who died within the year. The nine-year-old Tutankhaten became ruler and was coaxed into returning to Thebes. He changed his name to Tutankhamen, restoring the cult of Amen, and closing the door on a period called the Amarna Heresy.

Akhenaten has been credited by some scholars as the originator of Egyptian monotheism, although this issue is still in dispute. (For a discussion of the worship of Aten refer to the entry on the god.)

A variant spelling is Ikhnaten.

ALEXANDER THE GREAT (B.C. 356–323) The great Macedonian leader reached Egypt in the autumn of B.C. 332. According to one legend he consulted the oracle of Jupiter-Amen in the Siwa Oasis. Amen recognized Alexander as his son, and promised him control over the entire world. A short time later Alexander was crowned king of Egypt in the Temple of Ptah at Memphis. On his way to the shrine of Jupiter-Amen he made a stop at Rhacotis, a small fishing village and former frontier post of the Pharaohs. Realizing the advantages of the site, he decided to build a new city, to be called Alexandria. The layout of the city was geometric, with wide streets on a rectangular grid. The plan was drawn up by Deinocrates, an architect from Rhodes, and Cleomenes of Naucratis, who was in charge of its execution. According to legend the city was in the shape of a Greek garment. The perimeter was indicated with seeds which birds promptly ate. This seemingly bad omen was interpreted as a positive sign by Alexander. Later, he left the city and died in Asia. Ptolemy, one of Alexander's generals, was responsible for returning his body to Egypt and he erected a magnificent tomb for his leader in Alexandria. When Julius Caesar was in Egypt he asked to see the tomb of Alexander. The Emperor Caracalla is reported to

Amam

have stolen Alexander's sword from his body. Despite repeated rumors, the burial place of Alexander and the Ptolemies has yet to be discovered.

ALEXANDRIA see Alexander the Great.

AMAM A fantastic beast whose name means "the devourer." It has the forequarters of a crocodile, the hindquarters of a hippopotamus, and the body of a lion. When the Ba, or soul, was weighed in the judgment of the dead, the Amam would be waiting at the base of the scales to eat the heart of the deceased who failed to pass the

Amen-Ra

judgment. Variant spellings are Amamet and Am-mit.

AMAMET see Amam.

AMAN see Amen-Ra

AMARNA HERESY see Akhenaten and Aten.

AMARNA LETTERS see Tell el-Amarna.

AMEHETP see Amenhotep I.

AMEN-RA Composite god made up of Amen, whose name literally means "hidden," and the sun god Ra.

At first Amen was merely a god of local importance. However, after the princes of Thebes gained sovereignty over Egypt, making their city the new capital of the country, Amen became a prominent god in Upper Egypt and was looked upon as "King of the Gods." At that time Amen's sanctuary at Karnak was a comparatively small building, consisting of a shrine surrounded by a few small chambers and a forecourt with a colonnade on two sides. When the Theban princes became kings of Egypt, their priests declared their god Amen not only another form of the great creator sun god who was worshipped under such names as Ra and Khepera, but they gave him all the attributes that were ascribed to the sun gods and proclaimed him as the greatest of them all. When Amen was coupled with Ra, forming the composite god Amen-Ra, in the Eighteenth Dynasty, he became the mysterious creative power that was the source of all life in heaven, earth, and the underworld. Eventually the priests of Amen claimed that there was no other god like Amen, who was the "one one" and had "no second." This concept resembles that of the Hebrews, who said, "Yahweh our God is one Lord" (Deuteronomy 6:4).

In Egyptian art Amen-Ra is usually portrayed as a man with a beard, with a headdress of double plumes, various sections of which are colored alternately red and green, or red and blue. Around his neck he wears a broad collar or necklace, and his close-fitting kilt or tunic is supported by elaborately worked shoulder straps. His arms and wrists are decked with armlets and bracelets. In his right hand is the ankh, symbol of life, and in his left the scepter. The tail of a lion or bull hangs from his tunic. Sometimes Amen-Ra is given a hawk's head surmounted by the solar disk encircled by a serpent. When Amen appears with his wife, Amunet, he is often portrayed as a frog-headed man and she as a uraeus-headed woman. When Amen is shown with the uraeus, Amunet is depicted with the head of a cat. Variants of his name are Aman, Ammon, Am, Amon, Amun, and Hammon.

AMENET see Amunet.

AMENHOTEP, SON OF HAPU Egyptian sage on whom divine honors were bestowed and minister of Amenhotep III (c. B.C. 1379–1417). He was known for his wisdom and for the beautiful temples built under his supervision. Many magical texts and stories were attributed to him, and it was said that he was a devotee of Thoth, the scribe god who was credited with the authorship of the *Book of the Dead*. His fame continued to grow in later Dynasties. In Egyptian art Amenhotep, son of Hapu, is usually portrayed as a scribe with a roll of papyrus on his knees.

AMENHOTEP I (B.C. 1557–1530) Deified Pharaoh, worshipped with his mother, Ahmes-Nefertari, at the necropolis west of Thebes. He is said to have saved the life of a workman bitten by a snake, and after his death was invoked for protection. He is portrayed as a bearded man with a black body. The Greeks rendered his name as Amenophis I. A variant spelling of the Egyptian is Amehetp.

AMENOPHIS I see Amenhotep I.

AMENT A name for the goddess Isis, meaning "hidden," from Amenet, the feminine gender of Amunt, who assisted in transforming the bodies of the blessed dead into those who would live in the realm of Osiris.

AMENTET The West, the land of the setting sun, where the dead assembled waiting for the boat of the sun god Ra to pass. When the god appeared, those who had been his worshippers on earth, and who were fortunate enough to have secured the magical words of entry, were able to embark on the sun god's boat. Then accompanied by Ra they made their journey through Tuat, the underworld, passing through the realms of Osiris and Seker, gods of the dead. (Osiris was sometimes known as Amentet, as in one section of the *Book of the Dead*.)

They finally appeared on the eastern horizon at daybreak, where they were able to wander about. At sunset, they again joined Ra to continue their trip through Tuat. The Greeks called this journey Amenthes.

AMENTHES see Amentet.

AMKIHIU The souls of the blessed who have been fortunate enough to obtain admission into the boat of the sun god Ra as he crosses through the night heavens. In life they were devoted followers of Ra, and the reward for this is renewed youth and a new birth on earth.

AMMIANUS MARCELLINUS (fourth century A.D.) Author of *Roman History,* which contains descriptions of various Egyptian monuments and natural aspects of the Nile Valley.

AM-MIT see Amam.

AMMON see Amen-Ra.

AMON see Amen-Ra

AMONET see Amunet.

AMU see Fa.

AMULET Object intended to protect the human body from evil. The word amulet comes from the Arabic meaning "to bear" or "to carry," indicating that amulets were worn and carried about on the person. The ancient Egyptians placed many amulets on their own bodies as well as on their dead. A specific amulet rested on each part of the deceased's body as protection against serpents, worms, mildew, and decay.

AMUN see Amen.

AMUNET Goddess, consort of Amen at Karnak, who is often portrayed with the crown of Lower Egypt. Variant spellings of her name are Amonet and Amenet.

ANAT Egyptian goddess of Syrian origin, called the "lady of heaven" and "mistress of the gods." Her cult was introduced by Rameses II (B.C. 1304–1237). Originally Anat was a war goddess, with numerous cities in Syria dedicated to her worship. In Egyptian art she is portrayed as a woman seated on a throne or standing upright. When seated she grasps a shield and spear in her right hand and a club in her left, indicating her warlike nature. When standing she is dressed in a panther skin and holds a papyrus scepter in her right hand and the ankh, emblem of life, in her left. She wears a white-feathered crown that sometimes has a pair of horns attached at the base. Variant spellings are Annuthat and Antit.

ANHEFTA A protective spirit in the ninth section of Tuat, the underworld.

ANHER see Onouris.

ANHERT see Onouris.

ANHORET see Onouris.

ANHUR see Onouris.

ANIMALS Many Egyptian deities are associated with animals. Some gods, such as Horus, are depicted with the head of a hawk, while others, such as Hathor, are portrayed as cow-headed or as a cow. The following is a list of the animals associated with the various deities. Sometimes the same deity will be represented by different animals.

Ass
Set (in defeat by Horus)
Baboon
Thoth
Beetle
Khepera
Bull
Apis, Bata, Buchis, Mnevis, Onuphis, Serapis
Cat
Amunet, Bast, Mau
Cobra (see also *Snakes*)
Buto
Cow
Hathor, Isis (when identified with Hathor), Meh-urt, Nut (sometimes)
Crocodile
Horus Khenty Khat (when Horus defeats Set), Sebek, Set (in defeat by Horus)
Dolphin
Hat-mehit
Dog
Hapi, son of Horus, Thoth (when confused with the jackal)

Donkey
Set (in defeat by Horus)
Frog
Amen (as part of Ogdoad), Heket (as part of Ogdoad), Huh (as part of Ogdoad), Kuk (as part of Ogdoad), Nun (as part of Ogdoad)
Fish
Remi
Goose
Geb
Hawk
Amen-Ra, Harmachis, Haroeris, Harsaphes, Harsiesis, Hartomes, Horasematawy, Hormerti, Horus, Horus, the Hebenuite, Horus-Behdety, Khensu, Ra-Horakhty, Qebh, son of Horus, Soped
Heron
Utet
Hippopotamus
Taurt
Ibis
Aah, Toth
Jackal
Anubis, Heranubis, Tuamutef, son of Horus, Wepwawet
Lioness
Astarte, Sekhmet, Shehbui, Tefnut
Lynx
Maftet
Rabbit
Unnu, Wenenu, Wenenut
Ram
Amen, Ba-neb-djet, Bata, Harsaphes, Hutchaiui, Khnemu, Qebui
Snake
Amen-Ra (sometimes), Buto, Horasematawy, Hauhet, Kauket,

9

Mehen, Merseger, Naunet,
Nephthys, Qerhet, Ur-heka
Scarab
   Khepera
Sow
   Nut
Scorpion
   Serqet
Shrew-mouse
   Horus Khenty en Maatyu
Swallow
   Isis
Vulture
   Nekhebet
Wolf
   Wepwawet

ANKH   Egyptian hieroglyphic (stylization of a sandal strap) for "life," identified with the Greek Tau cross and the Christian *crux ansata*.

Various theories have been advanced to explain the symbolism of the ankh. According to some nineteenth-century scholars, the ankh is a symbol of the male and female generative organs, while for others the T and O shape represents an altar with an egg or vase upon it. Both theories have since been discredited. The early Egyptian Christians adopted the ankh which they had seen on so many monuments, believing that it prefigured the Christian cross. Sozomen, a fifth-century church historian, wrote that a great number of pagans embraced Christianity when the ankh was discovered on some Egyptian temples.

Christian symbolism explains the Tau cross, (the ankh symbol without the O) as an Old Testament prefiguration of the Christian cross. Some texts cite that the brazen serpent of Moses was suspended on a Tau cross (Numbers 21:9). According to another tradition, the Tau cross was the sign that the Israelites in Egypt marked in blood to protect them when Yahweh slaughtered the Egyptian children. This explanation seems plausible since the symbol was very common throughout Egypt. The Tau cross is often identified with the Egyptian hermit saint, Anthony the Abbot, and is worn by the Knights of St. Anthony, an order formed in 1352.

Ankh

ANKH-AAPAU   A monster serpent in the fifth section, or hour, of Tuat, the underworld, who lives upon the flames that emanate from its mouth.

ANKHAT: Title for the goddess Isis as the giver of life. It is also the name of a goddess.

ANKHI A monster serpent with a bearded mummiform god growing out from each side of its body.

ANNUTHAT see Anat.

ANPU see Anubis.

ANQUAT Title of the goddess Isis as producer of fertility in the waters.

ANTELOPE An animal sometimes associated with the evil god Set.

ANTHONY OF EGYPT, SAINT (A.D. 251–356) Egyptian monk, often called St. Anthony the Abbot, who is frequently pictured with the Tau cross, a form of the ancient Egyptian ankh, symbol of life. His feast day is January 17.

ANTIT see Anat.

ANTIU Four beings, each having four serpent heads, and armed, found in the tenth section of Tuat, the underworld.

ANUBIS The jackal-headed god of the dead. According to one myth, he was the son of the goddess Nephthys, who had tricked her brother, the god Osiris, into having intercourse with her. Anubis was abandoned by Nephthys at birth, and he was found and raised by Osiris's sister-wife, the goddess Isis. He accompanied Osiris

on his conquest of the world, and when Osiris was murdered and dismembered, he helped find his body and then embalmed it so well that it resisted the influences of time and decay. Thus, it was said, that burial rites were invented.

Subsequently, Anubis presided over funerals and guided the dead through the underworld into the kingdom of

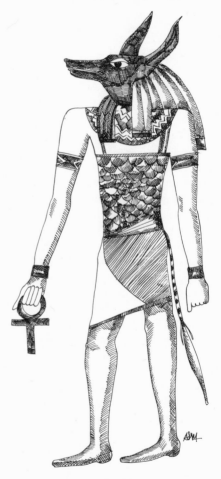

Anubis

11

Osiris. This function he shared with the god Wepwawet, or Ap-uat (whose name at one time was thought to be synonymous with Anubis). When the souls of the dead reached the other world, Anubis made certain that the heart of the deceased would be weighed fairly and watched that the body of the deceased was not accidentally committed to the monstrous Amam, "the devourer," who ate the dead.

The cult of Anubis continued during Greek and Roman times. According to Plutarch, the Egyptian jackal god was common to both the celestial and infernal regions. This dual role was reinforced in Roman times by Apuleius, who described in *The Golden Ass* (Book 11) a procession of the goddess Isis in which Anubis appeared with his jackal head and neck, a "messenger between heaven and hell, displaying alternately a face black as night and golden as day."

Anubis was portrayed as a jackal or a jackal-headed man, the jackal being known to prowl around the tombs of the dead. The name Anubis is the Greek rendering of the Egyptian Anpu.

ANUKET see Anukis.

ANUKIS Goddess, originally a water deity from the Sudan, who was worshipped with Khnemu and Satis at Elephantine. A Greek form of the Egyptian Anuket, her name means "to embrace" and may refer to the fact that she is believed to have fertilized the fields during the inundation. Anukisuas was at times identified as the goddess of lust. A red parrot was occasionally associated with the goddess. Anukis was portrayed as a woman wearing a crown of feathers.

APEP see Apophis

APERHER A god with a solar disk for a head from which protrudes two human heads, one wearing the white crown, the other the red crown of Egypt. He appears in the eleventh hour, or section, of Tuat, the underworld. His name may mean, "the lord of eternity."

APET see Taurt.

APIS Greek name for the Egyptian Hapi (Hape or Hap), the sacred bull of Memphis. It was said that Apis was born of a virgin cow that had been impregnated by the god Ptah. The calf was recognized by certain signs, such as a peculiar white mark on its neck and rump that resembled a hawk's wings and a scarablike hump under its tongue. The baby bull was brought to Memphis where each day it was let loose to roam in the courtyard of the temple for devotees to observe; his movements were believed to foretell the future. The day of the animal's birth was celebrated with a festival.

When the bull reached his twenty-fifth year, he was killed with great ceremony. He was drowned in a cistern, mummified, and entombed in an underground chamber of the temple

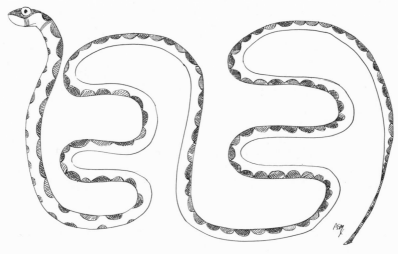

Apophis

where he was mourned for seventy days. This ritualistic killing may have been symbolic of the sacrificial slaying of the king, a rite common in pre-dynastic times. After the bull was dead, a new incarnation of the god was sought, and when the right calf was found, the process was begun again.

Originally Apis may have been a fertility god concerned with flocks and herds. At Memphis he became associated with Ptah, the god who fashioned the world, and with Osiris, the god whose blessed kingdom the dead hoped to enter. In Egypt, the cult of Apis was so important that Ptolemy I, in an effort to unite Greek and Egyptian worship, introduced the god Serapis, or Sarapis, into the country. A composite of Osiris and Apis, Serapis was honored by a cult that, along with the cult of the goddess Isis, later spread throughout the Roman Empire.

In Egyptian art Apis was portrayed as a powerful animal with massive limbs and body. A triangular piece of silver was fixed on his forehead, and a disk and the uraeus were placed between his horns. Above his legs figures of vultures with outstretched wings were outlined, and on his back, also outlined, was a rectangular cloth with an ornamental diamond pattern. Other sacred bulls were Mnevis and Buchis.

APOLLO Greek god of the sun, equated by them with the Egyptian gods Horus-Behdety and Menthu.

APOPHIS Greek form of the Egyptian Apep or Aaapef. A giant serpent and night demon. According to some accounts, he was a form of Set, god of evil and darkness. Each night Apophis did battle with the sun god Ra, whose spells and flames destroyed him. This nightly combat took place just before

Ra's ascension from Tuat, the underworld.

In the *Book of the Overthrowing of Apophis* a ritual is prescribed that was recited daily in the temple of the sun god, cataloguing in great detail the destruction that was to befall Apophis. The monster was to be speared, gashed, and every bone of his body separated by red-hot knives. His head, legs, and tail were to be scorched, singed, and roasted until the whole was shriveled and consumed by fire. The same fate also awaited Apophis's monstrous helpers, Sebau and Nak, as well as all his other spirits, shadows, and offspring of the night.

AP-UAT see Wepwawet.

APULEIUS, LUCIUS (second century A.D.) Latin author of *The Golden Ass*. In Book 2 he describes a festival in honor of the goddess Isis that gives a good picture of the Roman worship of the Egyptian goddess.

ARES Greek war god identified by them with the Egyptian god Anhur, whom they called Onouris.

ARI-HES-NEFER A lion-headed god whose statue was often placed on the doors of palaces and tombs to guard both the living and the dead from evil spirits.

ARITI see Nehata.

ARMANT see Hermonthis.

ARTISTS AND ARTISANS, GOD OF see Ptah.

ASAR see Osiris.

ASAR-HAP; ASAR-HAPI see Serapis.

ASBET A goddess associated in the Pyramid Texts with Isis and Nephthys.

ASET see Isis.

ASH-HRAU A five-headed monster serpent whose name means literally, "lots of faces." Ash-hrau resides in the sixth section, or hour, of Tuat, the underworld. Its body is bent into an irregular oval in such a way that its tail almost touches one of its heads.

ASP see Snakes.

ASS The Egyptians regarded the ass as both a demonic and a beneficent animal. In one text the deceased says, "May I journey forth upon earth, may I smite the Ass, may I crush the serpent-field Sebau; may I destroy Apophis in his hour. . . . " This identifies the ass with a host of demonic beings which must be overcome.

On the other hand, in the *Book of the Dead,* in a chapter entitled "Chapter of Driving Back the Eater of the Ass," the ass is a symbol of the sun god and is protected against Apophis, the monster.

AST see Isis.

14

ASTARTE Near Eastern mother goddess worshipped in Egypt. She was both the "mother of mankind" as well as a warrior goddess "clad in terror" who caused even the gods to tremble. She was often portrayed as a woman with the head of a lioness surmounted by the disk of the sun. She stood on a chariot drawn by four horses. Sometimes she is portrayed as a woman armed with a shield and club, riding a horse into battle.

ASTEN A form of the god Thoth.

ASTI-NETER see Nehata.

ASTRONOMY The ancient Egyptians believed that the stars were divine spirits around which the souls of the blessed dead collected. (Their ideas of the afterlife varied considerably.) In the early Pyramid Texts two classes of stars are given, the *Akhemu seku,* or "imperishable stars", and the *Akhemu urtchu,* the "stars which never rest."

The heavens were divided into four parts, and the stars were classed as "northern" and "southern." Among the former they placed Meskhet, the Big Dipper, and among the latter Orion and Sirius, or Sothis. The northern stars were associated with Set. Orion held the soul of Horus, and Sirius was identified with Isis. The moon was associated with Thoth and later as the abode of Osiris. The sun and the moon were the eyes of either Ra or Horus. The Egyptians knew five planets, Mercury, Venus, Mars, Saturn, and Jupiter.

ATCHET Goddess associated with the sun god Ra, and in some accounts considered his female counterpart. Her name may mean "the nurse" in the sense of nursing a child.

ATEF CROWN see Crowns.

ATEM see Tem.

ATEN A sun god, symbolized by the solar disk. His worship was advanced by Akhenaten who came to the throne as Amenhotep IV (B.C. 1372–1355).

The origin of the worship of Aten is obscure. He may originally have been a form of the sun god honored locally near Heliopolis. It was under the rule of Amenhotep IV, who changed his name to Akhenaten, which may mean "glory of Aten," that the cult of Aten was advanced.

When the worship of the new sun god was opposed by the priests of Amen-Ra, who was then the reigning sun god, Akhenaten left his capital of Thebes and constructed a new one at what is now Tell el-Amarna. Here in this new capital the king and his wife Nefertiti, the "beautiful one has come," brought about an artistic revolution in Egyptian art. Stressing naturalistic forms as opposed to stylized ones, the art of this period broke with the conservatism that had long been in vogue. For example, Akhenaten was portrayed realistically, even to the distortions of his body (for example, his distended stomach). One of the most famous works of this period is the

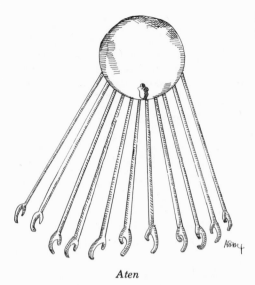

Aten

painted head of Nefertiti (now in the Egyptian Museum, West Berlin.

Akhenaten's reign, which lasted for a little more than fifteen years, came to an abrupt end. There is some speculation that the king and his wife were murdered. All known records of his reign were destroyed by the priests of Amen-Ra. Akhenaten's successor, his son-in-law Tutankhaten, had his name changed to Tutankhamen, the "living image of Amen," and under the direction of the priests he restored the worship of Amen-Ra.

Akhenaten has been called the first individual in history, as well as the heretic king. He has been credited by some scholars as the originator of Egyptian monotheism. However, it is not evident in any of the hymns to Aten that the god was believed to be the only god. One of the most majestic hymns to the god, ascribed to Akhenaten himself, opens thus:

> Thy rising is beautiful in the horizon of heaven,
> O thou Aten, who hadst thine existence
> in primeval time.
> When thou riseth in the eastern horizon
> thou fillest every land with thy beauties,
> Thou art beautiful to see, and art great, and art like crystal,
> and art high above the earth.
> Thy beams of light embrace the land, even every land which thou hast made.
> Thou art as Ra, and thou bringest (thyself) unto each of them,
> and thou bindest them with thy love.
> Thou art remote, but thy beams are upon the earth.

Although the extract from the *Hymn to Aten* gives an idea of the views of Akhenaten and his followers concerning Aten, it is impossible to gather precise information about the details of the belief or doctrine relating to Aten. Incense was burnt several times during the day and hymns were sung to the god, accompanied by harps and other instruments. The offerings to the god consisted of fruits and flowers. There was no animal sacrifice. The worship was joyous, and the surroundings pictured by the artists of this period were bright and cheerful.

The religious revolution of Akhenaten inspired the novel *The Egyptian* (1949) by Mika Waltari, which deals with the failure of Akhenaten to convince the court and people to worship Aten.

Variant spellings are Aton, Adon, and Eton.

ATHENE Greek goddess of war, wisdom, and liberal arts, identified by the Greeks with the Egyptian goddesses Isis and Neith.

ATHOR see Hathor.

ATHPI see Fa.

ATHYR see Hathor.

ATLAS In Greek mythology the Titan who fought against Zeus and was condemned to carry the weight of the world on his shoulders. He was equated by the Greeks with the Egyptian god Shu, whose name has been translated as "he who holds up."

ATMU see Tem.

ATON see Aten.

ATUM see Tem.

AUSAR see Osiris.

AUSARES see Osiris.

B

BA The soul, or that part of a person that had eternal existence after death.

The Ba, closely associated with the Ka (each person's double) and the Ab, or heart, was one of the principal elements of the life in man. The Ba amulet was in the form of a man-headed hawk wearing a beard. After death, the Ba was believed to visit its body in the tomb. Many graves had narrow passages in the pits so that the Ba might find its way there. In the Pyramids of Meroe, openings were left in the stone coverings near the apex so that the Ba might enter them, and a ledge to stand on was placed beneath each opening.

In the *Book of the Dead* the Ba is seen visiting its body, to which it presents the symbol shen, symbolic of eternal life. The final union of all souls with their bodies was believed to take place in the heavenly Anu Heliopolis. Small figures of the Ba made of gold and inlaid with semiprecious stones were placed on the breast of the mummy in the hope of preserving it from decay.

BABA One of the names of the evil god Set.

Ba

BABOON The baboon was sacred to the moon and thus to moon gods such as Thoth, who was sometimes portrayed as a baboon. In the *Book of the Dead* the deceased's heart is placed on a scale upon which sits a baboon. The baboon was to report to Thoth when the pointer was in the middle of the beam.

Sacred baboons were kept in temples dedicated to moon gods; they were believed to be spirits of the dawn who were transformed into baboons as soon as the sun had risen and they had sung a hymn in its honor.

BACIS (bull) see Buchis.

BA-₁ EB-DJET Sacred ram of Mendes whose name means "soul, lord of Busiris." The sacred ram was distinguished by certain marks, as were other Egyptian sacred animals. When the proper ram was found he was led in a great procession to Mendes, which was his city of worship, and enthroned in the temple. In some texts he is considered a form of the sun god Ra, in others of Osiris and Ptah. His wife was the dolphin goddess Hat-mehit.

Ba-neb-djet is depicted as a ram with flat branching horns surmounted by a uraeus. He is sometimes portrayed with four heads, that of Ra, Shu, Geb, and Osiris. The Greeks identified Ba-neb-djet with their gods Priapus and Pan, both associated with fertility and male sexual power.

Variant spellings are Ba-neb-Tatau, Ba-neb-Tet, Ba-neb-Tettu, and Banedbdetet.

BA-NEB-TATAU see Ba-neb-djet.

BA-NEB-TET see Ba-neb-djet.

BA-NEB-TETTU see Ba-neb-djet.

BANEDBDETET see Ba-neb-djet.

BAST Cat goddess worshipped at Bubastis.

She was the protector of pregnant women as well as a pleasure-loving goddess who reveled in music and dance. She also protected men against disease and evil spirits. She was generally considered the personification of the beneficial, fertilizing power of the sun, while her counterpart, the lioness goddess Sekhmet, represented the fierce, destructive power of the sun.

Bast became an important national deity about B.C. 950, and her festival was among the most popular in Egypt. According to Herodotus in his *History* (Book 2), vast numbers of men and women were in attendance, arriving by barge. There was singing and dancing, people clapped their hands, or played castanets. Women shouted abuses and even exposed themselves from the barges to those along the shore as they approached. At Bubastis the feast was celebrated with abundant sacrifices and festivities. Dead cats were carefully mummified and buried. It was said that more than 700,000 devotees attended the festival of Bast, and that more wine was consumed than in all the rest of the year.

In the Bible the Hebrew prophet Ezekiel (30:17) refers to Bast's city, which he calls Pi-beseth. He says that the young men who are Bast's adherents, will "fall by the sword" and be carried into captivity for their worship of her.

In Egyptian art Bast was usually portrayed as a woman with the head of a cat. In her right hand she often held a sistrum for her music, in her left an aegis with the head of a cat or lioness on top of it. A variant spelling is Bastet.

Bast

BASTET see Bast.

BATA A pastoral god whose cult image was a mummified bull or ram. Some scholars believe that *The Tale of Two Brothers*, sometimes called *Anpu and Bata*, is actually about the gods Anubis and Bata. A variant spelling is Bet.

BEARD For the ancient Egyptians the beard was considered sacred. Each Pharaoh wore a false beard that was believed to have its own life and was worshipped as a god. The gods were said to have "beards like lapis lazuli."

BEER Egyptian beer was produced from barley, which was made into bread and then soaked in water. The beer was the liquid that was drained from the bread. Beer was used by the living, and offerings of beer were made at the tomb.

BEETLE see Scarab and Khepera.

BEHDETY Epithet for Horus, meaning "He of Behdet," a form of the god worshipped at Behdet, a district of ancient Edfu. The Greeks called the city Appollinolis Magna and equated Behdety with their god Apollo.

BELZONI, GIOVANNI BATTISTA (1778 – 1823) Italian circus muscle man who became an Egyptian archaeologist. His methods, which often upset other Egyptian explorers, made him one of the most famous archaeologists of the time.

BENEN A guardian of the eighth section Tuat, the underworld, whom the sun god Ra passed in his boat.

BENTY Species of ape which seems to screech at dawn, like the proverbial rooster. His action was interpreted by the ancient Egyptians as a prayer heralding the coming of the rising sun.

BENU A fantastic bird identified by the Greeks with the phoenix. It was

Bes

portrayed as a huge golden hawk with a heron's head. The Benu was said to have created itself from fire which burned at the top of the sacred persea tree of Heliopolis. It was essentially a sun bird, symbol of both the rising sun and the dead sun god Osiris, from whose heart, in one account, the bird sprang. The Benu not only signified the rebirth of the sun each morning but became a symbol of the resurrection of man. The *Book of the Dead* provides a formula to enable the deceased to take the form of the Benu.

According to the Greek historian Herodotus (Book 2), the Benu made its appearance once every 500 years. His plumage was colored part gold and part red, and in size and form he resembled an eagle. He came from Arabia with the body of his father enclosed in an egg of myrrh, which he brought to the temple of the sun and buried there.

BES Dwarf god who was a patron of art, music, and childbirth, as well as a god of war and a strangler of antelopes, bears, lions, and serpents.

The dual nature of Bes in Egyptian belief is reflected in the various images of the god. Usually he is portrayed as a dwarf with a huge bearded head, protruding tongue, flat nose, shaggy eyebrows and hair, large projecting ears, long thick arms, and bowed legs. Around his body he wears an animal skin whose tail hangs down, usually touching the ground behind him. On his head he wears a tiara of feathers, which suggests his primitive nature.

In later Egyptian art, however, Bes is given a handsome body, since he absorbed the character of the sun god and became identified with Horus the Child as well as Ra and Temu. As Horus he wore a lock of hair on the right side of his head, which is the symbol of youth. All these images suggest the various phases of the sun during the day.

Bes was frequently portrayed on steles, vases, and amulets, often in ithyphallic form. His image was hung over headrests as a charm to keep away evil spirits. His female counterpart was Beset.

BESET Female counterpart of the god Bes who was patron of art, music, and childbirth.

BESI A god found in the tenth section of Tuat, the underworld, who pours flames onto a standard surmounted by the head of a horned animal.

BET see Bata.

BIBAN EL-HARIM see Valley of the Queens.

BIBAN EL-MOLUK see Valley of the Kings.

BIBLE, THE Sacred collection of writings made up of the Old and New Testaments. Egypt plays a major role in the Bible, being mentioned some 680 times. It is the land where Abraham goes (Genesis 12:10), where Joseph is sold (Genesis 37:36), where Jacob and his family settle (Genesis 46), and where the Israelites live in bondage and are delivered by Moses, while the Egyptian army is destroyed in the Red Sea (Exodus 14:15-30). In the New Testament Jesus is taken by Joseph and Mary to Egypt to escape from Herod, who wished to kill the child (Matthew 2:14). Two images of Egypt emerge from the Bible: a rich and vast land noted for its human wisdom, and a land of idolatry and magic. Isaiah writes that when Yahweh comes "the idols of Egypt shall be moved at his presence, and the heart of Egypt shall melt in the midst of it" (Isaiah 19:1). The prophet does, however, see a time when Egypt will worship Yahweh and the Lord will say, "Blessed be Egypt my people" (Isaiah 19:25).

BIRDS The Egyptians often pictured the Ba, or soul, as a bird with the head of a human being. Bird features were also assumed by various gods: the hawk was associated with Horus, Ra, and other deities; the ibis with the god Thoth; the goose with Geb; and the swallow was sacred to Isis since it was in this form that she flew around the tamarisk tree which enclosed Osiris's coffin at Byblos. The fantastic bird, the Benu, which corresponds to the phoenix, was portrayed as a huge golden hawk with a heron's head.

BITJE A monster serpent with a head at each end found in the ninth section of Tuat, the underworld.

BKHA (bull) see Buchis (bull).

BLACK see Colors.

BLIND HORUS see Horus Khenty en Maatyu.

BLUE see Colors.

BLUE WAR CROWN see Crowns.

BOAT, SACRED see Seker Boat.

BOOK OF THE DEAD Title commonly given to the collection of funerary texts which the Egyptians composed for the benefit of the dead, to guide their souls through the underworld. The collection consists of incantations, hymns, prayers, and magical words and formulas. The texts do not form a unified work, nor do they belong to any one period. They are miscellaneous in character and tell nothing of the lives or works of the individuals with whom they were buried.

The Egyptians possessed many funerary works, but none of them bore a name that could be translated as the *Book of the Dead*. This title was given by the tomb robbers in Egypt in the early nineteenth century, who discovered buried with the mummies rolls of papyrus, which they called *Kitab al-Mayyit,* "book of the dead man" or *Kitab al-Mayyitun,* "book of the dead." The robbers, however, knew nothing of the contents of the rolls; they were merely saying that what they found in the coffin was a "dead man's book."

In the graves of predynastic Egypt, vessels of food, and weapons were found buried with the dead, indicating that the early dwellers in the Nile Valley believed in some form of life in the tomb. The graves contain no inscriptions, and the bodies are often severed, reflecting the belief that the dead had the power to haunt the living if their bodies remained whole. The dynastic Egyptians, however, attached supreme importance to preserving and protecting the body, particularly from the terrifying demons who were believed to infest the region through which the dead had to go from this world to the beneficent kingdom of the god Osiris. To insure the deceased's safety, the priests composed a large number of funerary texts, which were said to have been inspired, or actually written, by the god Thoth.

There is no one definitive version of the *Book of the Dead*. The early texts were believed to have been derived from primitive, predynastic Egyptian beliefs. These texts, commonly known as the Pyramid Texts, are among the earliest known body of religious writing preserved anywhere in the world. They present a system of theology devised by the priests of the sun god.

In the Theban Recension of the *Book of the Dead* the texts (sometimes referred to as the Coffin Texts) were written on rolls of papyrus, frequently as long as 50 to 100 feet, and painted on coffins. They were divided into sections or chapters, each of which had a distinct title but no specific arrangement. This Recension was used from the Eighteenth to the Twenty-first Dynasties. A still later version is the Saite Recension of the *Book of the Dead*. In this collection, which was used from the Twenty-sixth Dynasty to the end of the Ptolemaic period, the number and order of the texts were standardized.

BOOK OF THE PYLONS Ancient Egyptian book called *Shat En Sbau* describing the Tuat, the underworld. It presents Osiris as the greatest of the gods, and forms a guide for the dead to enable them to make their way through Tuat successfully and in comfort. Tuat is here divided into twelve sections corresponding to the twelve hours of the night.

BOUTO see Buto.

BREAD The dead as well as the living ate bread; it was one of the main offerings made at tombs. During the time of the New Kingdom, some forty different kinds of breads and cakes were known.

BUCHIS A sacred bull worshipped at Hermonthis who was believed to be an incarnation of the warrior god Menthu. He was also called the "living soul of Ra," as well as the "bull of the mountains of sunrise and sunset." Buchis was black and his hair grew in a contrary way from that of all other animals. The bull was believed to change his color every hour of the day, and he was seen as the image of the sun shining in Tuat, the underworld. In Egyptian art Buchis wore a disk between his horns from which rose plumes and the uraeus. On his hindquarters was the sacred symbol of the vulture with outspread wings. Variant spellings of his name are Bacis and Bkha.

BUCKLE OF ISIS see Thet.

BULLS see Cattle.

BULLS, SACRED see Apis, Buchis, and Mnevis.

BURIAL RITES AND CUSTOMS see Funeral Customs.

BURIAL SITES see Tombs.

BUTO Greek name for the uraeus or cobra goddess Wadjet (Uatchet), protector of Lower Egypt. Buto was believed to be a form of the goddess Hathor and was identified with the appearance of the sky in the north at sunrise. Her twin sister Nekhebet was the goddess of Upper Egypt.

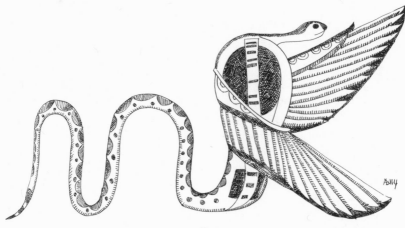

Buto

Buto helped the goddess Isis hide from the evil god Set who wished to destroy Horus, the son of Isis and Osiris. Isis had retreated to the floating island of Chemmis, filled with papyrus swamps, to give birth to her son Horus, who would in time avenge his father's death. Set never succeeded in finding the hiding place of Isis because Buto arranged the papyrus and other plants to screen her from view. As a further camouflage she shook her hair over Horus. For saving Horus, who the Greeks identified with their god Apollo, Buto was associated by the Greeks with their Latona, the mother of Apollo.

In the *Book of the Dead* Buto is usually given the role of the destroyer of the foes of the deceased. During the ceremonies that accompany the embalming, the priest addressed the mummy, saying, "The goddess Buto cometh unto thee in the form of the living uraeus, to anoint thy head. . . . "

Buto is sometimes portrayed as a woman wearing the crown of Lower Egypt upon her head. In one hand she holds the papyrus scepter, around which is twined a snake. In some pictures she bears the crown of Lower Egypt in her right hand and is about to place it on the head of the Pharaoh. Often she appears as a winged serpent with the crown of Lower Egypt upon her head.

A variant spelling of her Greek name is Bouto. Other names by which she is rendered in English are Uatchura, Inadjet, and Edjo.

C

CALENDAR The Egyptians devised a calendar which consisted of 365 days, divided into 12 months of 30 days, plus five additional days, the epagomenal days, which were the birthdays of the gods: day 1–Osiris, day 2–Horus, day 3–Set, day 4–Isis, day 5–Nephthys. There were three seasons to the year: the inundation, winter, and summer. A typical day would be written year 6 (that is the sixth year of the reign of the Pharaoh), month 3 of winter, day 13. There was no leap year.

In various magical texts which have come down to us from ancient Egypt, we find that certain days were listed as lucky while others were listed as unlucky. Thus the calendar of the month of Thoth (which was divided into three sections) notes the symbol of luck three times for day 1, but the symbol of good luck is noted only twice on day 7, and the symbol of bad luck noted once. The nineteenth day is marked wholly lucky, because: "It is a day of festival in heaven and upon earth in the presence of Ra. It is the day when flame was hurled upon those who followed the boat containing the shrine of the gods; and on this day the gods gave praises being content. . . . "

But the day of the 26th is marked wholly unlucky, because, "This was the day of the fight between Horus and Set." The various calendars of lucky and unlucky days, however, do not always agree.

CANNIBALISM The eating of human flesh, often for cultic purposes. Scholars do not agree on the function of cannibalism in ancient Egyptian culture. According to some sources, cannibalism was only practiced during famine; elsewhere, it is cited as an early cultic rite. One of the Pyramid Texts tells of King Unas "rising like a god who liveth upon his fathers and feedeth upon his mothers. . . . " Further on, the dead king is likened to a vigorous bull which feeds upon what is produced by every god and upon those who come from She-Sasa, the Fiery Lake, to eat words of power. In conclusion it says Unas eats men and feeds upon the gods. The Roman comic poet, Juvenal, in his satire *On the Atrocities of Egypt,* credits the Egyptians with eating human flesh—but Juvenal was violently opposed to all that was not Roman, and his report may be considered somewhat biased.

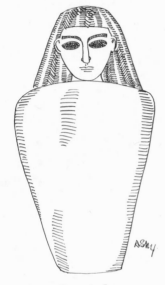

Canopic Jar

CANOPIC JARS Containers for the viscera of the dead which were removed during mummification. At the end of the New Kingdom, the canopic jars were decorated with the heads of the Four Sons of Horus. Mesthi, or Imsety, guarded the liver and was portrayed human-headed; Hapi, guarded the lungs and was portrayed dog-headed; Tuamutef, or Duamutef, guarded the stomach and was portrayed jackal-headed; and Qebhsennuf, or Qebsnuf, who guarded the intestines, was portrayed hawk-headed. The four jars were in turn guarded by four goddesses, Isis, Nephthys, Neith, and Serket. Late canopic jars often have the head of the god Osiris. The god was often worshipped in the form of a human-headed jar.

The name "canopic" was given by scholars to these jars since they found many of them in the Egyptian city of Canopus, 12 miles from Alexandria. The Greeks had named the city after Canopus, the pilot of the vessel of Menelaus, who was believed to have been buried there after being killed by a serpent.

CARNARVON, LORD (1866-1923) George Edward Stanhope Molyneux, Fifth Earl of Carnarvon. Along with Howard Carter, Carnarvon discovered the tomb of Tutankhamen in 1922. He died in Egypt of pneumonia and blood poisoning, the result of a mosquito bite. At the tomb a tablet with the inscription: "Death will slay with his wings whoever disturbs the peace of the pharaoh," was cited by some as a curse which caused the death of Carnarvon. The tablet, however, has never come to light and was never catalogued.

CARTER, HOWARD (1874–1939) British Egyptologist who discovered the tomb of Tutankhamen in the Valley of the Kings in 1922. He made his first visit to Egypt when he was 17. In 1899 he was appointed Inspector General of the Antiquities Department of the Egyptian Government. In 1908 he joined the Fifth Earl of Carnarvon in his exploration of Thebes. On

November 4, 1922, the tomb of Tutankhamen was discovered. Carter
published three volumes on his work
between 1923 and 1933. Several editions of the work are available.

CARTOUCHE A loop of rope with a
knot at one end, stylized in Egyptian
art to contain the name of the king. It
symbolized "that which the sun
encircles," meaning that the king
ruled the entire universe. The cartouche was used for two of the five
names given to the Pharaoh.

CAT The object of an important cult
in ancient Egypt. In Bubastis, the city
of the goddess Bast, who held the cat
as sacred, one particular cat was regarded as an incarnation of the deity.
The cat was also seen as a personification of the sun god. The *Book of the
Dead* mentions a cat that took up a
position by the persea tree in
Heliopolis on the night the foes of
Osiris were destroyed. In the commentary that follows, it is stated that the
"male cat" was the god Ra, and that its
name was Mau. One scene portrays
the cat cutting off the head of the serpent of darkness.

In ancient Egypt cats were accorded
the same respect as humans. When a
cat died, it was embalmed, treated
with spices and drugs, and laid in a
specially prepared coffin. According to
Greek sources, anyone who killed a
cat—wittingly or unwittingly—was
condemned to death. The writer
Diodorus tells of one offender, a Ro-

man, who was murdered by an angry
mob.

Herodotus in his *History* (Book 2)
writes that, "When a conflagration
takes place a supernatural impulse
seizes on the cats. For the Egyptians,
standing at a distance, take care of the
cats, and neglect to put out the fire; but
the cats making their escape and leap-
ing over the men, throw themselves
into the fire; and when this happens
great lamentations are made among
the Egyptians. In whatsoever house a
cat dies of a natural death, all the family shave their eyebrows only; but if a
dog die, they shave the whole body and
the head. All cats that die are carried
to certain sacred houses, where being
first embalmed, they are buried in the
city of Bubastis."

The lynx, a large wildcat with a
small patch of hair on the tip of each
ear, was also deified by a cult. In one
early text the animal attacks evil serpents and is described as a friend to the
dead. The lynx god, known as Maftet,
participated in the overthrow of the
monster serpent Apophis.

CATTLE Bulls and cows figured
prominently in the ancient Egyptian
view of life. Many of the gods were
portrayed in either bull or cow form,
among them Apis, the most famous
bull, and Hathor, the great goddess,
who was often depicted as a cow. In
Egypt the cow was honored as the
giver of milk, a divine food. Hathor
was called the "cow which is the sky,
which watches over the world of the

dead and which gives milk to Pharaoh. . . . "

CHAMPOLLION, JEAN FRANÇOIS (1790–1832) French Egyptologist who deciphered hieroglyphics in his famous work, *Précis du système hiéroglyphique* of 1822. He paved the way for modern advances in the study of ancient Egypt by demystifying its written records.

CHILDBIRTH, PATRON DEITIES OF Various deities were associated with birth in Egyptian mythology. The most important are: Bes, Beset, Heket, Meshkent, Nekhebet, Taurt.

CHILD, HORUS see Harpokrates.

CHILDREN According to the Greek historian Herodotus, in his *History* (Book 2), the ancient Egyptians believed that children possessed special gifts for divination. One account of the myth of Isis and Osiris has the goddess, who is searching for her husband's body, ask some children playing at the mouth of the Nile if they have noticed anything unusual. They tell her they have seen an elaborate chest. Later the chest was found to contain the body of Osiris, placed there by Set and his evil accomplices. From that time forth children were looked on with special favor in matters relating to divination.

CHEPERA see Khepera.

CIRCUMCISION That the ancient Egyptians practiced the removal of part or all of the male foreskin is evidenced by their mummies. Yet the exact symbolic significance of circumcision, a ritual mentioned in very few texts, remains unclear. However, it was probably intended as an offering, a shedding of blood dedicated to a god of generation or virility.

A male was circumcised when he reached puberty. Although the custom was not universally adopted by the Egyptian lay people, all priests were circumcised for ritual purification. Egyptian soldiers would often cut off the foreskins of their enemies to bring them back as a proof of victory. The Bible, 1 Samuel 18:25-27, notes that the same practice was observed by King David's men.

CLEOPATRA (B.C. 69–30) Last Queen of Egypt, seventh Macedonian princess to bear the name. By the will of her father, Ptolemy Auletes, she was to share the throne with her brother, who eventually ousted her. Julius Ceasar restored Cleopatra to the throne and she bore him a son, Caesarion, who was later killed by Augustus.

She became the mistress of Mark Antony, who killed himself after suffering defeat by Augustus. Not wishing to endure shame and the mercy of Augustus, Cleopatra committed suicide by either an asp bite or poison. She has fascinated generations of writers such as Shakespeare in *An-*

tony and Cleopatra and George Bernard Shaw in *Caesar and Cleopatra.*

COBRA GODDESS OF LOWER EGYPT see Buto.

COFFIN The mummiform case contained within the sarcophagus first used in the Middle Kingdom. Coffins were made from a variety of materials. One coffin often fitted into another, and the entire group was placed inside the sarcophagus.

COFFIN TEXTS Name given to magical formulas for the dead found inside the wooden coffins of the Middle Kingdom. The coffin texts were based on the formulas originally written for the king but they were adapted for the common people, to help them in the next world.

COLORS As in other civilizations, colors had symbolic connotations in ancient Egypt:

Gold, the color of the skin of the gods, as shown in many portrayals of the deities.

Black, the color of the pitch used to cover the mummy, was a symbol of resurrection and rebirth. Anubis, the god who watched over the dead, was depicted as a black-faced jackal, while Osiris, god of the dead and resurrection, was sometimes represented as black, and Min, god of fertility, portrayed with an erection, was also shown as black.

Green, the color of plant life, was also a symbol of resurrection. Osiris is often shown with a green body and face.

White is the color of the White Crown of the South, and the color of joy.

Red, except when shown on the Red Crown of the North, was an evil color, associated with the evil god Set. Often when the name of Set appeared in a text it was written with red ink. Men with red beards were considered evil.

Blue, the color of water appears on the Khepresh, the Blue War Crown, worn by the Pharaoh.

COMPANY OF GODS see Ennead.

COMPOSITE GODS A god who combines the characteristics of two or more gods, such as Amen-Ra, made up of the god Amen and the god Ra.

COW see Cattle.

CRAFT GOD, THE see Ptah.

CREATION MYTHS The Egyptians did not have one widely accepted creation myth but many explanations that were often in conflict with one another. There were various methods by which life was brought about, and many deities were credited with the act of creation because each city ascribed the central role to its own major god or goddess. In some myths life is brought forth when the god merely utters a word; in others, man is moulded by the deity out of clay;

and in still others, life is generated from the god's masturbation. The following are major deities associated with creation: Amen-Ra, Aten, the Ennead or Company of Gods, Geb, Hathor, Horus, Huh and Hauhet, Iusas and Nebhet Hotep, Khepera, Kuk and Kauket, Nun and Naunet, Nut, the Ogdoad, Ptah, Ra, Shu, Tefnut, Tem, and Thoth. Each of these gods or goddesses appears under a separate entry in this book.

CROCODILE In Egyptian belief the crocodile played a dual role, as both a beneficent and a demonic being. In some myths he was identified with the evil god Set, who was a foe of Osiris. In other myths the crocodile is credited as an aid to Osiris, said to have borne the god's body across the lake on his back. Some texts report that Horus, the son of Osiris, took the form of a crocodile in order to search for the pieces of his father's mutilated body. In another myth Set, in the form of a crocodile, is blamed for attempting to destroy Isis and Horus.

The god Sebek was portrayed as a crocodile and identified with both Ra and Horus as a sun deity. Herodotus in his *History* (Book 2) tells us that the city of Crocodilopolis was devoted to the worship of this god. Sacred crocodiles were kept and attended to with elaborate care. When they died, they were "embalmed and placed in sacred coffins. On the other hand, the people of the region of Elephantine have so little regard for crocodiles that they eat them."

CROCODILE GOD   see Sebek.

CRONOS Greek god of the world and time identified by the Greeks with the Egyptian earth god Geb.

CROOK The shepherd's crook was carried by both the gods and Pharaoh as a symbol of power.

CROWNS Various crowns and headdresses appear on Egyptian deities. The most common are:

Pschent, or Double Crown: Symbol of the unification of Upper and Lower Egypt, consisting of the red crown of Lower Egypt and the white crown of Upper Egypt.

Red Crown: Symbol of Lower Egypt which has a wicker stinger at its front.

White Crown: Symbol of Lower Egypt, in the shape of a mitre.

Khepresh, or Blue War Crown: Symbol of war with a bulbous shape and a snake in front of it.

Atef Crown or Headdress: Resembles the shape of the white crown but has a small sun's disk on top and is flanked on either side by feathers.

Hemhemet Crown: Made up of three Atef crowns, side by side, mounted on ram's horns.

Ram's Horns Crown or Headdress: Consists of ram's horns, either horizontal or curved. Often it serves as a base for one of the other crowns.

Various other combinations are found such as Amen's Crown, which consists

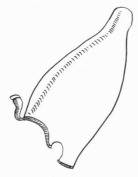

White Crown

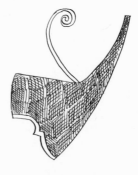

Red Crown

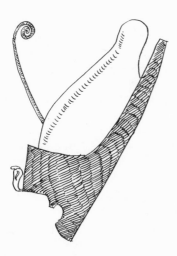

Double Crown

Amen's Crown

of two feathers on a base similar to the Red Crown, or the Vulture Headdress of the queens and goddesses, which has a vulture as its base. Sometimes it is surmounted by a sun's disk and horns.

D

DARKNESS, DECAY, AND DEATH, GODDESS OF see Nephthys.

DAYS, LUCKY AND UNLUCKY see Calendar.

DEAD, ISLAND OF see Sekhet-Aaru.

DEATH see Coffin, Funeral Customs, Mummy, Osiris, Sarcophagus, and Tombs.

DEATH GODS Various gods were associated with death in Egyptian belief. The main gods were Anubis, who watched over the burial of the dead, Osiris, the god of death and resurrection who promised eternal life to his worshippers, and Seker, a death god who was sometimes combined with Osiris.

DECANS Tables of the constellations drawn up by the ancient Egyptians as a means of telling time at night. A given decan appearing in the same place in the sky indicated a certain hour.

DED see Tet.

DEMOTIC see Hieroglyphics.

DESHRET The "Red Land," name given by the ancient Egyptians to the desert areas that surrounded the irrigated land.

DESTINY, GOD OF Shai.

"DEVOURER, THE" see Amam.

DHOUTI see Thoth.

DIONYSUS Greek god of wine and ecstasy often identified by the Greeks with the Egyptian god Osiris.

"DIVINE MOTHER" see Hesat.

DJED see Tet.

DJEHUTI see Thoth.

DJESER see Zoser I.

DJET see Thet.

DOG Although there was a cult of the dog at Cynopolis, this animal was not regarded as a god. Herodotus writes in his *History* (Book 2) that when a dog died, members of the house would "shave the whole body and head. . . . All persons bury their dogs in sacred vaults within their own city." The consumption of any wine, or corn, or other food that happened to be in the house when the animal died was forbidden. After the dog's body had been embalmed, it was buried in a tomb.

According to the ancient writer Diodorus, a dog was the guardian of the bodies of Osiris and Isis, and dogs guided Isis in her search for the body of Osiris, protecting her from savage beasts. However, this writer may have confused the jackal, sacred to Anubis, with the dog.

DOLPHIN GODDESS see Hatmehit.

DONKEY Sometimes the evil god Set was identified with the donkey.

DOOMED PRINCE, THE Literary folktale about a prince who attempts to escape his fate. The translation is by William Flinders Petrie in his *Egyptian Tales.*

There once was a king to whom no son was born; and his heart was grieved, and he prayed for himself unto the gods around him for a child. They decreed that one should be born to him. And his wife, after her time was fulfilled, brought forth a son. Then came the Hathors to decree for him a destiny; they said, "His death is to be by the crocodile, or by the serpent, or by

the dog." Then the people who stood by heard this, and they went to tell it to his Majesty. Then his Majesty's heart sickened very greatly. And his Majesty caused a house to be built upon the desert; it was furnished with people and with all good things of the royal house, that the child should not go abroad. And when the child was grown, he went up upon the roof, and he saw a dog; it was following a man who was walking on the road. He spoke to his page, who was with him, "What is this that walks behind the man who is coming along the road?" He answered him, "This is a dog." The child said to him, "Let there be brought to me one like it." The page went to repeat it to his Majesty. And his Majesty said, "Let there be brought to him a little pet dog, lest his heart be sad." And behold they brought to him the dog.

Then when the days increased after this, and when the child became grown in all his limbs, he sent a message to his father saying, "Come, wherefore am I kept here? Inasmuch as I am fated to three evil fates, let me follow my desire. Let God do what is in his heart." They agreed to all he said, and gave him all sorts of arms, and also his dog to follow him, and they took him to the east country, and said to him, "Behold, go thou whither thou wilt." His dog was with him, and he went northward, following his heart in the desert, while he lived on all the best of the game of the desert. He went to the chief of Naharaina.

And behold there had not been any

born to the chief of Naharaina, except one daughter. Behold, there had been built for her a house; its seventy windows were seventy cubits from the ground. And the chief caused to be brought all the sons of the chiefs of the land of Khalu, and said to them, "He who reaches the window of my daughter, she shall be to him for a wife."

And many days after these things, as they were in their daily task, the youth rode by the place where they were. They took the youth to their house, they bathèd him, they gave provender to his horses, they brought all kinds of things for the youth, they perfumed him, they anointed his feet, they gave him portions of their own food; and they spake to him, "Whence comest thou, goodly youth?" He said to them, "I am son of an officer of the land of Egypt; my mother is dead, and my father has taken another wife. And when she bore children, she grew to hate me, and I have come as a fugitive from before her." And they embraced him, and kissed him.

And after many days were passed, he said to the youths, "What is it that ye do here?" And they said to him: "We spend our time in this: we climb up, and he who shall reach the window of the daughter of the chief of Naharaina, to him will be given her to wife." He said to them, "If it please you, let me behold the matter, that I may come to climb with you." They went to climb, as was their daily wont: and the youth stood afar off to behold; and the face of the daughter of the chief of Naharaina was turned to

them. And another day the sons came to climb, and the youth came to climb with the sons of the chiefs. He climbed, and he reached the window of the daughter of the chief of Naharaina. She kissed him, she embraced him in all his limbs.

And one went to rejoice the heart of her father, and said to him, "One of the people has reached the window of thy daughter." And the prince inquired of the messenger, saying, "The son of which of the princes is it?" And he replied to him, "It is the son of an officer, who has come as a fugitive from the land of Egypt, fleeing from before his stepmother when she had children." Then the chief of Naharaina was exceeding angry; and he said: "Shall I indeed give my daughter to the Egyptian fugitive? Let him go back whence he came." And one came to tell the youth, "Go back to the place thou camest from." But the maiden seized his hand; she swore an oath by God, saying, "By the being of Ra Harakhti, if one takes him from me, I will not eat, I will not drink, I shall die in that same hour." The messenger went to tell unto her father all that she said. Then the prince sent men to slay the youth, while he was in his house. But the maiden said: "By the being of Ra, if one slay him I shall be dead ere the sun goeth down. I will not pass an hour of life if I am parted from him." And one went to tell her father. Then the prince made them bring the youth with the maiden. The youth was seized with fear when he came before the prince. But he embraced him, he kissed him all over, and said: "Oh, tell me who thou art; behold, thou art to me as a son." He said to him: "I am a son of an officer of the land of Egypt; my mother died, my father took to him a second wife; she came to hate me, and I fled a fugitive from before her." He then gave to him his daughter to wife; he gave also to him a house, and serfs, and fields, also cattle and all manner of good things.

But after the days of these things were passed, the youth said to his wife, "I am doomed to three fates—a crocodile, a serpent, and a dog." She said to him, "Let one kill the dog which belongs to thee." He replied to her, "I am not going to kill my dog, which I have brought up from when it was small." And she feared greatly for her husband, and would not let him go alone abroad.

And one went with the youth toward the land of Egypt, to travel in that country. Behold the crocodile of the river, he came out by the town in which the youth was. And in that town was a mighty man. And the mighty man would not suffer the crocodile to escape. And when the crocodile was bound, the mighty man went out and walked abroad. And when the sun rose the mighty man went back to the house; and he did so every day, during two months of days.

Now when the days passed after this, the youth sat making a good day in his house. And when the evening came he lay down on his bed, sleep seized upon his limbs; and his wife filled a bowl of milk, and placed it by his side. Then came out a serpent from his hole, to bite the youth; behold his wife was sitting by him, she lay not down. Thereupon the servants gave milk to the serpent, and he drank, and was drunk, and lay upside down. Then his wife made it to perish with the blows of her dagger. And they woke her husband, who was astonished; and she said unto him: "Behold thy God has given one of thy dooms into thy hand; he will also give thee the others." And he sacrificed to God, adoring him, and praising his spirits from day to day.

And when the days were passed after these things, the youth went to walk in the fields of his domain. He went not alone, behold his dog was following him. And his dog ran aside after the wild game, and he followed the dog. He came to the river, and entered the river behind his dog. Then came out the crocodile, and took him to the place where the mighty man was. And the crocodile said to the youth, "I am thy doom, following after thee. . . ."

(Here the papyrus breaks off.)

DOUBLE CROWN see Crowns.

DOUBLE OF A PERSON see Ka.

DREAMS As with other ancient peoples, the Egyptians believed that the gods often made their will known through dreams. There are various

Egyptian texts on such matters. In one the future Thutmosis IV dreams that a god told him to remove the sand from in front of the Sphinx and he would be made ruler of a united Egypt. The young prince did as commanded in the dream and eventually was made king of a united Egypt.

Another legend tells of a dream in which Nut-Amen saw two serpents, one on his right side and one on his left. When he awoke he asked for an interpretation of the dream. He was told: "The land of the South is thine, and thou shalt have dominion over the land of the North: the White Crown and the Red Crown shall adorn thy head. . . . " Inspired by his dream Nut-Amen invaded Egypt, and he was successful. He dedicated part of his spoils to the god Amen who had granted him the dream.

The Egyptian magicians often interpreted dreams and claimed the ability to bring about dreams through magical words or ritual acts. One Egyptian text reads: "To obtain a vision from the god Bes. Make a drawing of Bes, as shown below, on your left hand, and envelop your hand in a strip of black cloth that has been consecrated to Isis and lie down to sleep without speaking a word, even in answer to a question. Wind the remainder of the cloth round your neck. . . . "

Another text tells the person to "Take a clean linen bag and write upon it the names given below. Fold it up and make it into a lamp wick, and set it alight, pouring oil over it. . . . Then in the evening, when you are going to bed, which you must do without touching food, do thus. Approach the lamp and repeat seven times the formula given below: then extinguish it and lie down to sleep. . . ."

DRINK, GOD OF   see Tchabu.

DUAMUTEF   see Tuamutef.

DUAT   see Tuat.

DWARF GOD   see Bes.

E

EAST WIND, GOD OF see Henkhisesui.

EDJO see Buto.

EEL Eels were sacred in Upper Egypt, where their mummified remains have been found.

EGYPT The ancient Egyptians often called their land *Kemi* or *Kemit,* meaning "black land," because of its rich soil. In Arabic the name is *Mirs* or *Mizr,* meaning "red mud." The common name for Egypt in the Bible is *Mizraim,* though it is sometimes called "the land of Ham" (Psalm 105:23) as well as Rahab, the "proud" or "insolent" (Psalm 87:4). The English word Egypt is derived from the Middle English word *Egipte,* which in turn comes from the Old English *Egypte,* it in turn from the Latin, *Aegyptus,* and that in turn from the Greek *Aiguptos.* The Greeks derived their word, it is believed, from *Hikuptah,* a variant of *Hat-kaptah,* which means "Temple of the *Ka* of Ptah," the name of the city of Memphis which was dedicated to the god Ptah.

EGYPTOLOGY The study of ancient Egypt goes back to the Egyptians themselves. For example, Khaemwaset, a son of Rameses II, devoted his life as a priest in the sanctuary of Heliopolis to Egypt's past. The Greeks followed with one of the earliest accounts of Egyptian life, written by Herodotus in his *History.* His entire second book is devoted to their civilization. Other writers of the ancient world who mention Egypt include Juvenal, Tacitus, Plato, Ammianus Marcellinus, Josephus, Eusebius, Julius Africanus and Clement of Alexandria.

From about the fifteenth century A.D., European visitors to Egypt described its monuments in various travel guides. Europeans en route to the Holy Land saw Egypt through the Old Testament's portrayal of it as an enemy of Yahweh and his cult. By the seventeenth century the traveler was not so much a pilgrim, as an explorer drawn to a strange and fantastic land. George Sandys, an Englishman, visited Egypt in 1610 and produced drawings of the pyramids as well as a written account of his travels. Other voyagers continued to visit Egypt and write about their adventures. The event that had the greatest effect on Egyptology, however, was the invasion of Egypt by Napoleon. *La Description de l'Egypte,* a series of volumes dealing with the ancient monuments was produced by a group of scholars. At the same time the Rosetta Stone was discovered and was later used to help decipher the Egyptian hieroglyphs.

After Napoleon, many travelers came to Egypt, often with dishonest intentions, to plunder the monuments. However, the new wave of visitors included many scholars, who helped to bring about a better understanding of ancient Egypt. Among them was William Flinders Petrie who worked for the Egyptian Exploration Fund. Currently, interest and travel in Egypt are very high. There are many attempts presently being made to preserve the remains of this once great ancient civilization.

EILEITHYIA Greek goddess of childbirth, daughter of Zeus and Hera, who made childbirth easy or difficult. The Greeks identified her with the Egyptian goddess Nekhebet.

ELEPHANT The elephant was not generally a cult figure, but may have been regarded so in predynastic times. The island opposite Syene was called Elephantine because the rocks nearby looked like elephants, or because it was a depot of the ivory trade.

ELOQUENT PEASANT, THE TALE OF see Peasant and the Workman, The.

ELYSIAN FIELDS see Sekhet-Aaru.

ENNEAD, OR COMPANY OF GODS Cosmological system of grouping gods that was arranged by the priests of Heliopolis, a center of worship in Egypt. The Ennead contained nine gods, but at times the number varied according to circumstances. Three Companies of Gods evolved, of which the first two were known as the Great Enneads and the Lesser Enneads. The gods of the Great Ennead were Tem, Shu, Tefnut, Seb, Nut, Isis, Set, Nephthys, Thoth and Horus. Osiris, the great man god, was omitted in one list but included in another.

The Heliopolitan Ennead was accepted generally throughout Egypt, but the Heliopolitan priests knew that it was important to leave room for those gods of both the north and the south of Egypt, as well as lesser gods who were identified with the main gods of the Heliopolitan list. When the doctrine of Heliopolis was adopted in another home in Egypt, the chief local god usually was merged with the leading Heliopolitan deity, and a composite god was formed who became the head of the new Ennead.

EPAGOMENAL DAYS Five days at the end of the Egyptian calendar year which were the birthdays of the gods. These were:

Day 1
Osiris
Day 2
Horus
Day 3
Set

Day 4
Isis
Day 5
Nephthys

ERMENT see Hermonthis.

ESET see Isis.

ETERNITY AMULET see Shen.

ETON see Aten.

EUSEBIUS (fourth century A.D.) Greek Christian writer who preserved some of the writings of Manetho, the Egyptian priest who wrote a *History of Egypt.* Quotations from Manetho are scattered throughout Eusebius's work.

EVIL, GOD OF see Set.

EXODUS The "going out" of the Hebrews from their bondage in Egypt under the leadership of Moses. The date of the event is not known, but estimates range from B.C. 1580 to 1215. The Exodus is often referred to in the Bible as the outstanding manifestation of Yahweh's love for his people.

EYE OF RA see Utchat.

F

FA One of twelve gods, the "bearer," or "carrier," who carries on his head the serpent Mehen to the eastern part of the sky in the eleventh section or hour of Tuat, the underworld, leading the boat of the sun god Ra. The other gods are Ermenu, Athpi, Netru, Shepu, Reta, Amu, Ama, Shetu, Sekhenu, Semsem, and Mehni.

FALCON see Hawk.

FAMILY The family was most important in ancient Egyptian society. Men of all classes were known to marry their blood sisters—primarily, it seems, as a means of keeping property within the family. The myth of Osiris who married his sister Isis, and his brother Set, who married another sister, Nephthys, supported this practice. In *Isis and Osiris* Plutarch tells us that Osiris also had intercourse with his sister Nephthys, and the god Anubis was born of this union.

The religious texts describe the spirits of the Tuat, or the Underworld or Other World, rejoicing in marriage, though no mention is made of offspring. One early text tells of a king who married a young and beautiful woman in the Kingdom of Osiris, the land of the dead, and also married the goddess Isis. He carried a woman off from her husband whenever he pleased, and made her his wife.

The mother played an important part in the scheme of family life. Kinship was reckoned on the mother's side, and whereas the father's name is often not recorded on a funeral work, the name of the mother is frequently noted. The *Maxims of Ani* advises that offerings should be made to fathers and mothers alike who rest in their tombs, but that a man should take most care in the treatment of his mother, who has suckled him for three years, and carried bread and beer to him every day that he attended school. The writer says: "Give thy mother no cause to be offended at thee, lest she lift her hands to the God, Who will hear her complaint and will punish thee."

Adultery was prevalent in ancient Egypt. One text tells of the adulterous wife of Aba-aner who was burned by royal command, at the north wall of the palace. In the folktale *The Tale of*

Two Brothers, when Anpu hears of his wife's adultery he returns home to kill her, and throws her body to dogs or jackals.

Prostitution was also common. In the *Maxims of Ani* the reader is told to be on guard against strange women from outside the town, as well as women whose husbands are out of town. "Do not look at her, do not follow her, have no commerce with her. She is like a whirlpool in a current leading man knoweth not where. To listen to her is an abominable and deadly thing."

Nevertheless, the courtesan and concubine were recognized members of ancient Egyptian society. On one coffin the inscription asks that the deceased be allowed to see "his concubines whom it is his heart's desire to meet."

FATE AND FORTUNE, PERSONI-FICATIONS OF see Shai and Renenet.

FERTILITY AND CROPS, GOD OF see Min.

FINGERNAILS For many ancient societies fingernails, as well as hair, symbolized the entire person or personality. Thus, to avoid injury, any action, such as cutting the nails, had to follow a prescribed ritual and occur at a specific time. One was careful not to let his fingernails come into the possession of his enemies since they could be used for black magic. An Egyptian manual for priests advises that a priest should cut his nails in imitation

of the god Thoth, and the manner in which he cut his nails on a certain occasion.

FISH Mummified fish have been found in Egypt where a fish cult existed in the city of Oxyrhynchus. The fish was believed to have swallowed the phallus of Osiris when his evil brother Set hacked the body of the god to pieces.

Treatment of various fish differed throughout ancient Egypt. In one city a certain fish would be taboo, while in another it was honored and mummified. According to Greek sources, the mormyrus fish, worshipped at Oxyrhynchus, once caused a war when its cultists retaliated against a neighboring town for eating the fish.

FLAIL The royal insignia, or Nekhekh, symbol of power and terror,

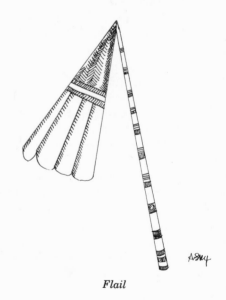

Flail

derived from the manual threshing device, which consisted of a long wooden handle or staff, and a shorter free-swinging stick attached at its end, which was used to beat wheat.

FOLKTALES see Tales.

FOOD OF THE GODS The gods as well as men lived on food, and frequent reference is made in Egyptian texts to the food of the gods. The gods fed themselves with celestial food which was supplied to them by the Eye of Horus, meaning that they existed on rays of light that fell from the sun. Thus they became beings whose bodies were made wholly of light.

In one myth the gods are said to live upon a "wood, or plant of life," which may have grown near the great lake in Sekhet-hetep, a fertile region of the gods and the dead. In other texts we are told how they ate and drank "bread of eternity" and "beer of eternity." There is also mention of a fig tree and a heavenly vine, the fruit of which was eaten by the beatified. Bread came from the Eye of Horus when it shed its light on the olive tree.

FROG A symbol of generation, birth, and fertility, around which a cult evolved. The frog goddess was Heket and the four male primeval gods of the Ogdoad, which was a group of eight gods who made the world, were portrayed as frog-headed.

FUNERAL CUSTOMS The Egyptians paid elaborate attention to the burial of the dead and the cult that surrounded the act. The funeral of a king or a member of the royal family, or that of a wealthy person, was very magnificent.

The ancient Greek historian Diodorus wrote that when a king died all the inhabitants of the country wept and tore their garments. The temples were closed and the people did not offer sacrifices or celebrate any festival for seventy-two days. During that time crowds of two or three hundred men and women would go about the streets with mud on their heads and with their garments knotted below their breasts, singing dirges. They did not eat wheat or any animal food, and abstained from wine. No one would wash or make love.

When the seventy-two days ended, the body was placed in a coffin at the entrance to the tomb. At this time everyone had the right to make an accusation against the person, even if the deceased were a king. The priests then pronounced a funeral oration over the body, telling of the noble works of the deceased.

We are not sure if this account by Diodorus is entirely accurate. From various Egyptian works we learn that professional mourners were hired, who beat their breasts and poured dust over their heads. In a typical funeral held at Thebes the deceased's body, with his or her belongings, was placed in a boat to cross the Nile. The mummy was accompanied by two women representing Isis and Nephthys. Other boats carried the family and other

47

mourners. When the boats reached the west bank of the river, the mummy was placed on a sledge drawn by two cows. The mourners then gathered together to walk to the necropolis, while the priests burned incense over the bier and recited ritual texts. When the company arrived at the tomb a new series of rituals ensued. One was the ceremony of the Opening of the Mouth, which was to restore the person's body to life. This was followed by the widow kneeling before the coffin and weeping. Then the coffin and the man's belongings were placed inside the tomb, and the entrance closed. The mourners then gathered for a funeral banquet as a communion with the dead person.

FUNERARY TEXTS Name given to various texts dealing with the dead and the afterlife, such as the *Book of the Dead*.

The texts were created to grant eternal life to the dead. The magic words were written on the walls of the tombs or on the furniture and the papyri which were placed in the tombs. At first the texts were written for the Pharaoh alone—who was certain to enter into eternal life. In time, however, the hope of eternal life was granted to all. Some of the oldest funerary texts were discovered in the pyramids and date from the end of the Old Kingdom. Other texts have been found from the Middle Kingdom. Perhaps the best-known collection of funerary texts is the *Book of the Dead*. There are, however, others, such as *The Book of the Opening of the Mouth* and *The Book of Breathings*.

G

GANDER   see Goose.

GEB God who personified the earth's surface.

He was the brother-husband of the sky goddess, Nut. According to one myth, Geb was separated from Nut by the god Shu at the behest of the sun god Ra, who was angered by their closeness. In such a way, the sky above and the earth below were created. However, Geb was left inconsolable by the separation and he cried so fiercely that his wailing could be heard day and night and his tears filled the oceans and seas.

Geb was often depicted lying under the feet of Shu, raised on one arm with one knee bent. In this form he symbolized the mountains and waves of the earth's surface. He was also portrayed as a man wearing a goose on his head, which was the hieroglyph of his name and was sacred to him. In some places he was called Kenkenwer, or "the great cackler," because it was said he laid the egg from which the world sprang. Most frequently, however, Geb was identified as the father of the great Osirian gods—Osiris, Isis, Nephthys, Set and Horus—and as

Geb

such, was known as "father of the gods" or "chief of the gods." In classical Greek times, he was identified with Cronus, who was the father of the great Olympian gods.

Variants of his name are Qeb, Keb, and Seb.

GENITALS, PROTECTOR OF see Sia.

GIRDLE OF ISIS see Thet.

GOLD Aside from its secular uses, gold was regarded as divine by the ancient Egyptians who believed it was "the flesh of the gods." Hathor, one of the greatest goddesses, was thought to be an incarnation of gold. Many cult objects were either made of gold or covered with gold leaf. In painting the color yellow was often used in place of gold.

GOOSE The goose or gander was a symbol of the god Amen and of Geb, the earth god who was sometimes called Kenken-wer, or "the great cackler," because it was said he laid the egg from which the world sprang. Among the Egyptians goose was a favorite dish, and was frequently offered in temples. Herodotus in his *History* (Book 2) says that a portion of the daily food of the priests consisted of goose flesh.

GRASSHOPPER The ancient Egyptians associated the grasshopper with happiness. In the *Book of the Dead* the deceased says, "I have rested in the Field of Grasshoppers," and an earlier text tells how the king will "arrive in heaven like the grasshopper of Ra."

GRAVES see Tombs.

GREAT CACKLER Title sometimes applied to the earth god Geb because it was said he laid the egg from which the world sprang.

GREEN see Colors.

H

HADES Greek god of the underworld identified by the Greeks with the Egyptian god Osiris.

HAIR Egyptian priests often shaved their heads, whereas many of the lay people wore wigs over their natural hair. Children often wore a long twist of hair curls over the right temple. The young god Horus, or Horus the Child, is often portrayed in this manner as is the moon god Aah. The hieroglyph for the lock of hair came to mean "child."

HAMMON see Amen.

HAP God of the Nile who became identified with all the great primeval creation gods and eventually was said to be the creator of everything. At a very early period Hap absorbed the attributes of Nun, the primeval watery mass from which the god Ra emerged on the first day of creation. As a result, Hap was regarded as the father of all beings. He held a unique position in Egyptian religion, although he was not in any theological system developed by the priests.

The light of Ra brought life to men and animals, but without the waters of Hap every living thing would perish. While many other mythologies repre-

Hap, God of the Nile (North)

51

sent water as being feminine, Hap is usually portrayed as a fat man with the breasts of a woman to indicate his powers of fertility. When he represents both the south and north Nile, Hap holds two plants, the papyrus and the lotus, or two vases, from which he pours out water. His name is also spelled Hapi or Hapy.

HAPI One of the four sons of Horus and Isis who guarded the lungs and was portrayed as dog-headed.

HAPI-ASAR see Serapis.

HAPY see Hap.

HAPY-WET God of the Nile in Heaven, believed to be a form of the god Khnemu united with the god Ra.

HARE-HEADED GOD see Unnu.

HARENDOTES Epithet in Greek for the Egyptian Har-en-yotet, meaning "Horus protector of his father." It refers to the role of Horus as avenger of the death of his father, Osiris, at the hands of Set.

HAR-EN-YOTET see Harendotes.

HARMACHIS Greek name form of the Egyptian Horakhty meaning "Horus who is on the Horizon." Under this form he appears as the Great Sphinx near the Pyramid of Cheops. Often Harmachis is combined with the god Ra to form the composite god Ra-

Harmachis or Ra-Horakhty. In this form he is portrayed as a man with the head of a hawk.

HAROERIS Greek form of the Egyptian Har Wer, or "Horus the Elder," or "Horus the Great," worshipped at Letopolis. According to some texts Haroeris was the son of Ra and Hathor, though Plutarch in his account, *Isis and Osiris,* makes him the son of Geb, the earth god, and Nut, and brother of Osiris. Haroeris was worshipped with his female counterpart, Ta-sent-nefert, and their son P-neb-taui, who is portrayed with a disk upon his head and a lock of hair at his side indicating his youth. In Egyptian art Haroeris is portrayed as a hawk-headed man often wearing the double crown of Upper and Lower Egypt.

HARPER, THE SONG OF THE see Song of the Harper.

HARPOKRATES Greek name form for the Egyptian Heru-p-khart meaning "Horus the Child," or "the Infant Horus." When portrayed alone he is pictured nude with the sidelock of youth and the Double Crown of Upper and Lower Egypt. One hand is touching his lips or he sucks his thumb, which the Greeks misinterpreted as a symbol of discretion, and made Harpokrates the God of Silence. Often Harpokrates is shown being suckled by his mother, Isis.

Harpokrates

HARSAPHES Greek name form of the Egyptian Hershef, a ram god portrayed as a ram-headed man who was a god of fertility and associated with water. Originally a local god of Heracleopolis Magna in the Faiyum, when he became a national deity he was identified with Horus as well as with Amen. His name means "He who is on his lake."

HARSIESIS Greek name form of the Egyptian Hor-sa-isit, meaning "Horus, the son of Isis." Under this form Horus was one of the most popular deities in Egypt. He was conceived by his mother, Isis, after she had magi-

cally had intercourse with the dead body of her husband, Osiris. Harsiesis was born prematurely on the floating island of Chemmis in the marshes not far from Buto. During his childhood he was protected by his mother from Set, the murderer of Osiris, who wished to destroy Harsiesis. Eventually, Harsiesis battled Set and was the victor. Under the form of Harsiesis the god is variously portrayed, sometimes as hawk-headed, and carrying instruments of death.

HARTOMES Epithet meaning "Horus the Lancer," referring to the god Horus in his role of attacking the evil god Set, who had killed Osiris, his father. Hartomes is portrayed as a hawk-headed man in the act of driving a long spear into an unseen foe or beneath the ground.

HAR WER see Haroeris

HATHOR Cow goddess whose name literally means the "house of Horus." According to one myth she stood in the form of a cow upon the earth in such a way that her four legs were the pillars holding up the sky and her belly was the firmament. Each evening Horus, as the sun god, flew into her mouth in the form of a hawk and each morning appeared again reborn. Consequently, Horus was said to be both her husband and her son.

Hathor was one of the oldest known goddesses of Egypt, symbolizing the great mother or cosmic goddess, who conceived, brought forth, and maintained all life. She not only nourished the living with her milk,

Hathor

the fields with an intoxicating brew which when she drank made her incapable of perceiving mankind.

Hathor's main temple was at Dendera, where she was worshipped with Horus of Edfu and their son Ihi, who was portrayed as an infant playing the sistrum (a musical instrument, somewhat like a rattle, whose sound was said to drive away evil spirits) at her side. Great festivals were celebrated in her temple, the most important being the festival of her birth, held at the new year, which ended with a drunken orgy. Her temple became known as a palace of enjoyment and a house of intoxication, and gave rise to her title as mistress of merriment and dance, as well as her popularity as a goddess of love, whom the Greeks identified with Aphrodite.

In later Egyptian mythology, Hathor became the representative of all the great goddesses in Egypt, and shrines in her honor were erected throughout the land. The most famous were the seven Hathors—Hathor of Thebes, Hathor of Heliopolis, Hathor of Aphroditopolis, Hathor of the Sinaitic Peninsula, Hathor of Momemphis or Ammu, Hathor of Herakleopolis, and Hathor of Keset.

As the cow goddess of Tuat, she was portrayed in Egyptian art wearing a long pendant collar around her neck and the Menait, emblem of joy and pleasure, on her back. She was also depicted as a woman wearing on her head a pair of horns within which rested the solar disk, as a woman with the head of a cow, and as a cow walk-

but was said to supply celestial food for the dead in Tuat, the underworld.

Hathor, however, also had her destructive aspects. One myth tells how at the instigation of the sun god, who had grown old and wanted to punish mankind for plotting to do away with him, she began to slay the human race. She enjoyed the slaughter so much that the other gods, alarmed, flooded

54

ing out from a funeral mountain. Variant spellings of her name are Athyr and Athor.

HAT-MEHIT Dolphin goddess, wife of Ba-neb-djet, the ram of Mendes.

HATSHEPUT (B.C. 1504–1483) Woman Pharaoh, daughter of Thothmes I, often portrayed with the false beard associated with kingship. She built the magnificent tomb-temple at Deir-el-Bahri and ruled for twenty years with her lover Senmut. In order to establish her position as ruler she had inscribed on the walls of the Deir-el-Bahri complex the tale that she was the daughter, not of Thothmes, but of the god Amen and Queen Aahmes. The text describes how the god in the form of Thothmes made love to Aahmes, telling her: "Hatsheput shall be the name of this daughter whom I have implanted in your body. She shall exercise beneficent kingship in this entire land. My spirit shall be hers. . . . "

At her death, however, her successor, who was kept in complete subjection during her reign, tried to erase her memory by destroying her many statues and erasing her name from her various monuments. Hatsheput means "foremost in nobility."

HAWK The cult of the hawk or falcon is one of the oldest in Egypt. The hawk was identified with various sky or sun gods, such as many of the Horus gods as well as Ra. He was also identified with Osiris, the god of the dead.

The main center of worship was at Hieraconpolis or Hawk City. According to the Greek historian Herodotus, in his *History* (Book 2), the punishment for killing a hawk was death.

HEADREST AMULET see Weres.

HEALING, GOD OF see Khensu.

HEARING, GOD OF see Setem.

HEBS see Nehata.

HEB-SEB see Seb.

HEKET Frog goddess who presided over conception and birth. She was said to be present at the birth of every king of Egypt. According to one myth, Heket assisted the goddess Isis in bringing her brother-husband Osiris back to life and in conceiving a child by him.

Since the frog was seen in great numbers a day or two before the rise of the Nile, it was regarded as a symbol of new life and prolific generation. A frog amulet—sometimes a frog at the end of a phallus—was carried by Egyptians to guarantee fertility. Variant spellings of Heket are Heqet, Heqtit, and Heqt.

HELEN OF TROY In Greek mythology, heroine abducted by Paris and the cause of the Trojan War. According to the Homeric poems Helen never went to Troy but was taken to Egypt, with her shadow or double in Troy.

55

Richard Strauss's opera, *Die Aegyptische Helena* ("The Egyptian Helen") recounts the tale. The libretto was written by Hugo von Hofmannsthal, and the work was first performed in 1928. In the opera Menelaus, the husband of Helen, plans to kill her after the war for being unfaithful to him, but a magic potion given by an Egyptian sorceress Aithra makes him forgive Helen.

HELIOPOLITAN ENNEAD see Ennead.

HEMETCH A serpent demon mentioned in a magical formula of Unas, a king of the Sixth Dynasty.

HEMHEMET CROWN see Crowns.

HENEB God who presided over grain and other products of the land, although Osiris, the god of death and resurrection, also presided over grain.

HENKHISESUI God of the east wind portrayed as a snake-headed man with four wings.

HENMEMET Lesser divine beings, the people of heaven. The word is also a generic term for mankind as differentiated from beasts and deities.

HEN-NETER see Priests.

HENNU BOAT see Seker Boat.

HENTIU Spirits in the twelfth section, or hour, of Tuat, the underworld,

who raise their hands in adoration of Osiris. They are believed to be forms of Osiris, and greet him with "Live, thou ruler of the thick darkness! Live, O thou who are great in all things. . . . " The allusion is to the death and burial of Osiris.

HENT-NUT-S see Perit.

HEPHAESTUS Greek god of smiths identified with the Egyptian god Ptah, the craft god.

HEPTET A goddess, the embracer, who is believed to have assisted in the resurrection of Osiris. She had the body of a woman with the head of a bearded snake. She wore on her head a pair of horns surmounted by a solar disk, the Atef crown, and uraei with disks and horns. In each hand she held a knife.

HEQET; HEQT; AND HEQTIT see Heket.

HER-HEQUI One of the four divine sovereign chiefs in the fifth section, or hour, of Tuat, the underworld, when the sun god Ra passes in his serpent boat.

HERI-SEP-F see Mates.

HERMANUBIS Greek name for the Egyptian Heru-em-Anpu, a composite god made up of Horus and Anubis. Hermanubis is portrayed as a jackal-headed man, which makes it almost impossible to distinguish him from Anubis, who is portrayed in the same manner.

HERMES TRISMEGISTUS A Greek name for the Egyptian god Thoth meaning, "Hermes, three times great, or very, very, very great." The Greeks, who identified Thoth with their god Hermes, believed that he was the first of the magicians to leave his followers a series of sacred books whose formulas had the power of commanding "all the forces of nature" and subduing "the very gods themselves." There is a poem by Longfellow titled "Hermes Trismegistus."

HERMONTHIS Ancient Egyptian city in North Egypt, South of Thebes, in which the Buchis Bull was worshipped. It was prominent in Roman times and dedicated to the god Montu. Modern Armant or Erment is on the ancient site.

HERMOPOLIS MAGNA Ancient Egyptian city in South Egypt on the Nile, chief seat of worship of Thoth, the scribe of the gods.

HERODOTUS (c. B.C. 485–425) Greek historian called by Cicero "the father of history." His work, *The Persian Wars,* often simply called *History,* is in nine books. Egypt is covered in Book 2. He is believed to have visited Egypt about B.C. 450. While scholars have questioned the accuracy of some of Herodotus' reports, his work was the main source of information on ancient Egypt until the

nineteenth century, when interest in the study of this civilization was spurred by Napoleon's Egyptian campaigns.

HERON Sacred bird believed to house the soul. In the *Book of the Dead* there is a spell to help the deceased person effect transformation into a heron.

HER-PEST A form of the god Horus as victor over the great "male hippopotamus," the symbol of the evil god Set. His victory over Set is portrayed in the Ptolemaic Temple at Edfu.

HER-SHA-A see Pesi.

HERSHEF see Harsaphes.

HERT-KETIT-S A lion-headed goddess who presided over the pit Hatet, in the eleventh section, or hour, of Tuat, the underworld. She belches fire on wretched creatures who are then hacked to pieces by a large knife which she holds in both hands.

HERT-NEMMAT-SET A woman fiend in the fourth pit of the eleventh section, or hour, of Tuat, the underworld, who punished the shadows and heads of the damned.

HERT-SEFU-S A woman fiend in the fifth pit of the eleventh section, or hour, of Tuat, the underworld, who punished the shadows and heads of the damned.

57

HERU see Horus.

HERU-EM-ANPU see Hermanubis.

HERU-KHU One of the four divine sovereign chiefs in the fifth section, or hour, of Tuat, the underworld, when the sun god Ra passes in his serpent boat.

HERU-P-KHART see Harpokrates.

HERY-SHA-DUAT A god whose name means "He who is over (is in charge of) the Field of the Tuat," or the underworld. He has nine *sekhtiu* or "field laborers" who perform all the work connected with ploughing and watering the fields in Tuat.

HESARET see Hesat.

HESAT The divine cow whose function was to nurse the children of the deities. She eventually became the Divine Mother and was considered the mother of the Mnevis Bull. A variant spelling of her name is Hesaret.

HETCH-MET One of the four divine sovereign beings in the fifth section, or hour, of Tuat, the underworld, when the sun god Ra passes in his serpent boat.

HETCH-NAU A monster serpent, with two heads, one at each end, who guards Osiris in his form as Osiris-Seker.

HETEMET-KHU see Nehata.

HIERATIC see Hieroglyphics.

HIEROGLYPHICS A system of writing used in ancient Egypt made up of phonograms or sound values and ideograms or picture signs with no sound values. The text is written in horizontal lines (read in either direction) or vertical columns, from top to bottom. The sequence of reading is indicated by the direction in which the figures of the humans and the animals face. Hieroglyphs were fully developed by about B.C. 3100. Since they were difficult to use in everyday writings, such as legal and business documents, a cursive script which simplified the pictorial hieroglyphs, called Hieratic, came into use. This in turn was replaced by Demotic, another cursive script, although Hieroglyphs and Hieratic were still used for religious texts. For centuries the meaning of the hieroglyphs was lost until they were deciphered by the French scholar Jean François Champollion in the nineteenth century.

HIPPOPOTAMUS In Egyptian belief the hippopotamus played a dual role, both as a beneficent being, as in the case of the goddess Taurt, who was portrayed as a female hippopotamus and aided those in childbirth, and as a demonic being, as a form of the evil god Set. A form of the god Horus, called Her-tchema, meaning "Horus the piercer," refers to his role of spearing Set while in the form of a hippopotamus. (In the Tutankhamen find is a statue of a man, who may be the king holding a harpoon or lance poised at an invisible foe which may have been a figure of the hippopotamus.) In Edfu, sacred harpooners were maintained whose duty it was to kill hippopotamuses. Edfu contained the great Temple to Horus who was the victor over Set.

HIPPOPOTAMUS GODDESS see Taurt.

HONEY A symbol of resurrection in ancient Egypt, honey was believed to have come from the tears of the sun god Ra when he wept. The tears formed a bee who in turn made the honey.

HORAEMATAWY A form of the god Horus meaning "Horus the uniter of the Two Lands." In this form Horus is said to be the son of the goddess Hathor. He is portrayed as a hawk-headed man, or a serpent, or a man, wearing various headdresses. He is believed to have sprung out of a lotus which blossomed in the heavenly abyss at the beginning of the year.

HORAKHTY A form of the god Horus meaning "Horus who is on the Horizon." Often he is combined with the god Ra to form the composite god, Ra-Horakhty, or in his Greek name form, Ra-Harmachis. In this form he is portrayed as a hawk-headed man.

HORMERTI A form of the god Horus, portrayed as a man with a hawk's head, above which are the horns of the god Khnemu and the solar disk encircled by a uraeus. In one hand he holds the Udjat, and is called "Horus of the Two Eyes."

HOR NUBTI Epithet of Horus, meaning "Horus the vanquisher of Set," and referring to his victory over the evil god Set.

HOR-SA-ISIT see Harsiesis.

HORSE There are no horse-headed native deities in Egyptian mythology, since the horse was introduced late into Egyptian life, possibly at the time of the Hyksos invaders. The foreign goddess Astarte, whose cult was adopted in Egypt, was called Mistress of Horses.

HORUS Sky god often portrayed as a hawk or hawk-headed. Originally Horus (whose name is a Latin form of the Greek word for the Egyptian Heru of Hor) was a local god worshipped in the delta region of the Nile. Eventually his cult spread throughout Egypt and was carried into Roman times.

The hawk was one of the first animals to be part of a cult in ancient Egypt. Heru means "he who is above" or "that which is above," making the hawk a personification of the sky and the sun. In predynastic times there were several hawk gods, the most important being at Hierakonpolis in Upper Egypt, where Horus took the form of a solar disk with wings. When

59

the kings of the North moved into Lower Egypt, uniting the two lands, Horus became known as the Uniter of the South and the North.

Horus was sometimes said to be the son of the goddess Hathor, whose name means "house of Horus," and each evening he would fly into the goddess's mouth to emerge reborn each morning. In the most famous myth associated with him, however, Horus is the son of the god Osiris and the goodess Isis and avenges his father's murder by defeating the demonic god Set in a series of battles, Osiris thus being identified with the dead king and Horus with the living king.

Sometimes the living king was said to embody within himself both Horus, the spirit of light, and Set, the spirit of darkness, reflecting the eternal strife that is always present in the universe. In his role as the defeater of Set, Horus is variously portrayed as a mounted warrior with the head of a hawk and as a hawk-headed man with a large pointed spear being driven into a foe. In one version of the myth, Horus's left eye, which signified the moon, was wounded in his battle with Set (giving rise to one explanation for the moon's various phases). The eye was healed by the god Thoth and representations of the restored eye were used as an amulet.

A manuscript, written in Thebes in the twelfth century B.C., contains the myth of "The Contest of Horus and Set for the Rule," sometimes called, "The Contending of Horus and Set." The work is written in a colloquial style and has much in common with the folktale. In the following version, which is based on various literal renderings of the text, a colloquial English is used.

After the murder of Osiris by his evil brother Set, the slain king went to the Underworld where he was crowned King of the Living and the Dead, but the land of Egypt was left without a king. So Horus, the son of Osiris and Isis, appeared before the assembly of the gods which was presided over by Ra, the sun god, to be recognized as the new king.

The first to speak in the court was Shu, god of the atmosphere and a son of Ra.

. "Horus should be crowned king since Osiris his father was king before him. That's only fair and just," Shu said.

"Yes," replied Thoth, the ibis-headed god, and secretary of the court. "Horus is the rightful heir to the throne of Egypt."

When Isis, Horus's mother, heard the verdict, she was very pleased.

"Bring the good news to my husband Osiris in the Underworld," she told the North Wind. "Tell him his son Horus will be crowned king."

So they took the royal crown and placed it on Horus's head.

"Wait," Ra cried out. "Who gave you authority to crown Horus?"

"It's too late. We have already crowned him," the gods responded.

Then Set, who was also present and

wished the crown for himself, became very angry.

"Horus and I can settle the matter between us. Let Horus step outside with me. If he defeats me, then make him Pharaoh. If I defeat him, then crown me king."

"No," cried Thoth. "That is not the way to settle a legal matter. We must follow what is just. How can we make Set the king when he is only the brother of Osiris, while Horus is the son of Osiris?"

Ra, however, was angry at the decision since he favored Set, not Horus.

"Well," said the god Onuris, "what are we to do? We can't stay here all night arguing over the matter."

"I have a solution," Ra said. "Let's call on the god Ba-neb-djet to decide the matter."

So the gods sent for Ba-neb-djet, who refused to decide the matter, saying, "I'm not qualified. Send a letter to the Great Goddess Neith and do whatever she says."

So Ra dictated a letter to Thoth. It read as follows:

Great and Divine Mother Neith: I am writing to ask you what should be done about the feud between Horus and Set for the kingship of Egypt. Everyone here is tired of the matter. Nobody, however, knows how to decide the issue. Will you give us your decision?

The answer came back quickly. It read as follows:

Horus should be made king since Osiris his father sat upon the throne before him. If he isn't made king I will destroy Egypt by letting the heavens fall upon it! Set, however, as compensation should have his possessions doubled and your two daughters given to him as his wives.

When Thoth read the letter before the assembled gods, they looked at one another and said, "The goddess is right."

"No," Ra cried out, turning to Horus. "You're not fit to be king. Why you're a weakling, a mere boy who still feeds at his mother's breasts."

This outburst angered the monster god Baba, who turned to Ra, saying, "How can anyone take you seriously? Why, no one even worships you anymore. Your temples are deserted and covered with dust."

When Ra heard this insult he fell down and started to cry. When the other gods saw this they became angry at Baba.

"Now look what you've done," they said. "Get out of here. You're making matters worse."

So Baba left and the other gods soon followed, leaving Ra sulking on the floor. When Hathor, his mother, heard her son was crying, she came to cheer him.

"Look," she said as she lifted her skirts and showed Ra her vulva. When Ra saw what his mother did he burst out laughing, got up, and reconvened the court. When the court reassembled, he said to Horus and Set, "Each of you speak your piece."

So Set spoke first.

"I am the great god Set. Each day I defeat the monster Apophis when he tries to destroy the boat of Ra as it crosses the heavens. No other god can do this. Therefore I should be made king."

The gods realized that if the sun were destroyed, they also would be destroyed. So they said, "Yes. Set is right. Make him king."

But Onuris and Thoth spoke up.

"How can you make Set king when he is only the brother of Osiris, while Horus is the rightful son of Osiris."

"How can we give the throne to a mere lad," answered Ba-neb-djet, "when a strong god like Set should have it."

"We will never settle this matter," the gods cried out in despair.

Horus then spoke to his mother Isis. "It's no good. They are trying to cheat me of my rightful place on the throne."

Isis then became so angry that she cursed all of them.

"Don't be angry!" the gods cried out. "We'll settle the matter and the rightful one will be made king."

When Set heard this he became furious at the gods.

"I'll kill each and every one of you," he cried out. "Get her out of the court."

So Ra said, "We will move the court to Central Island and continue our deliberations there. Tell Anty the Ferryman not to let any woman that looks like Isis across the river."

Then all the gods left the courtroom and crossed over to Central Island.

Isis, however, was determined to follow them. She came to Anty the Ferryman disguised as an old bent woman, wearing a gold ring.

"Will you ferry me across to Central Island, for I have some food for my little boy who has been taking care of some cattle there? He hasn't eaten for days and must be very hungry."

"They told me not to let any woman across," Anty replied.

"Didn't they say that you weren't to let Isis across?"

"What will you give me if I ferry you across?" he asked.

"I'll give you a loaf of bread."

"A loaf of bread," he laughed. "What kind of a payment is that?"

"Then I'll give you this gold ring."

Anty agreed to the bargain and took Isis across the river. When she reached the other side she could see the gods sitting at lunch in Ra's pavilion. Set was there and saw Isis coming. When Isis saw that Set had seen her, she uttered an incantation, and transformed herself into a beautiful young girl. When Set saw her, he immediately lusted after her. He left his meal and followed her.

"My beautiful young girl," Set said when he caught up with her. "Come and stay with me."

"My lord," she replied. "I am a widow of a herdsman. I bore him an only male child. After my husband's death my boy came to take care of the cattle, but a stranger came, telling my son, 'I'll beat you and take away your father's cattle.' I need someone to defend my son's rights."

"What! Shall the cattle be given to a stranger when the son is alive?" Set cried out.

Immediately Isis changed herself

into a kite bird and flew to the top of a tree.

"You have condemned yourself by what you have said," Isis cried out.

Then Set began to cry when he realized what happened. He went to Ra and told the whole story.

"You have convicted yourself," Ra told Set.

"Bring Anty the Ferryman here," Set said, "and punish him for allowing that woman to cross."

So they brought Anty and cut off his toes as punishment. Then the gods left Central Island and crossed over to the other side of the river. When they reached the other side, Ra said, "We still haven't settled the matter. If this goes on we will be here for eternity. We will place the crown upon Horus and proclaim him king and settle the matter."

When Set heard this he burst into anger at all the gods.

"Don't be angry with us," the gods said to Set. "The matter was decided by Ra, not us."

So they took the crown and placed it on Horus.

"It's not fair. I am the brother of Osiris and I should be king. Let Horus and me settle the matter between ourselves."

Ra then changed his mind and agreed with Set's proposal.

"Come," Set said to Horus. "Let's change ourselves into two hippopotamuses and plunge into the water. Whoever can stay longest under the water will be made king."

So the two gods transformed themselves into hippopotamuses and submerged themselves. When Isis saw this she said, "Set will kill my boy Horus."

To prevent this Isis brought some yarn and made a rope. Then she took a pound of copper, melted it, and made a harpoon. Attaching the harpoon to the rope she threw it into the water. The harpoon hit Horus by mistake.

"Mother, mother," he cried out. "The harpoon has hit me."

Then Isis cried out, saying to the harpoon, "Let loose from him." And the harpoon let loose from Horus.

Isis then threw the harpoon into the water again, and this time it struck Set.

"What are you doing to me, Isis?" Set cried out. "I am your brother. Do you wish to destroy your own blood?"

Isis then felt sorry for Set and called out to the harpoon, "Let loose of him." And the harpoon let loose of Set.

When Horus saw that his mother had saved the life of his evil uncle, he took an axe and chopped off her head. He then took her head and went to hide on a mountain. Isis, however, changed her headless body into a statue of flint with no head.

When Isis appeared before the gods, Ra said, "Who is this woman who has come here without a head?"

"It is Isis," said Thoth. "Her son Horus has decapitated her."

"He must be punished for such a crime," Ra said.

So the gods left in search of Horus. Meanwhile Set found Horus asleep under a tree. He seized him, plucked out his eyes, and buried them on the mountain, where they illuminated the earth. Horus's eyeballs became like the bulbs which grow into the lotus.

Set returned to Ra and lied, saying, "I could not find Horus."

Later Hathor found Horus weeping in the desert. She captured a gazelle and milked it.

"Open your eyes so I can put milk in them," she said to Horus.

Then Horus opened his eyes and she put the milk into them.

"Now open your eyes again," she said. Horus opened his eyes and his sight was restored.

When Hathor and Horus returned to court, she told Ra all that had happened.

"Please, let's not quarrel any more," Ra said to Horus and Set. "Let's eat and drink and have some peace."

Then Set turned to Horus. "Come to my house and we'll have a party."

So Horus accepted and left with Set. When it was time to go to sleep the two went to bed together. During the night Set had an erection and thrust his penis between Horus's legs in an attempt to rape him. But Horus put his hands between his thighs, catching Set's semen.

Next morning Horus went to his mother Isis and told her what Set had done.

"See what Set has done," he said, opening his hands and showing Set's semen.

Isis let out a shriek. With a copper knife she immediately cut off Horus's hands, throwing them into the marsh

water. Then she provided Horus with new hands, equally as good.

Then Isis fetched some fragrant ointment and applied it to Horus's penis, causing it to become stiff. She then told Horus to insert his penis into a pot and let his semen flow into the soil of the pot.

The next morning Isis carried the pot with Horus's semen in it to the garden of Set. She asked the gardener, "What kind of vegetable does Set eat?"

"He doesn't eat any vegetable but lettuce," said the gardener, "since it makes him potent."

So Isis took the semen of Horus and placed it on the lettuce. Later Set came to have his daily ration of lettuce, ate some and immediately he became pregnant from Horus's semen.

Later when Set met Horus he said, "We still haven't settled the matter of who will be king. Let's return to court and have it out."

Horus agreed. The two appeared again before the gods.

"Speak your peace," the gods said.

"I am king," said Set, "since last night I sodomized Horus."

Then all the gods looked at Horus with disgust and spit in his face.

Horus, however, laughed at all of them.

"Set is a liar. Let Set's semen be called and let's see where it comes from. Then call my semen and see where it comes from."

So Thoth placed his hands upon Horus's arms and said, "Come out semen of Set."

But Set's semen did not answer from

Horus's body, but from the marsh where Isis had thrown Horus's semen-covered hands.

Then Thoth placed his arm on Set. "Come out, semen of Horus," he said. "Where shall I come out from?" the semen asked.

"Come out of his ear," replied Thoth.

"But I am divine fluid."

"Then come from the top of his head," Thoth answered.

Suddenly the semen came up from Set's head in the form of a golden disk. Set tried to seize the golden disk but Thoth took it away and placed it on his own head.

Then all the gods said, "Horus is right. Set is wrong."

But still Set would not accept the verdict.

"It's not settled yet," he cried out. "We will have a boat race. Whoever wins the race will be made king."

So Horus built a ship of cedar, plastered over with gypsum, and placed it in the water. Set, seeing Horus's boat, thought it was made of stone. So he went to the mountains and cut off a rocky peak and made a stone boat. When he placed it in the water it sank. Set then transformed himself into a hippopotamus and caused Horus's boat to sink. But Horus took a harpoon and aimed it at Set.

"Don't throw it at him," the gods cried out. So Horus didn't and went downstream to Sais. He spoke to the goddess Neith.

"Let the judgment be made between Set and me."

In the meantime the gods had gathered again. Shu said to Ra, "The crown belongs to Horus."

Thoth said, "Let's send a letter to Osiris and let him decide the matter between his son and his brother."

So a letter was sent to Osiris asking what should be done. Osiris responded immediately: "Why should my son be defrauded? I make you all strong by providing you with barley and wheat."

When Osiris's answer arrived Ra was sitting in his palace with the rest of the gods. The letter was read aloud. Ra, angry at what Osiris had written wrote back: "What if you had never come into being? What if you had never been born? Do you think the barley and wheat would not exist?"

Osiris replied: "Yes. You rule the gods, but you let justice slide down to the underworld! Remember this: The land is mine, filled with fierce spirits whom I control. No god or goddess has more power than I do. I have ultimate authority—the stars, the gods, and all life are eventually destined to come to my land—the land of the West."

When Osiris's answer reached the gods it was quickly read aloud to all by Thoth.

"It's all true what Osiris says," they said.

Yet, Set again challenged Horus to one more battle. But Horus defeated Set who was brought in chains before the gods. Isis presented Set to the gathered assembly.

Ra looked at Set.

"Why didn't you follow the verdict of the gods instead of having to do battle again?"

Horus

"I am defeated," Set replied. "Let Horus be called and let him be made king."

So Horus was called and placed on the throne of his father Osiris.

"You are the good king of Egypt, the beloved land," they all shouted.

Isis cried out, "You are the beautiful king. You illumine the whole earth with your splendor."

"What are we to do with Set?" Ptah asked.

"Let me adopt him as my son," said Ra. "His voice will thunder in the sky and he shall be feared by all."

Then all the gods and goddessess

were pleased and there was joy in the land for Horus was made king.

Various other forms of Horus are Harpokrates, Harsiesis, Harmachis, Haroeris, and Horus-Behdety.

HORUS-AAH   A composite god made up of Horus and the moon god Aah.

HORUS-BEHDETY   A form of the god Horus, meaning "He of Behdet," a district of ancient Edfu, called by the Greeks Appollinolis Magna. They equated Horus-Behdety with their god Apollo.

The myth surrounding this form of Horus was written on the temple of Edfu. After having aided the king Ra-Harakhte (a form of the god Ra and Horus combined) Horus-Behdety flew up to heaven in the form of a winged disk, being called "Great God, Lord of Heaven." From heaven he was able to see the enemies of his father. He chased them in the form of a winged disk and slaughtered them. After this victory the god Thoth declared Horus, the son of Ra, the sun god, and declared that his name should be Horus-Behdety, that is, Horus of Edfu. Then Horus suggested to Ra that he come to see the dead enemies of his father.

Ra, escorted by Hathor and the goddess Astarte, "mistress of horses," went to see the dead. When Ra saw what Horus had done he said, "This is a very pleasant life," and named a temple in Horus's honor, called

"Pleasant Life." Then Thoth said, "This was the spearing of my foes," and they called the city Edfu Teb from that day. Then he said to Horus, "Thou art a great protector," and the boat of Horus was then called "Great Protector."

Then Ra and Horus went into Ra's boat. Horus slew the enemies of Ra, such as crocodiles, along the way. Then Horus took the form of a winged disk and placed himself in the bow of the boat of Ra. The enemies of Ra tried again to defeat the god, but Horus, aided by his "blacksmiths," slaughtered most of them, while others fled at Tchetemet, or "slaughter."

A third battle ensued and again Horus was the victor. Those who remained moved on, but Horus followed them, capturing 142 whom he bound in chains, as well as a "male hippopotamus." He then slew the rest and gave their entrails to his companions to eat. As proof of his victory he stood upon the hippopotamus, and was

Horus-Behdety

called Her-pest, or "He who is on the back."

The enemy, however, was still not undone. Another battle ensued. In this one Horus captured 381 rebels whom he slew in the bow of Ra's boat, giving one to each of his companions.

When the evil god Set saw that his cohorts were being destroyed he entered the battle. Horus captured Set and threw a lance into him. Then he cut off his head, as well as the heads of Set's companions.

Horus dragged the body of Set throughout the land, but Set turned himself into a snake and hid in a hole.

Horus then turned himself into a pole on the top of which was a hawk's head and stopped up the hole. Some of the followers of Set were still free, so Horus went again in pursuit of them. He slew 106, while others fled to the sea. Horus then changed himself into a lion, with a man's head surmounted by the triple crown. He brought back 142, and slew them, tearing out their tongues.

When this was done Ra told Horus that he wished to travel farther upon the sea to kill the remainder of his foes who had turned into crocodiles and hippopotamuses. Horus, however, told Ra it was impossible to sail farther on the sea since one-third of the enemy was in the water. Then Thoth recited certain magical spells to protect the boat of Ra which set sail. Finally, Horus and his companions destroyed the remaining enemies on land. When this was done Horus turned himself into the winged sun disk with uraei, two serpents who might consume with fire any rebels who remained. The sun disk with snakes was called Uruatchti, and portrayed the goddesses Nekhebet and Uatchit.

In Egyptian art Horus-Behdety is often portrayed as a hawk-headed man carrying in his hands some weapons, indicating his victory over Set.

HORUS, FOUR SONS OF The children of Horus and Isis who guarded the organs of the dead. The four sons were Mesthi, or Imsety, who guarded the liver and was portrayed with a human head; Hapi, who guarded the lungs and was portrayed as jackal- or dog-headed; Tuamutef, or Duamutef, who guarded the stomach and was portrayed as jackal-headed; and Qebh-sennuf, or Qebsnuf, who guarded the intestines and was portrayed as hawk-headed. The organs of the dead were placed in special jars, called Canopic jars, each jar having a head on it in the shape of one of the four sons.

HORUS GODS Name given to the various gods of ancient Egypt who bear the name Horus. Many of the gods were originally separate deities but in time, the various Horus Gods were blended into Horus and the distinctions blurred.

HORUS, THE HEBENUITE A form of the god Horus in which he is portrayed as a hawk-headed man on the back of an antelope, symbolizing his victory over the evil god Set. Hebenuite was the metropolis of the sixteenth nome of Upper Egypt.

HORUS KHENTY EN MAATYU A form of the god Horus, which may mean "Horus at the head of those who see not." It was popularly called "Blind Horus." This form appeared when the evil god Set blinded him. The shrew-mouse, a symbol of darkness, was identified with this form of Horus.

HORUS KHENTY KHAT A form of the god Horus in which he is portrayed with the head of a crocodile on a human body. He wears upon his head the horns of Khnemu and the Atef crown. The name may mean, "Horus at the head of the belly."

HORUS NETCHER NEDJE ITEF A form of the god Horus meaning "Horus the god, he who avenges his father." The name refers to Horus's role in defeating the murderer of his father Osiris, the evil god Set.

HORUS THE ELDER see Haroeris.

HORUS THE GREAT see Haroeris.

HU Egyptian god of the sense of taste. He was born from the drops of blood that flowed from Ra when he mutilated himself. Hu was not only the personification of the sense of taste in gods and men, but was also the personification of the divine food on which gods and men fed.

In the *Book of the Dead* the deceased says, "I have taken possession of Hu in my city, for I found him therein" and "Hu is in my mouth." In some passages, however, it is difficult to decide whether Hu refers to the god Hu or to the divine food *hu*. In Egyptian art Hu is portrayed as a man with the sign of his name above his head.

HUH AND HAUHET Two primeval deities, male and female, who, according to the priesthood of Hermopolis, made up part of the Ogdoad, the eight gods who created the world. Huh was portrayed as frog-headed and Hauhet as serpent-headed.

HUTCHAIUI God of the west wind portrayed as a ram-headed man with four wings, or as a ram-headed beetle.

HYKSOS Generic term for a group of peoples from the Syrian-Palestine area who ruled over the Delta part of Egypt in the Fifteenth and Sixteenth Dynasties. Their chief god was Set. Their name is derived from the hieroglyphs for "rulers of the desert uplands," though in ancient times it was misinterpreted as meaning "shepherd kings." Some scholars maintain that the biblical Joseph and his brothers came to Egypt during the time of the Hyksos.

HYMNS AND PRAYERS Numerous hymns and prayers have come down to us from ancient Egypt. Perhaps the most famous is the Hymn to Aten, which portrays a loving god for all humankind. Other hymns, however, are lacking in any personal feeling, often merely listing the various titles of the god and the cities in which he is worshipped. Thus, it is fruitless to look for the richness and depth that is found in the Old Testament Book of Psalms. Aside from the many for the public, various personal hymns and prayers have also been preserved. They are often, however, little more than magical incantations.

I

IB see Ab.

IBIS This bird was associated with the moon god Thoth who was also the scribe of the gods. The animal was regarded by the Egyptians as the enemy of snakes, especially the "winged serpents" which they believed to exist. Herodotus in his *History* (Book 2) says that he saw bodies of winged serpents in a gorge. "The story goes," he writes, "that with the spring, the winged snakes come flying from Arabia toward Egypt, but are met in this gorge by the birds called ibises, who forbid their entrance and destroy them."

IBIS-HEADED GOD see Thoth.

ICHNEUMON The mongoose was honored by the ancient Egyptians since it was believed to be immune from snake bites and destroyed the eggs of crocodiles; it was also associated with the rising sun. If, according to one ancient writer, Diodorus, the ichneumon did not eat the crocodile's eggs the land of Egypt would have been overrun by them. Bronze figures of ichneumon have been found in several tombs.

IKHNATEN see Akhenaten.

ILLNESS see Medicine.

IMAGES Egyptians believed that statues were substitutes for the person they represented and were erected in tombs and temples. Thus, if the mummy was destroyed, the image acted as a replacement for the Ka of the dead person. When statues were erected in temples it was believed that the person continued to live in the image.

IMHOTEP Deified Egyptian sage who lived at the court of King Zoser. Imhotep was celebrated in his own lifetime, and after his death was venerated until it was said that he was the son of the god Ptah. He replaced Nefertem in the triad of gods worshipped at Memphis and eventually his worship eclipsed even that of his divine father, Ptah. Besides his fame as a sage, he was also known as a master builder, having built the Step Pyramid for King Zoser I. In Egyptian art Imhotep is usually portrayed as a priest with shaved head reading a scroll while seated. The Greeks knew him as Imuthes, or Imouthes, or "he who comes in peace."

IMIUT An early god whose name means "He who is in his wrappings." The title refers to the fetish of the god, consisting of a vessel or vase supporting an upright pole to which a headless inflated animal skin was attached by the tail, tipped with a papyrus flower. The blood of the animal is often shown pouring into the vessel. The pole upon which it hung represented the lotus stem and bud. The fetish of Imiut was later associated with Anubis and Osiris, both gods of the dead.

Imiut

IMOUTHES AND IMUTHES see Imhotep.

IMSETY see Mesthi.

IMY-HEMEF Gigantic serpent, about fifty feet long, who lived on the top of Bakhau, the Mountain of the Sunrise. His name means "Dweller in his flame."

INADJET see Buto.

INCENSE The use of incense formed an important part of cultic worship among the Egyptians. Each substance used in the composition of incense was supposed to possess magical properties, and the smell produced by burning them together was thought to be favored by the gods. The smoke was believed to form a material vehicle on which the words of the prayers recited by the worshipper would rise to heaven. When they reached the god or goddess, the odor which accompanied the words would cause the deity to grant the supplicant's petition.

INFANT HORUS, THE see Harpokrates.

IPHTIMIS Name given by the Greeks to the Egyptian god Nefertem, a sun god of Memphis, also god of perfumes.

ISIS Goddess, sister-wife of Osiris and mother of Horus. Her name is the Greek form of the Egyptian Ast, or Eset.

Isis was the great and beneficent goddess and mother. Her influence and love pervaded heaven, earth, and the abode of the dead. She was the personification of the female creative power that conceived and brought forth every living creature and thing. She used her power not only in creating new things, but in restoring what was dead. She was also the noblest example of a faithful and loving wife and mother, and it was in that role that she was most highly honored by the Egyptians.

In numerous passages in the Pyramid Texts, it is stated that Osiris, Isis, Set, and Nephthys were deified members of a family of human beings. According to Plutarch, when Osiris was killed by his evil brother Set, who threw his coffin into the river, Isis found the box and hid it, but Set discovered the hiding place, cut up Osiris's body and scattered the pieces throughout Egypt. Isis recovered the dismembered parts, and with the help of the god Thoth restored her brother-husband and had intercourse with him, conceiving a child, who was called Horus.

In the *Book of the Dead*, there are many allusions to Isis's loving care of Osiris, but little is said of her devotion to her son Horus, whom she reared to become the avenger of his father's murder. The Metternich Stele (found in Alexandria in 1828 and given to Prince Metternich by Mohammed Ali) reports that the goddess in her wanderings and sorrows cried out, "I, even I, am Isis, and I came forth from the

house wherein my brother Set has placed me." Set was not satisfied by murdering his brother Osiris; he took further vengeance by shutting Isis up in a prison. While Isis was confined, she was visited by Thoth, the prince of both heavenly and earthly law, who offered advice that would protect her and her unborn son. After Thoth had helped her to escape, she later exclaimed, "I came forth from the house at eventide, and there also came forth with me my seven scorpions, who were to accompany me, and to be my helpers. Two scorpions, Tefen and Befen, were behind me, two scorpions, Mestet and Mestetef, were by my side, and three scorpions, Petet, Thetet and Maatet, showed me the way."

The seven scorpion goddesses led Isis to a village near the Papyrus Swamps, where a rich woman, from whom she sought shelter closed the door in her face (this story is similar to the Christian legend of Joseph and Mary who were refused shelter). Enraged at the treatment Isis had received, one of the scorpion goddesses, Tefen, stole into the woman's house, stung her child to death, and set the house afire. Isis took pity on the woman's grief and restored her child to life, and a flood of rain extinguished the fire. A peasant woman then invited Isis to her house and the goddess stayed there, while the woman who had rejected her suffered agonies of remorse.

A short time later Isis brought forth her child Horus on a bed of papyrus plants in the swamps. She hid the boy carefully, fearing that he might be stung by a venomous reptile. One day she set out to obtain provisions and other necessities for her son in the city of Am. When she returned, she found him lying dead, foam on his lips, the ground around him soaked with tears from his eyes and realized that he had been killed by Set, in the form of a scorpion. Isis's cries brought out all the neighbors, but no one could help her. Finally, on the advice of Nephthys, her sister, she appealed to the sun god Ra. The sun stood still in the heavens and Thoth (a form of Ra in the legend) descended to earth to comfort her and taught her a spell to restore Horus to life.

Isis uttered the magic words, and the poison flowed from her son's body, and as air entered his lungs, his sense and feeling returned, and the boy was restored to life. Thoth ascended to the heavens and the sun resumed his course amid great rejoicing.

When Horus grew up he fought against Set in a battle that lasted three days and three nights. Horus had gained the advantage but Isis, who was also Set's sister, took pity on her brother and uttered a spell that caused his fetters to fall away, and allowed him to escape. Horus was filled with anger at his mother, and revenged himself by cutting off her head. However, Thoth intervened and transformed the decapitated head of Isis into the head of a cow, which he attached to her neck.

From a number of passages in various Egyptian texts, it is evident that Isis was thought to possess great skill in magic. One of her great feats was recorded in the myth of Ra. Since most mythologies believe that to possess the true name of a god was to have power over that god, many deities had more than one name; that is, one by which they were generally known and another, which might be called the real name, that was kept secret lest it come into the hands of an enemy and be used against them. Isis once tried to make Ra reveal to her his greatest and most secret name.

"Cannot I by means of the sacred name of God make myself mistress of the earth and become a goddess of like rank and power to Ra in heaven and upon earth?" she asked herself. Using her magical skill, she made a venomous reptile out of dust mixed with Ra's spittle, and by uttering certain words of power over the reptile made it sting Ra as he passed through the heavens. The sun god, who was at the point of death, was forced to reveal his hidden name. Satisfied at last, Isis recited an incantation to drain the poison from Ra's limbs, and the god recovered.

In the *Hymn to Osiris* Isis's use of magic words helps restore Osiris to life, and in the Theban Recension of the *Book of the Dead* one entire chapter is devoted to the bestowing upon the deceased some of the magical powers of the goddess.

Isis was worshipped in shrines throughout Egypt, and was addressed by many different titles, such as "the divine one," "the greatest of all the gods and goddesses," "the queen of all gods," "the female Ra," "the female Horus," "the lady of the new year," "the maker of sunrise," "the lady of heaven" and "the light-giver of heaven." From various classical writers we learn that her worship even spread beyond Egypt—to western Europe, where she was identified with Persephone, Tethys, and Athene, as her husband Osiris was identified with Hades, Dionysus, and other foreign gods.

The chief temple of Isis in Rome stood in the Campus Marinus, where the goddess was called Isis Campensis. In *The Golden Ass* (Book 11) Apuleius describes a festival of Isis that was held in Rome in the latter half of the second century A.D. The writer refers to the goddess as *regina coeli*, "queen of heaven" (a title later used for the Virgin Mary) and identifies her with Ceres, Venus, and Persephone. For the Greeks, the holiest of all the sanctuaries to Isis was at Tithorea. Pausanias in his *Description of Greece* (Chapter 32) writes that a festival in her honor was held there twice a year, once in spring and once in autumn.

The associations of Isis continue—to the Syrians, who identified her with many local Syrian goddesses and the early Christians who borrowed some of her attributes to bestow upon the Virgin Mary. Several incidents of the wanderings of Mary with the Christ Child in Egypt as recorded in the Apocryphal Gospels echo the events from the life of Isis described in the texts found on the Metternich Stele.

In Egyptian art Isis is usually portrayed as a woman wearing the vulture headdress, and holding a papyrus scepter in one hand and the ankh, symbol of life in the other. Her symbol is the Thet, the knot or buckle of Isis, which is a sign of life and blood. Her crown is composed of a pair of horns with a solar disk between them, sometimes surmounted by a throne, called *set*, (the goddess's name is *Aset* in Egyptian). Isis is also shown wearing the double crowns of the south and the north, with the feather of Maat attached at the back; in another variation, her headdress consists of the horns and the solar disk, with two plumes. The horns are usually of the cow-goddess Hathor, although less frequently they are ram's horns under the double crown to associate Isis with her counterpart Osiris, who was represented by the ram of Mendes. When Isis is portrayed as a woman and not as a goddess, she wears an ordinary woman's headdress, but even then a uraeus is drawn in over her forehead to indicate her divinity. Sometimes the goddess is shown suckling Horus (much as the Virgin Mary is often portrayed with the Christ Child).

The symbol of Isis in the heavens was the star Sept, which was chosen because its appearance marked not only the beginning of the new year, but also the advance of the inundation of the Nile. As the light giver of this season of the year she was called Khut; as the mighty earth goddess her name was Usert; as the great goddess of Tuat, the underworld, she was Thenenet; as the power that shot forth

Isis

the bodies of the blessed dead to live in the kingdom of Osiris she was Ament, or "hidden" goddess.

ISIS-SOTHIS   see Satis.

ISRAEL The relations between Egypt and Israel are an important part of the Old Testament, where Egypt is mentioned by name 680 times. The name Israel, however, appears only once in an ancient Egyptian work which commemorates a victory over Israel. It reads: "Israel is devastated, her seed no longer exists."

ITY   God of music, son of the Bull of Ra and the goddess Hathor. In some texts, Ity is called "the bull of confusion." He was portrayed as a man with the double crown of Upper and Lower Egypt and the sidelock of youth.

IUSAASET AND NEBT-HETEP see Iusas and Nebhet Hotep.

IUSAS AND NEBHET HOTEP Wives of the god Tem, who were given various roles. Iusas sometimes appeared as the sole parent of the first divine couple Shu and Tefnut. Other times, Iusas and Nebhet Hotep are merely female aspects of Tem, who is bisexual in some accounts.

Iusas was depicted as a woman holding a scepter in her right hand and the ankh, symbol of life, in her left. She wore a vulture headdress surmounted

the Nile flood she was Satis; as the embracer of the land and the producer of fertility by her waters she was Anquet; as the producer and giver of life she was Ankhat; as the goddess of cultivated land and fields she was Kekhet; as the goddess of the harvest she was Renenet; as the goddess of the food that was offered to the gods she was Tcheft; and as the great lady of the underworld who assisted in restoring by a uraeus, and a disk between a pair of horns. Nebhet Hotep appears to have been a double of Iusas, since in some accounts the name Iusas-Nebhet Hotep is translated as "mistress of the gods."

Variant spellings are Iusaaset and Nebt-Hetep.

J

JACKAL From earliest times the Egyptians identified the jackal with the dead and the tombs of the dead, where they had seen the animal roam. The principal jackal gods were Anubis and Wepwawet. In many of the tales of the ancient writers the jackal was confused with the dog.

JUPITER-AMEN Form of Amen, combined with the title of the Roman sky god, Jupiter. Alexander the Great visited the god's temple in the Siwa Oasis in B.C. 332. The oracle called Alexander, "son of Amen." Shortly afterwards Alexander was crowned King of Egypt.

JUSTICE, GODDESS OF see Maat.

JUVENAL (c. A.D. 55–140) Roman satirist, who spent some time in Egypt. Juvenal hated all that was not Roman, and considered the Egyptian world view barbaric. In his fifteenth satire, sometimes titled *On the Atrocities of Egypt*, he ridicules Egyptian beliefs, especially their animal cults and he accuses the Egyptians of cannibalism. The great English poet, John Dryden translated five of Juvenal's satires, and Dr. Johnson imitated two of the most famous in his poems "London" and "Vanity of Human Wishes."

K

KA   The double or the abstract personality of a man or woman. The Ka could separate itself from or unite itself to the body at will and could move freely from place to place. A dead man's Ka had to be preserved if his body was to become everlasting. Funeral offerings, such as meats, cakes, wines, and unguents, were made to the Ka, and when food was not available, offerings were painted on the walls, accompanied by the recitation of specific prayers. The tombs of the early Egyptian had special chambers in which the Ka was worshipped and received offerings, and the priesthood included a group called "priests of Ka," who performed services in honor of the Ka. According to one version of the creation myth that appears in the Pyramid Texts, after the sun god spit out the gods Shu and Tefnut, he put his arms about them so that his "Ka might be in them." The Ka is closely associated with the Ba, the soul.

KA-HEMHEM   A lion god who appears in the sixth section, or hour, of Tuat, the underworld.

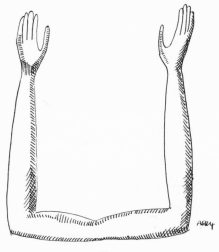

Ka

KAI   One of the four earthly forms of Osiris found in the sixth section, or hour, of Tuat, the underworld.

KARNAK   see Thebes.

KEB   see Geb.

KEFI   A guardian of the tenth section of Tuat, the underworld, as the sun god Ra passes in his boat.

KEKHET   A title of Isis as the goddess of cultivated land and fields.

KEMET Name given to ancient Egypt, meaning the "black land," because of the richness of the soil. A variant spelling is Qemet.

KENKEN-WER Title meaning "great cackler" and applied to the earth god Geb because it was said he laid the egg from which the world sprang.

KHA-A A god who carries a bow in the tenth section, or hour, of Tuat, the underworld. He helps the sun god Ra in his journey toward the east, and defends him by slaying his enemies.

KHAIBIT The shadow of a man. Like the Ka and Ba, the Khaibit was believed to be able to separate itself from the physical body and move about freely. In the *Book of the Dead* the Khaibit and the Ba are closely associated in the phrase, "May I look upon my soul [Ba] and my shadow [Khaibit]."

KHAT The whole physical body of man. The word, according to some scholars, conveys a concept of the body as an entity that is liable to decay. In the *Book of the Dead* the khat is mentioned in reference to the mummified body of the deceased; the preservation of the body was extremely important. On burial day prayers and ceremonies were offered so that the khat might have the power to change into the sahu, or spiritual body, and in this form could ascend to heaven to live with the gods.

KHENSU An early moon god of healing and regeneration. His name means "navigator" or "he who crosses the sky in a boat," and he was identified as a form of the moon god Thoth.

Khensu was an aid to women and cattle in fertility and conception, but he was best known as a god of healing, called Khensu Nefer-hetep, who possessed absolute power over the evil spirits that infested the earth, sea, and sky.

One myth tells of the king of Thebes praying to a statue of Khensu Nefer-hetep on behalf of the daughter of the prince of Bekhten. The god listened to the king's plea, nodded his head (the statue of the god was provided with a movable head which the priests manipulated), and promised to imbue his divine power in the statue which was to be sent to the city of the sick princess. The statue arrived in Bekhten and through its magical powers the princess was exorcised of the demon. The demon then spoke to Khensu, acknowledging the god's superior power, and spent a happy day with the god and the prince of Bekhten. At night, the demon returned to his own dwelling place, and Khensu left for his home in Thebes in the form of a hawk.

In Egyptian art Khensu is usually portrayed with the body of a man and the head of either a hawk or a man; he is standing or seated on a throne. His headdress is the lunar disk in a crescent, or the solar disk with a uraeus, or the solar disk with plumes and a uraeus. Sometimes he holds the ankh, emblem of life.

Variants of his name are Khonsu, Chons, Chunsu, and Khons.

KHENSU-HUNNU see Khensu-pakhart.

KHENSU-NEFER-HETEP The god Khensu in his form as protector against evil spirits, god of love, and god of fertility. He was portrayed with the double crown of Upper and Lower Egypt, the ankh, sign of life, and the scepter of royalty.

KHENSU-PA-KHART A form of the god Khensu as "Khensu the Babe," sometimes called, Khensu-Hunnu, "Khensu, the Child."

KHENSU-RA A form of the god Khensu combined with the sun god Ra, portrayed wearing a solar disk on his head and holding a stylus in his right hand.

KHEPERA The god who represented the rising or morning sun and was closely associated with the scarab, the sacred beetle of ancient Egypt.

Khepera was among the original creation gods and like the rising sun with which he is identified, he was said to be self-created, born of his own substance. According to one myth he copulated with his own shadow and

from his semen came Shu, the air, and Tefnut, moisture; and from the union of Shu and Tefnut came Seb, the earth, and Nut, the sky; and they in turn bore the great gods Osiris, Isis, Set, and Nephthys. These nine deities formed a group worshipped in a cosmological system known as the Ennead or Company of Gods. In another creation myth, the sun god Ra was said to have created himself in primeval time in the form of the god Khepera.

Khepera was portrayed in Egyptian art as a beetle-headed man or as a man whose head was surmounted by a beetle, or sometimes simply as a beetle. The worship of the beetle dates back into the early days of Egypt, and the identification of Ra with the beetle god, a later modification, is an example of the grafting of new religious beliefs onto old ones.

The beetle was usually identified as the scarab and was held as a symbol of resurrection and fertility. There are various explanations of its association with Khepera. Since the beetle became visible in great numbers on the surface of the mud of the Nile, the beetle was thought to have created itself from its own matter, as the sun seemed to create itself each morning. Other sources trace the association to the large balls, consisting of beetle eggs in a mass of dung, which the beetle industriously rolled about with its hind legs for long distances before burying in a hole. The ball of the beetle was identified with the ball of the sun that appeared to roll daily across the sky

Khepera

Roman soldiers wore the likeness of the beetle on a ring.

Variant spellings of the god's name are Kheperi, Khepri, Kheprer, and Chepera.

KHEPRESH   see Crowns.

KHEPRI   AND   KHEPRER   see Khepera.

KHERT NETER   A title for Tuat, the underworld, meaning "divine subterranean place." Sometimes the name is given as Neter-khertet.

KHESFU   A god who carries a javelin in the tenth section, or hour, of Tuat, the underworld. He helps the sun god Ra slay his enemies as Ra journeys toward the east.

KHET   "Steps" amulet that symbolized the support on which the god Shu stood when he separated the earth goddess Nut from the sexual embrace of the earth god Geb. Shu used the steps because he was not tall enough to reach Nut whose outstretched arms and legs represented the arch of heaven. The "double-steps" amulet, which resembled the Step-Pyramid of Sakkara in form, was identified with the steps on which the god Khnemu stood when acting as creator god.

and was the source of life.

Since beetles were believed to be the incarnation of Khepera, beetle amulets were worn to attract the power of the god and secure his protection. In Egyptian funerary practice beetles or beetle amulets, often inscribed with a text from the *Book of the Dead*, were buried with the mummies to help insure their resurrection. In Roman times when going to battle

KHETI   A monster serpent in the eighth section of Tuat, the underworld, who belches forth fire used to punish those who have gone against the rites connected with Osiris. On his back stand seven gods.

KHMUN see Khnemu.

KHNEMIU Four divine beings wearing red crowns, found in the eleventh section of Tuat, the underworld.

KHNEMU Ram-headed god of creation and fertility, worshipped on the isle of Elephantine in the Nile River.

Although the Egyptian views of Khnemu changed, ancient texts show that he maintained an exalted position among the gods. His image continued to appear on Gnostic gems and papyri for some two or three centuries after the birth of Christ.

Khnemu's name literally means "moulder." He was said to have moulded on his potter's wheel the great cosmic egg that contained the sun. He was known further as the potter who fashioned man and the gods and in certain texts he was said to preside over children in their mother's womb and infuse them with health.

Originally a local water god of the Cataract region, and perhaps a personification of the Nile, Khnemu was later regarded as the Nile god of all Egypt. He united within himself the souls of the great gods Ra, Shu, Geb, and Osiris, and was thus portrayed with four rams' heads upon a human body, which, according to some sources, represented fire, air, earth, and water.

One of the myths of Khnemu tells of a seven-year drought that came upon Egypt in the reign of Tcheser, a king of the Third Dynasty. Legend has it that the drought was a punishment for neglecting the god. When the country had nearly been destroyed by famine, the king went to the temple of Khnemu to make offerings. Khnemu appeared, and, claiming he was the Nile, promised to inundate the land, provided the proper worship was restored to him. The king readily agreed, and Khnemu made the waters of the Nile flow from his two caverns, and prosperity returned to the land.

Khnemu was usually represented as

Khnemu

85

a ram-headed man, with long wavy horns adorned with plumes, a disk and a uraeus. Because of his importance, he was worshipped in many forms throughout Egypt.

A variant spelling of his name is Khnum. To the Greeks he was known as Khnoumis.

KHNEMU KHENTI NETCHEM-TCHEM ANKHET A form of the god Khnemu, meaning "Khnemu, Lord of the House of Sweet Life."

KHNEMU KHENTI PER-ANKH A form of the god Khnemu, meaning "Khnemu, Governor of the House of Life."

KHNEMU KHENTI-TAUI A form of the god Khnemu, meaning "Khnemu, Governor of the Two Lands," that is, Upper and Lower Egypt.

KHNEMU NEB A form of the god Khnemu, meaning, "Khnemu, Lord."

KHNEMU NEB-TA-ANKHTET A form of the god Khnemu, meaning "Khnemu, Lord of the Land of Life."

KHNEMU NEHEP A form of the god Khnemu meaning "Khnemu the Creator."

KHNOUMIS see Khnemu.

KHONS see Khensu.

KHORP HEMTIU Title of the chief priest of the temple of Ptah, meaning "Chief of the Artificers."

KHUT A name for the goddess Isis as light giver.

KITAB AL-MAYYIT AND KITAB AL MAYYITUM see *Book of the Dead.*

KNOT OF ISIS see Thet.

KUK AND KAUKET Two primeval deities, male and female, who, according to the priesthood of Hermopolis, made up part of the Ogdoad, the eight gods who created the world. Kuk was portrayed as frog-headed and Kauket as serpent-headed.

L

LATONA   Mother of the Greek god Apollo who was equated with the Egyptian goddess Buto, the protector of Lower Egypt.

LAW, GODDESS OF   see Maat.

LETTERS TO THE DEAD   Title given to letters, usually written on pottery bowls, which were placed in tombs with food offerings. The letters were thought to convey messages from the living to the dead, since the Egyptians didn't fully accept death as an end to the communications and experiences of the living.

LETTUCE   The ancient Egyptians believed that lettuce was an aphrodisiac. It was fed to the sacred white bulls of Min, the god who was the bestower of sexual powers, and to Set, who was said to grow lettuce in his garden.

LIBRARY, GODDESS OF   see Sefkhet-Aabut.

LION   The cult of the lion, associated with the sun gods Ra and Horus, is one of the oldest and most important in

Egypt. Its chief center of worship was at Leontopolis in the Northern Delta; sacred lions were possibly kept here and in various centers of worship. One of the oldest gods in Egyptian mythology is Aker, a lion god who was supposed to guard the gate of the dawn through which the sun god passed each morning.

In the *Book of the Dead* the Akeru gods are portrayed as two lions seated back to back, supporting between them the horizon with the sun's disk upon it. In later religious writings they are called Sef and Tuau, that is, "Yesterday" and "Today." Since the Egyptians believed that the gates of morning and evening were guarded by lion gods, they placed statues of lions at the doors of palaces and tombs to guard both the living and the dead.

LITERATURE, GODDESS OF   see Sefkhet-Aabut.

LOTUS   The lotus, depicted in its various forms, had great significance for the Egyptians. It was the symbol of Upper Egypt, as well as a symbol of rebirth, and was sacred to Nefertum, the Lord of Perfumes. Gods, such as

Lotus

Horus, are often shown seated on a lotus, because of the myth that "a great lotus came out of the primordial waters" at creation.

LOVE, GOD OF see Khensu-Nefer-hetep.

LOWER EGYPT The northern area of Egypt, often called the Red Land or the North, which centers around the Delta. This region was once a separate state, ruled from the ancient capital of Buto. The protective god of Lower Egypt was Horus and the protective goddess Buto, the snake or cobra goddess. The crown was the red crown, and the plant the papyrus.

LUCK, GOD OF see Shai.

LUST, GODDESS OF see Anukis.

LUXOR see Thebes.

LYNX see Maftet.

M

MAA   see Maat.

MAA-AB   A guardian of the sixth
section of Tuat, the underworld, whose
name means "right of heart."

MAAHES   Lion-headed god at Leontopolis, who was the son of Ra
and Bast. He was portrayed as a
man with the head of a lion wearing
the Atef crown, or as a lion devouring
a captive. In some texts he is identified with Horus the Younger.

MAAT   Goddess who was the personification of the physical and moral
law of the universe.
   Both Maat and her male counterpart Thoth took part in the creation of
the world. While Maat assisted the
sun god Ra as he traveled in his course
from east to west each day, Thoth
helped turn the "thoughts" of the sun
god into material objects. In one myth,
Maat embraced Ra "both at morn and
at eve." In her role as the regulator of
the path of the sun, Maat was called
"daughter of Ra" or "eye of Ra." She
was also known as "lady of heaven,"
"queen of the earth," and "mistress of
the underworld."

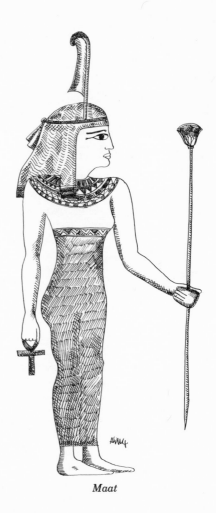

Maat

89

The goddess appears in the *Book of the Dead* in the dual form of Maati, or the Maat goddesses of the South and North of Egypt. Along with the 42 Assessors or Judges, she listened to the confessions of the dead in the Judgment Hall in a ceremony where the dead were obliged to recite a list of forty-two denials of various sins known as the "Negative Confession."

Maat was more than just a goddess—she was the embodiment of an important concept for the Egyptians. The literal English translation of this concept would be "straight," but depending on the context, it can mean right, true, truth, real, genuine, righteous, steadfast, and unalterable; there is no single word in English that embraces all the meanings of this term. One Egyptian text describes the goddess Maat by saying, "Great is Maat, the mighty and unalterable." It has been said that as a moral power Maat was the greatest of the Egyptian goddesses.

In Egyptian art Maat is portrayed in human form wearing a headdress with an ostrich feather attached to it. However, in some depictions she holds the feather in her hand, and she is sometimes shown headless, with the feather taking the place of her head.

Variant spellings of her name are Maa, Maet, Maht, and Maut.

MAET see Maat.

MAFTET Name given to the sacred lynx. In the *Book of the Dead* the Maftet, or lynx god, was regarded as a friend of the dead and was said to have taken part with other gods in overthrowing the monster serpent Apophis. The Maftet was also believed to protect the mummy in its tomb from attack by serpents.

MAGIC Ancient Egypt was known for its magic, which was of two kinds—one employed for beneficent ends, the other for evil. The priest or layman skilled in magic was given special respect, regarded as a very great and mysterious being, who by pronouncing certain words or names of power could heal the sick, cast out evil spirits, and even restore the dead. The forces of nature, such as the wind and storms, the rivers and seas, were also under his control. No god or spirit or evil being could resist the power of magic words.

The best account of the workings of Egyptian magic can be found in the Hebrew Old Testament in the story of the conflict of Aaron and Moses against the Egyptian priests. The Bible (Acts 7:22) describes Moses as "learned in all the wisdom of the Egyptians" and he "was mighty in words and in deeds." From the phrase "mighty in words," some scholars have inferred that Moses, like the goddess Isis, possessed words of power which he could use to control a variety of natural forces. Thus in Exodus (7:10-13) Moses turns a rod into a snake and Aaron's rod, or serpent, swallows up the rods or serpents of the various Egyptian priests. At the magical words of Moses his brother Aaron lifted his rod up over the waters which became blood. He then stretched his rod over the waters and frogs appeared. When Moses sprinkled ashes "toward heaven" they became boils. His final deed was the death of the Egyptian firstborn. The difference between the power of Moses and the Egyptian priests is that Moses' actions were at the command of Yahweh, whereas the Egyptian priests sought to control their gods by invoking the magic words.

Like many other ancient peoples, the Egyptians believed in signs, in amulets to protect against evil, and in rites to ensure health or eternity to the living or dead. The days of the week were considered either lucky or unlucky, and, most important, fate was inescapable. In the *Tale of the Doomed Prince* the prince was killed because he was unable to avoid his evil destiny.

MAGIC, DEITIES OF Ur-heka and Weret Hekau were, respectively, the god and goddess of magic. In a depiction of the creation, done on papyrus in the Twenty-first Dynasty, the god Shu is shown holding up the goddess Nut above the body of the earth god Geb, while Ur-heka kneels at the left of the picture. The goddess of magic was said to make the pharaoh's crown "great in magic."

MAGIC FLUTE, THE see *Zauberflöte, Die.*

MAHT see Maat.

MAMMISI Misnomer applied by the French scholar Champollion to the annex to a temple where the annual rite of the birth of a child god was enacted. The word is from Coptic and means, "place of birth."

MANDULIS see Merul.

MANETHO (Third century B.C.) Egyptian priest and historian noted for his *History of Egypt.* Manetho divided the history of the kings into various Dynasties which are still used by historians, though the dating for each period has changed. His writings, however, have been lost and only survive in part in quotations from other sources.

MARIETTE, AUGUSTE (1821–1881) Egyptologist who worked for the Louvre Museum and went to Egypt in 1859, where he discovered numerous sites at Memphis and Gizeh. In 1858 he was made keeper of the monuments of the Egyptian government. He excavated the Sphinx and the temples of Dendera and Edfu.

MARRIAGE see Family.

MARS The planet Mars was under the protection of the god Ra.

MASPERO, GASTON (1846-1916) French director-general of the Egyptian Service of Antiquities and the author of several works on ancient Egypt. One of his most popular works is *Les contes populaires de l'Egypte an-*

cienne, published in 1882, in which a number of Egyptian folktales are translated into French.

MASTABA   The name given by the Arabs to a massive rectangular building found in Egypt placed over a burial pit in the sand. The word is from the Arabic. The proportions of the building reminded the Arabs of the long, low seat or bench called mastaba, that was common in their homes. The mastaba was intended to protect the body of the deceased from the elements and from thieves. The four sides of the building are symmetrically inclined toward the center. The exterior surfaces are not flat, for each course of masonry, formed of rows of stones, was placed a little behind the one on which it stood. The top of the mastaba is flat. The entrance is sometimes on the south side, but never in the west, which faces the land of the dead.

Inside there is a small room or chamber, which contains the false door through which the Ka, or double, of the deceased may pass. The second room, called *Serdad* or *Sardab,* Arabic for cellar, contained the statue of the deceased in which his Ka would reside, and the pit or cellar, where the body lay.

MATES   A demon who waited for the dead to pass by the Sheni or torture chamber in the underworld. A god with the face of a greyhound and the eyebrows of a man, Mates remained unseen and was easily able to seize and tear out the hearts of those who passed by. In some texts he is called Beba, in others Heri-sep-f.

MATET   The boat that the sun god Ra used in the morning, to start the day. Matet means "becoming strong."

MAU   The great cat who cuts off the head of Apophis, the monster of darkness. He is equated with the sun god Ra, who destroys darkness.

MAUT   see Maat.

MAU-TAUI   A name for Thoth in his role as guardian of the Hall of Maati where the dead are judged. When the deceased wishes to be admitted to the Hall, he is asked, "Who is the god that dwelleth in this hour?" He must respond, "Mau-taui." "And who is this?" the deceased is questioned, and answers, "Mau-taui is Thoth." Thoth next inquires about the deceased's reason for coming into the Hall.

Satisfied with the responses to these and some further questions, Thoth then inscribes or records the name of the deceased on a slab, and he is allowed to enter the Hall.

MEDICINE   The ancient Egyptians were noted for their skill in medicine. According to Homer's *Odyssey* Egyptian doctors were the most accomplished in the world. In his *History* (Book 2) Herodotus states that the Egyptians were specialists in curing many diseases.

However, in spite of its acclaim, much of ancient Egyptian medicine

Meh-urt

was based on religious beliefs rather than science. The Egyptians thought that sicknesses were either sent by the gods or engendered by good and evil spirits. One text tells of a man who offended the goddess Mert-sekert, and had difficulty in breathing, for "she pursueth whosoever sinneth against her." The goddess removed the sickness and sent "sweet air" that was easy to breathe after the man pleaded for her assistance. He said, "She made me to forget my suffering, and I had air to breathe." His problem may have been bronchitis or asthma.

In another text, a man writes a letter to his dead wife saying: "What harm did I ever do to thee that I should come to the terrible plight I am in? What harm have I done to thee that thou shouldst lay thine hand upon me, seeing no evil hath been done to thee?" The letter may have been written after the husband consulted a magician about an illness or depression. This suffering was undoubtedly attributed to the man's dead wife.

One of the most important medical documents, the "Papyrus Ebers," contains various remedies which often rely on popular folk cures. The Papyrus is believed to have been written about B.C. 1500, although it reflects practices of the Old Kingdom.

MEHEN The great serpent who surrounds the sun god to protect him in his boat from the monster serpent Apophis. When he is shown crossing the heavens through the night, the sun god often appears as a ram-headed man wearing the solar disk. Around the sun god is a cabin and the serpent Mehen, who protects him, coils around the cabin.

MEHNI see Fa.

MEH-URT The Celestial Cow, the goddess who gave birth to the sky when nothing else existed. Her name literally means "the great flood." Meh-urt is portrayed as a cow who represents Heaven's Ocean, which the

93

Greeks called Methyer. In some texts she is associated with Isis and described as the protector of the dead.

Variant spellings of her name are Mehturt and Mehueret.

MEHUERET   see Meh-urt.

MEHTURT   see Meh-urt.

MEMNON, COLOSSUS OF   Popular name given by the Greeks to one of two gigantic statues of Amenophis III, which were located at Thebes. In Greek mythology Memnon was the handsome son of Tithonus and Eos, the dawn. During the Trojan War Memnon went to the assistance of King Priam and was slain by Achilles. His mother, Eos, was inconsolable at his death, and, according to myth, wept for him every day. The Greeks identified Memnon's kingdom with Egypt and thus conferred the name Colossus of Memnon on one of the statues of Amenophis III. The statue was known for a mysterious sound which issued from it at sunrise. The sound was said to occur when Eos kissed her son at daybreak and the hero greeted her kiss with a musical acknowledgment. However, the statue lost its mysterious sound when it was partly restored.

MEMPHIS, GOD OF THE NE-CROPOLIS   see Seker.

MEN-A   see Nehata.

MENAT   Counterpoise or weight used to balance the necklace of some gods, such as Ptah. It also served as an amulet.

MENES   Name given in Greek legend to the first king of Egypt, Meni. Menes is mentioned in Herodotus' *History* (Book 2) as the first human to rule after the gods had left Egypt. He founded the city of Memphis, built a temple to the god Ptah, and raised a dike to protect Memphis from the overflow of the Nile. According to some accounts he was eaten by a hippopotamus. His name is sometimes given as Narmer.

MENI   see Menes.

MENI-RET   One of the four earthly forms of Osiris found in the sixth section, or hour, of Tuat, the underworld.

MENKHET   see Nehata.

MENMENU   A monster surmounted by disks on its back, with three serpent heads with fourteen stars on each head and fourteen human heads. The Menmenu was found in the fourth section, or hour, of Tuat, the underworld. It fed on whatever it could find.

MEN-SHETA   A god bending over a staff in the seventh section of Tuat, the underworld. Men-sheta means "establisher of what is secret."

MENTHU   A sun god noted for his warlike character worshipped at Thebes. He appears to have been a personification of the destructive heat of the sun. It is likely that Menthu was originally a god of local importance, who was absorbed into the worship of Amen-Ra, becoming the composite god, Menthu-Ra. In Egyptian art he is portrayed as a hawk-headed man, holding in one hand the ankh, emblem of life, and in the other a scepter. His head is adorned with two plumes, the disk of the sun, and the uraeus. In later dynastic times he is pictured with the head of a bull. The Greeks identified him with Apollo. Variant spellings of his name are Mentu, Mont, and Muntu.

MENTU   see Menthu.

MER   see Pyramid.

MERCURY   The planet Mercury was under the protection of the god Set.

MERSEKHNET   see Meshkent.

MESHKENT   Goddess associated with childbirth, whose name means "the place where one delivers." She was often portrayed as two bricks, for Egyptian mothers crouched when giving birth and leaned on two bricks. She is sometimes portrayed as two bricks that terminate in a human head. At the time of death Meshkent appeared; she testified on the character of the deceased before Osiris, the judge of the dead. Variant spellings of her name are Meskhenet and Mersekhnet.

MERSEGER   Greek name form of the Egyptian Mert-sekert, a snake goddess of the necropolis at Thebes. Merseger means "the lover or friend of him who makes silence," referring to Osiris, god of the dead, as the maker of silence. Mert-Sekert was associated with the funerary mountain at Thebes, where she was known as "the peak," and she protected the tombs in the desert. In one Egyptian text she appeared in the form of fresh air to bring relief to a sufferer with a respiratory ailment, who had confessed his sins to her and begged her forgiveness.

In Egyptian art she is variously portrayed as a snake-headed woman and a human-headed snake, with a disk and horns upon her head. A variant spelling of her name is Mertseger.

MERTSEGER   see Merseger

MERT-SEKERT   see Merseger.

MESKHENET   see Meshkent.

MESKHET   The name the Egyptians gave to the constellation commonly known as the Big Dipper.

MESTHI   One of the four sons of Horus and Isis, who guarded the liver and was portrayed with a human body. A variant of his name is Imsety.

METES   A guardian of the eleventh section of Tuat, the underworld, as the sun god Ra passes in his boat.

MILK In ancient Egypt milk was the food of both gods and mortals. A king was often shown sucking the breasts of a goddess, to indicate his entry into the divine world. Milk was offered on the 365 altars of the shrine of Osiris.

Min

MIN God of fertility, crops, and bringer of rain. The chief centers of his worship were at Coptos and Panopolis. He was honored at harvest festivals, and was then offered the first sheaf of the harvest by the king. According to some sources he was also worshipped as a god of roads and travelers and was evoked by caravan leaders before they set out through the desert. In Egyptian art Min is portrayed as a man with an erect phallus, holding a flail in his right hand. On his head he wears a crown surmounted by two tall plumes and a streamer descending from its back.

In later times Min was identified by the Egyptians with Amen-Ra and by the Greeks with Pan. He was also closely associated with Horus, who in some texts was addressed as Min-Horus.

MNEVIS (Bull) Greek name for the Egyptian sacred bull Wer-mer worshipped at Heliopolis. He was believed to be an incarnation of the sun and was often portrayed as a bull with a disk and the uraeus between his horns. He also appeared as a man with the head of a bull.

MONGOOSE see Ichneumon.

MONT see Menthu.

MONTH, GODDESS OF THE FIRST see Tekhi.

MOON The main gods associated with the moon were Aah, Khensu, and Thoth. Sometimes Thoth is portrayed as an ibis with a winged moon over his head. The moon was also believed to be one of the eyes of the god Horus, while the sun was the other.

MOSES AND AARON   see Magic.

MOTHER   see Family.

MUMMY   A term applied to the body of a human being, animal, bird, fish, or reptile which has been intentionally preserved. The word "mummy" is derived from an Arabic word which means "bitumenized thing," or a body preserved by bitumen. In his *History* (Book 2) Herodotus describes the Egyptian embalming practice:

When in a family a man of any consideration dies, all the females of that family besmear their heads and faces with mud, and then leaving the body in the house, they wander about the city, and beat themselves, having their clothes girt up, and exposing their breasts, and all their relations accompany them. On the other hand, the men beat themselves, being girt up in like manner. When they have done this, they carry out the body to be embalmed.

There are persons who are appointed for this very purpose; they, when the dead body is brought to them, show to the bearers wooden models of corpses made exactly like by painting. And they show that which they say is the most expensive manner of embalming, the name of which I do not think it right to mention on such occasion [Herodotus means the sacred

name of Osiris, god of the dead], they then show the second, which is inferior and less expensive; and then the third which is the cheapest.

Having explained them all, they learn from them in what way they wish the body to be prepared; then the relations, when they have agreed on the price, depart; but the embalmers remaining in the workshops thus proceed to embalm in the most expensive manner. First they draw out the brains through the nostrils with an iron hook, taking part of it out in this manner, the rest by the infusion of drugs. Then with a sharp Ethiopian stone they make an incision in the side, and take out all the bowels; and having cleansed the abdomen and rinsed it with palm wine, they next sprinkle it with pounded perfumes. Then having filled the belly with pure myrrh pounded, and cassia, and other perfumes, frankincense excepted, they sew it up again; and when they have done this, they steep it in natrum, leaving it under for seventy days; for a longer time than this it is not lawful to steep it.

At the expiration of the seventy days they wash the corpse, and wrap the whole in bandages in flaxen cloth, smearing it with gum, which the Egyptians commonly use instead of glue. After this the relations, having taken the body back again, make a wooden case in the shape of a man (that is, in the form of the god Osiris) and having made it, they enclose the body; and thus having fastened it up, they store it in a sepulchral chamber, setting it upright against the wall. In this manner they prepare the bodies that are embalmed in the most expensive way.

Those who, avoiding great expense, desire the middle way, they prepare in the following manner. When they have charged their syringes with oil made of cedar, they fill the abdomen of the corpse without making any incision or taking out the bowels, but inject it at the fundament; and having prevented the injection from escaping, they steep the body in natrum for the prescribed number of days, and on the last day they let out from the abdomen the oil of cedar which they had injected, and it has such power that it brings away the intestines and vitals in a state of dissolution; the natrum dissolves the flesh, and nothing of the body remains but the skin and bones. When they have done this they return the body without any further operation.

The third method of embalming is this, which is used only for the poorer sort. Having thoroughly rinsed the abdomen in syrmaea, they steep it in natrum for seventy days, and then deliver it to be carried away. [The embalmers mould the penis of the deceased erect, indicating the life-force for the next world.]

The Old Testament book of Genesis (50:2-3) reports that Jacob's embalming occupied forty days, but the period of mourning was seventy days. In Egyptian sources figures on the period of mourning vary. In one case the embalming is said to have taken sixteen days, the bandaging thirty-five days, and the burial seventy, making a total of 121 days. According to other sources embalming lasted seventy or eighty days, and the burial rites ten months.

In addition to the method described by Herodotus, the ancient Egyptians also preserved their dead in honey. Honey is often called a symbol of life in folklore from throughout the world. The body of Alexander the Great was preserved in "white honey which had not been melted."

The bodies of very poor Egyptians were preserved by either soaking in salt and hot bitumen, or in salt only. In the first process every cavity was filled with bitumen, and the hair disappeared. For a time the early Egyptian Christians embalmed their dead, but St. Anthony the Great told his two faithful disciples not to allow his body to be embalmed; he insisted on being buried under ground, in a place known only to them. He said, "At the resurrection of the dead I shall receive it [a new body] from the Savior incorruptible."

Mummies, or parts of mummies, were used as medicine for centuries in Europe. In Scotland in 1612 a mummy cost eight shillings a pound. When real mummies were not available, the bodies of criminals were used in their place. Sir Thomas Browne, the seventeenth century English author wrote: "Mummy is become merchandise...."

MUSIC, GOD OF   see Ity.

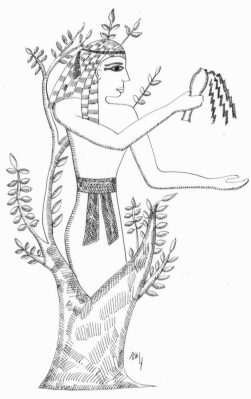

Mut

MUT Goddess, principal female counterpart of the solar deity Amen-Ra. Her name means "mother," but she was believed to possess both male and female reproductive organs. Mut is sometimes identified with Bast, the cat goddess, and sometimes with Sekhmet, the lion goddess.

In Egyptian art Mut is usually portrayed as a woman wearing on her head the united crowns of the South and North and holding in her hands the papyrus scepter and the ankh, emblem of life. Sometimes she is standing upright, with her large winged arms stretched out full-length. At her feet is the feather of Maat and on her head is the vulture headdress. However, this versatile goddess is occasionally portrayed with the head of a man or a vulture and with a phallus and the claws of a lion or lioness.

Her temple at Thebes has a horseshoe-shaped Sacred Lake and her sanctuary was in use for 2,000 years.

N

NAKITH One of the four goddesses who protect each of the four earthly forms of Osiris in the seventh section, or hour, of Tuat, the underworld. Her daily responsibility is to drive away the enemies of the sun god Ra and to hack to pieces the arch-serpent Apophis daily.

NAMES The ancient Egyptians attached great importance to names, for they believed that they had power over a god or person when they knew his true or real name. In the myth of "Isis and the Secret name of Ra," the goddess forces Ra to tell her his true or secret name, thus placing himself completely in her power. In texts on the creation we are often told that the creator god uttered his sacred name and the creation came about. It was believed that one could destroy a god or being by removing his name from hieroglyphic inscriptions. The Pharaoh Akhenaten tried to obliterate the god Ra by having his name chiseled out of monuments throughout Egypt. When Akhenaten's religious reform failed, his name was subjected to the same abuse by the followers of Amen.

NAOS A small, enclosed shrine for the statue of a god, often placed in the innermost part of the temple.

NARMER see Menes.

NARRATIVES see Tales.

NAU A monster serpent called the "bull of the gods," who had "seven serpents on his seven necks." He appears in Tuat, the underworld.

NAU-SHESMA A monster serpent with seven heads of seven snakes, who had authority over seven archers, or seven bows, in Tuat, the underworld.

NAUT A form of Nut as the night sky. In one text she is said to make "the gods refresh themselves beneath her shadow."

NEB Hieroglyph meaning "all" and found on amulets in various combinations with the ankh and other symbols.

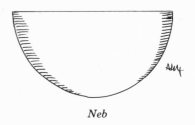

Neb

NEB-ER-TCHER A form of the sun god Ra, "the lord of the end," or the universe, who says, "I am he who came into being in the form of the god Khepera, and I was the creator of that which came into being. . . . " The title is also applied to Osiris, as both lord of the universe and as lord of his reunited body after death.

NEBT-KHU One of four goddesses in the eleventh section, or hour, of Tuat, the underworld. She sits upon a snake with one hand raised over her face. She never moves from her place, and lives on the voices of the snakes which come forth from her feet daily. The other three goddesses are Nert, Nebt-ankhiu, and Hentneteru.

NEB-PAT see Nehata.

NEBTHET see Nephthys.

NEBHET HOTEP see Iusas and Nebhet Hotep.

NEBT-MAT; NEBT-SHEF-SHEF-ET; AND NEBT-SHAT see Perit.

NECROPOLIS Greek for "city of the dead," applied to the burial areas near Egyptian cities, towns, and villages. The areas chosen were usually on the edge of the desert.

NEFERTEM A sun god of Memphis, who was also a god of perfumes. His name is believed to mean "Tem the Younger," denoting that he was the first incarnation of Tem at Heliopolis, the sun god who sprang up each dawn from a lotus, which was said to be the refuge of the sun during the night. Nefertem was later identified with a number of other gods, including Thoth and Horus. According to one myth, he was the son of Ptah, the craft god, and Sekhmet, a fierce lion goddess, the three forming the divine Memphis Triad.

In Egyptian art Nefertem is portrayed as a man holding the khepesh, a curved sabre, or the ankh, symbol of life, or the lotus scepter surmounted by plumes. The Greeks called him Iphtimis.

NEFER An amulet of the windpipe and stomach, often made of some semi-precious stone.

NEFERTITI (fl. 1372–1350 B.C.) The wife of Akhenaten, she worked closely with her husband to establish the worship of Aten in Egypt, but is not mentioned in reports of the last three years of the king's life. Explanations vary: some accounts claim that she died, and others that she removed herself from the king and lived in her own palace, apart from the main residence. Nefertiti means "the beautiful one has come."

Nefertiti is often shown with the

king and her six daughters (according to some contemporary scholars Akhenaten may not have been the girls' father). The famous head of Nefertiti in the Egyptian Museum of West Berlin is but one of her many fine portraits.

NEGATIVE CONFESSION A confession of sins *not* committed which was given in the Hall of Judgment before Osiris and the forty-two Assessor Judges. The Negative Confession took place before the rite of Weighing of the Heart, which decided the fate of the deceased. A list of the Negative Confession from the Eighteenth Dynasty has 42 declarations, as many as there were judges.

The forty-two declarations (some are repetitions) are:

1. I have not done iniquity.
2. I have not robbed with violence.
3. I have not done violence to any man.
4. I have not committed theft.
5. I have slain neither man nor woman.
6. I have not made light the bushel.
7. I have not acted deceitfully.
8. I have not purloined the things which belong to God.
9. I have not uttered falsehood.
10. I have not carried off goods by force.
11. I have not uttered vile (or evil) words.
12. I have not carried off food by force.
13. I have not acted deceitfully.
14. I have not lost my temper and become angry.
15. I have invaded no man's land.
16. I have not slaughtered animals which are the possessions of God.
17. I have not laid waste the lands which have been ploughed.
18. I have not pried into matters to make mischief.
19. I have not set my mouth in motion against any man.
20. I have not given way to wrath without due cause.
21. I have not committed fornication, and I have not committed sodomy.
22. I have not polluted myself.
23. I have not lain with the wife of a man.
24. I have not made any man to be afraid.
25. I have not made my speech to burn with anger.
26. I have not made myself deaf unto the words of right and truth.
27. I have not made another person to weep.
28. I have not uttered blasphemies.
29. I have not acted with violence.
30. I have not acted without due consideration.
31. I have not pierced (?) my skin (?) and I have not taken vengeance on the god.
32. I have not multiplied my speech beyond what should be said.

103

33. I have not committed fraud, and I have not looked upon evil.
34. I have never uttered curses against the king.
35. I have not fouled running water.
36. I have not exalted my speech.
37. I have not uttered curses against God.
38. I have not behaved with insolence.
39. I have not been guilty of favoritism.
40. I have not increased my wealth except by means of such things as are mine own possessions.
41. I have not uttered curses against that which belongeth to God and is with me.
42. I have not thought scorn of the god of the city.

But even when the deceased had satisfied the Forty-two Judges or Assessors, he could not pass out of the hall until he could identify the magical names of the various parts of the door that opened into the region of the blessed. When that feat was accomplished, the god Mau-taui posed the question, "Who is Mau-Taui?" Whereupon the dead answered, "Mau-taui is Thoth." Then Thoth asked the reason for his coming to the Judgment Hall, and the deceased replied that it was to have his name written down by Thoth. The ordeal continued on with more questions about the fitness of the deceased until Thoth was satisfied that the dead was worthy and allowed him to pass out of the hall into the blessed region.

NEHA-HRA A monster serpent, enemy of the sun god Ra, who is slain daily.

NEHATA One of twelve gods in the ninth section, or hour, of Tuat, the underworld, who, when greeted by the sun god Ra, begins to utter words of power, causing life and strength to arise in Osiris. The other gods are Teba, Ariti, Menkhet, Hebs, Nebti, Asti-neter, Asti-paut, Hetemet-khu, Neb-pat, Temtu, and Men-a.

NEHEM AWAY A personification of the beneficent aspect of the goddess Hathor. The name means, "The one who takes care of the deprived," referring to those who have been robbed or plundered. She was associated with the sistrum, a musical instrument that was said to drive away evil spirits and was often depicted with the head of Hathor as one of its elements.

NEHES A companion of the sun god whose name means "awake" or "awakening." The name was also applied to Set, the brother of Osiris, to indicate that he was the watchful serpent lurking in Tuat, the underworld.

NEHUI A bird-headed god in the twelfth section, or hour, of Tuat, the underworld. He carries a paddle and his daily duty is to raise up the disk of the sun.

NEIT   see Neith.

NEITH   Goddess of the city of Sais. Like a great many Egyptian deities Neith had a dual nature. She could be both fierce and gentle. She was a mother goddess, a nourisher and sustainer of life and a protector of the dead, as well as a deity of savagery and bloodlust, who when angry could threaten to have the heavens fall upon the earth.

Neith was originally worshipped as an ancient war goddess, who led the charge in battle. Her symbols, two crossed arrows and a shield, reflected her martial nature. With the advent of the Twenty-sixth Dynasty, Sais, her city, became the capital of Egypt, and Neith's importance increased considerably. A great festival, called the Feast of Lamps, was held in her honor, and according to Herodotus in his *History* (Book 2), her devotees burned a multitude of lights in the open air all night during the celebration.

Neith became associated with the creation myths, similar to the sky cow goddess Hathor, and, as a goddess of weaving and the domestic arts, she was said to have woven the world on her loom. Thus, she was sometimes called the first birthgiver, the mother who bore the sun before anything else existed. The following was inscribed on the wall of her temple: "I am all that has been, that is, and that will be."

In Egyptian art Neith was usually portrayed as a woman wearing the

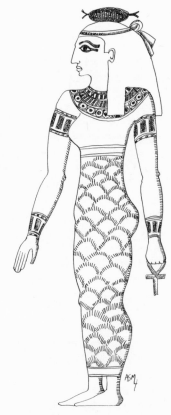

Neith

crown of the North on her head and holding a scepter in one hand and the ankh, emblem of life, in the other. Sometimes she is shown grasping a bow and two arrows. She is also portrayed as a cow with eighteen stars on one side and a collar with the ankh around her neck. In another depiction a crocodile sucks at each of her breasts, to indicate her power over the river Nile. The Greeks identified her with their goddess Athene.

Variant spellings of her name are Neit, Net, and Nit.

NEKENU A god who carries a javelin in the tenth section, or hour, of Tuat, the' underworld. He helps the sun god Ra, slaying his enemies, as Ra travels toward the east.

NEKHEBET Vulture goddess of Upper Egypt. She was said to be a form of the primeval abyss that brought forth light and was sometimes called "the father of fathers, the mother of mothers." She was also a symbol of nature and a patron of childbirth.

In Egyptian art she is usually portrayed as a woman wearing the vulture headdress surmounted by the white crown, the sign of her sovereignty over Upper Egypt, to which two plumes are attached. She sometimes holds the scepter in one hand and the ankh, emblem of life, in the other. The scepter is occasionally formed of a long-stemmed flower, which appears to be a water lily with a serpent twined around it. Nekhebet is also represented as a woman with the head of a vulture. The Greeks identified her with their goddess Eileithyia.

NEKHEKH see Flail.

NEMI A guardian of the tenth section of Tuat, the underworld, as the sun god Ra passes through in his boat.

NENUERBESTA A mummified god who stands at the beginning of the fourth section of Tuat, the underworld, as the sun god Ra passes through in his boat.

NEPHTHYS Greek name for the Egyptian goddess Nebthet, who personified darkness, decay, and death. She was the daughter of the earth, Geb, and the sky, Nut, and was the sister of Osiris, Isis, and Set.

In early Egyptian mythology Nephthys was usually regarded as the female counterpart of Set, the god of evil and darkness. According to one myth, she abandoned Set, with whom she had remained barren, for her brother Osiris, the god of light, and tricked Osiris into copulating with her, thereby conceiving Anubis, the jackal-headed god.

Later, however, she became the faithful friend of Isis and helped her sister collect the scattered limbs of Osiris, and reconstitute his body, after he had been dismembered by Set. In the Pyramid Texts and the *Book of the Dead* she is considered a friend of the dead.

Although Nephthys was a goddess of death, she was also the female counterpart of the ithyphallic god Min, who symbolized virility, reproduction, and regeneration. As such she symbolized the life that springs from death and was identified with the outlying desert region of the Nile, which was usually dry except at flood time.

Nephthys was skilled in magic and words of power, and as a healing deity, along with Isis and Osiris, she was one of the great gods of Mendes in the Delta region. She often appeared with Isis on the walls of coffins, with winged arms outstretched in a gesture of protection.

Nephthys

In Egyptian art Nephthys is portrayed as a woman wearing the symbol of her name on her head. Among her many titles were "mistress of the gods," "great goddess, lady of life," "sister of the god," and "lady of heaven, mistress of the two lands."

NEPER A grain god who was often combined with Osiris, god of the dead.

The composite god was called Osiris-Neper.

NEPMEH The seven gods who meet the sun god Ra in his boat in the first section of Tuat, the underworld.

NET see Neith.

NET The ancient Egyptians believed that in journeying from this world to the next the spirits of the dead would encounter evil beings who sought to entrap them in their nets. The priests composed a series of spells to avoid entrapment. Some of these spells have come down to us in the *Book of the Dead,* with pictures of the magical nets and the magical names of every part of the nets.

Lucky souls flew through the air toward their abode in the other world without mishap, but the less fortunate were caught in the net of the "fierce fowler whose fingers were hidden." The great fowler, who was called Her-f-ha-f, ferried the dead over the river of death.

NETCHER The hieroglyph for "god" which represents a pennant on a pole. The presence of Amen and other gods who were often invisible was indicated when the pennant blew in the breeze.

NETERT-EN-KHENTET-RA see Perit.

NETER-KHERTET see Khert Neter.

107

NETRU see Fa.

NI A god who has two birds' heads and carries a paddle in the twelfth section, or hour, of Tuat, the underworld. His daily duty is to raise up the disk of the sun.

NILE The annual flooding of this river, some 4,000 miles long, made Egypt a fertile land. The Nile begins in Africa, south of the equator, and flows northward out of the tropics into desert land. The Delta, shaped like the Greek letter $\triangle$, gave the name to the fertile region of Egypt. As the river flows toward the sea it passes through six cataracts, areas of jagged crags and ledges. The Nile is usually 10 to 12 miles wide.

The ancient Egyptians often referred to their homeland as "The Gift of the Nile," for the life of the land depended upon the river. The Nile was personified as the god Hapi. One hymn opens:

Hail, O Nile.
You show yourself in the land,
Coming in peace, giving life to
Egypt. . . .

For the Egyptians the Nile was the center of the world, where all life began.

NIT see Neith.

NO Name given in the Old Testament to the Upper Egyptian city of Weset, which the Greeks called Thebes.

NOMARCH Title of the governor of a "nome" or province. At certain times in Egyptian history the nomarch had great importance, functioning as a minor king in his region. During the Middle Kingdom, however, the power of the nomarch decreased.

NOME GODS The name given to the local god or gods in each nome, or province, of Egypt. According to Egyptian texts the country consisted of forty-two nomes, although classical Greek and Roman historians give different accounts. Each nome was represented by a particular god or group of allied gods. A temple dedicated to the nome god, where a body of priests divided the duties of serving him, was situated in the capital city of each nome.

The nome priests were subject to no external authority; in fact, the high priest possessed nearly as much power as the king. The same god was honored by many nomes, although the worship of each god in a province contained elements peculiar to that region. Horus, for instance, was worshipped in three nomes of Upper Egypt and two nomes of Lower Egypt. Each nome, however, varied the forms and titles it applied to its gods and goddesses.

NORTH WIND, GOD OF see Qebui.

NU see Nun.

NUMBERS As with many other ancient societies numbers played an important part in Egyptian belief. The symbolism of the important numbers are:

1. Uniqueness. The single cult object in the temple.
2. Binary form. Found in the layout of temples.
3. Plurality. The number of gods in a Triad. Plural of three means "many."
4. Cardinal points. Ritual acts were often performed eight times (twice four) for the country was made up of Upper and Lower Egypt (twice two).
5. Sacred number of the priests of Hermopolitan who called Thoth "the greatest Five."
6. Appears in the lunar calendar.
7. The seven Hathors, goddesses of birth and seven apertures in a person's head.
8. The eight gods of the Ogdoad.
9. The Ennead, the group of nine gods.

NUN AND NAUNET Male and female primeval dieties who the priesthood of Hermopolis included in the Ogdoad, which consisted of the eight gods who created the world. Nun was called the "father of the gods" and was basically an abstract concept: he had neither temples nor worshippers. There is a myth that Tem created Nun as his home and sailed over him each day in two magical boats, one called Mantchet, "becoming strong," the other Semket, "becoming weak."

In Egyptian art Nun was portrayed as a frog-headed man and Naunet, his female counterpart, as a snake. He was sometimes shown plunged up to his waist in water, with his arms supporting the gods who issued from his body. He was also depicted wearing a solar disk with plumes on his head. A variant spelling is Nu.

NUBT A goddess who in some texts is said to be the mother of Osiris.

NUBTI Epithet of Set common in the South of Egypt. Set was portrayed with one body and two heads, one of a hawk, the other of the "Set animal," which has not yet been identified. Horus, the victor over Set, is sometimes called Hor Nubti, or "Horus the vanquisher of Set." A variant of the name is Set-Nubti.

NUT Goddess who personified the sky and was the wife of the earth god Geb.

According to one myth Nut was Geb's twin sister and slept with him against the will of her husband, the sun god Ra. In revenge, Ra had the couple separated by Shu, who held up the sky, and declared that Nut could not bear children in any month of the year. However, the god Thoth took pity on her, and bested the Moon at checkers to win $1/72$ of its light, from which he was able to construct five new days. Because these days were not in the calendar, and did not fall under the jurisdiction of Ra, the goddess was

Nut

She is also described as a friend and protector of the dead in other Egyptian texts.

The sycamore was sacred to her. One text reads: "Hail, thou sycamore of the goddess Nut! Grant thou to me of the water and of the air which dwell in thee." In one myth, Ra passed between the goddess's two turquoise-colored sycamores at Heliopolis when he began his journey across the sky each morning. And in another myth the demon Apophis was killed by Ra at the sycamore of Nut. The branches of the sycamore tree became a place of refuge from the fiery heat of the summer sun. Weary travelers refreshed themselves in the tree's shade and ate of the tree's abundant fruit, on which the goddess herself subsisted. There is speculation that the sycamore of the goddess Nut served as the prototype of the sycamore that sheltered the Virgin Mary, when she sat and rested during her flight into Egypt with the Christ Child and Joseph.

In Egyptian art Nut was usually portrayed as a woman bearing a vase of water upon her head. She sometimes wears a headdress of horns and the disk of the goddess Hathor, and holds a papyrus scepter in one hand and the ankh, emblem of life, in the other.

able to conceive and give birth to five children—Osiris, Horus, Set, Isis, and Nephthys.

In the *Book of the Dead* there are several allusions to the meat and drink Nut provides for the deceased.

O

OBELISK A tall, four-sided shaft, often tapering at the top. Connected with the solar cults in Egypt, most obelisks were taken to other countries over the centuries.

The obelisks in London and New York City were dubbed "Cleopatra's Needle" by the general public.

OFFERING TABLE Low rectangular slab used for food offerings for the dead. The name and titles of the deceased as well as prayers were written on the offering table.

OGDOAD A group of eight gods who according to the priesthood of Hermopolis, a city in Upper Egypt, created the world. The power of these gods, who had ruled over the earth for a time, and then died and gone to the underworld, still manifested itself in the flow of the Nile and the sun's orbit across the sky. The eight deities were: Nun and his consort, Naunet; Huh and his consort, Hauhet; Kuk and his consort, Kauket; Amen and his consort, Amunet. The four male gods were portrayed with frog heads, and the four female gods with serpent heads.

In some accounts, instead of creating the world, the Ogdoad were pre-sented as the first beings to emerge from the receding Nile floodwaters. In later myths the Ogdoad was said to be the soul of Thoth, a god sacred to Hermopolis who was believed to be self-created.

ONNOPHRIS see Unnefer.

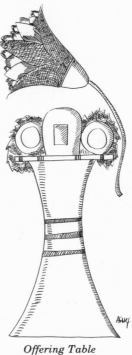

Offering Table

ONNOS see Unas.

111

Onouris

ONOURIS Greek name for the Egyptian war god Anhur, whom the Greeks identified with their god Ares. He was believed to be the personification of the warlike nature of the sun god Ra, and he was often coupled with the god Shu, who held up the heavens, and invoked under the composite god Onouris-Shu. In Egyptian art Onouris is portrayed in a headdress adorned with four straight plumes, wearing a long embroidered robe. He is often holding a lance. He is sometimes seen holding a cord by which he leads the sun. Variant English spellings of the Egyptian form of his name are Anhoret, Anher, and Anhert.

ONUPHIS Greek name form of the Egyptian Aa-Nefer, the bull which was said to house the soul of Osiris, god of the dead and of resurrection.

OPET see Taurt.

OPHOIS WEPWAWET see Wepwawet.

ORACLES Like the ancient Greeks, Egyptians believed that a god could speak through an oracle. Of the many methods used to learn the will of the gods, the most common was to ask a question of a statue of a god while in procession. If the statue moved forward the answer was "yes," and if the statue moved backward the answer was "no." Questions that required more than a "yes" or "no" answer were written out on tablets with possible responses. Then the manner in which the god's statue nodded indicated the correct answer.

OSIRIS God of the dead and of resurrection, who was the brother-husband of Isis, the father of Horus, and the brother of Set and Nephthys. His worship formed one of the great cults of ancient Egypt.

The Osirian myth, which cannot be found complete in any one Egyptian source, appears in numerous references in extant texts. It is assumed that Egyptians knew the myth so well that a complete narrative was thought unnecessary. The Greek writer Plutarch, who lived in the first century A.D., whose narrative *On Isis and Osiris,* was compiled from various oral and written sources, was responsible for making the Egyptian myth of the death and resurrection god well known to the Greeks and Romans.

The subject was also covered by other Greek writers, whose accounts sometimes differed from Plutarch, who, despite his errors in understanding Egyptian customs, remained the best known and most influential source. The following version of the myth, based mainly on Plutarch, uses for the most part the Egyptian transcriptions of the gods' names, except for the Greek form of Osiris (Ausar, Ausares), which is much better known than the Egyptian Asar, Ausar, or Ser.

According to Plutarch, when the sun god Ra discovered that his wife, the sky goddess Nut had been unfaithful with the earth god Geb, he cursed her with barrenness, ensuring that she would never bear a child during any day of the month in the year. However, the god Thoth, was also in love with Nut and was able to construct five new days from the 1/72 part of the Moon's light he had won in a checker game with that god. As these days did not come under the curse of Ra, Nut was able to bear Geb five children: Osiris on the first day; Horus on the second (although Horus is also called the son of Osiris); Set, the evil god, on the third; Isis, who became the wife of Osiris, on the fourth; and Nephthys,

the death goddess, on the fifth. The Egyptians considered the first, third, and fifth of these five new days unlucky.

When Osiris was born, a voice proclaiming the birth of the lord of creation was heard throughout Egypt. As king, Osiris devoted himself to civilizing his subjects; he taught them husbandry, instructed them in the worship of the gods, and established a code of laws. When Egypt was at last peaceful and flourishing, Osiris set out to bring his teachings to the other nations of the world.

Isis, Osiris' sister-wife, ruled the state during the king's absence. When he returned, his evil brother Set (identified by Plutarch with Typhon) and Aso, the Queen of Ethiopia, and seventy-two others plotted to assassinate him. The conspirators built a chest to conform to the measurements of Osiris' body. The box was brought into Osiris' banquet hall while he was eating, and he was tricked into lying down in it. Set and his cohorts closed the box, brought it immediately to the mouth of the Nile, and launched it out into the river.

These events occurred on the seventeenth day of the month of Hathor, when Osiris was in the twenty-eighth year of his reign. This day was subsequently marked on the calendar as triply unlucky; it was the day that Isis and Nephthys began their great lamentation for Osiris.

On hearing of this treachery, Isis cut off a lock of her hair as a sign of her mourning and set out to find her husband's body. When she discovered in

113

her wanderings that Osiris had slept with their sister Nephthys and that the offspring of the union was the jackel-headed god Anubis, Isis found Anubis and brought him to guard her. (Although the story goes that Osiris had not lusted after his sister, but had been tricked by her; Nephthys was in love with him.)

Isis learned that the chest containing Osiris had been carried by the waves to the coast of Byblos and lodged in the branches of a bush. A large and beautiful tree had quickly grown up, and the chest was now enclosed on every side and hidden from view. The king of Byblos had been attracted by the tree's unusual size, and had it cut down to make into a pillar for one of the rooms of his house. Isis learned of this and went to Byblos where she was taken to the palace to become nurse to one of the queen's sons. It is said that the goddess would transform herself into a swallow at every opportunity and hover around the pillar, bemoaning her fate. Each night she placed the queen's son into a special fire to consume his mortal parts, until the queen finally discovered her son in the flames and cried out. Isis revealed her story and begged for the pillar that supported the roof. The queen took pity and ordered that the pillar be cut open and the chest removed. When she saw the body of her dead husband, Isis cried out with such fierceness that one of the queen's children died of fright.

Isis set sail for Egypt, where, on arriving, she embraced the corpse and wept bitterly. She hid Osiris's body in a secluded spot and went to visit her son Horus (called Orus by Plutarch) at Per-Uatchit (Butos, in Plutarch). Set stumbled upon the chest when he was out hunting one night, realized what it contained, and proceeded to tear Osiris's body into fourteen pieces which he dispersed all over Egypt.

Twice bereaved, Isis set sail to collect the fragments of Osiris's body. Wherever she found her husband's remains, she erected a tomb to Osiris, and it is said that this is why there are so many of these buildings scattered throughout Egypt. Isis collected all the pieces of her husband except for the penis, which had been devoured by a fish. Isis then constructed a phallus to take the place of her husband's, and a festival was held in its honor.

After some time Osiris's spirit returned from the dead and appeared to his son Horus, encouraging him to avenge his father's death. Horus then engaged Set in a great battle that lasted for three days, but when he finally won, Isis took pity on her brother and let him go free. Enraged, Horus cut off his mother's head, which the god Thoth replaced with a cow's head. (The goddess is thus sometimes shown as cow-headed.) Two more battles ensued between the combatants when Set appeared before the gods and accused Horus of being a bastard and Thoth defended Horus. Horus again proved victorious.

This is the general outline of the Osirian myth as reported by Plutarch. Osiris was the man god (he was first a human and later deified) who had con-

Osiris

dead and the god of the living. He may also have represented the sun after it set, and as such symbolized the motionless dead. In some later texts he is identified with the moon. The Egyptians claimed that Osiris was the father of the gods who had given birth to him, and the father of the past, the present, and the future (immortality).

In Egyptian art Osiris is usually portrayed as a mummy, wearing a beard and with the white crown upon his head and the Menat, an amulet associated with virility and fecundity, hanging from his neck. He sometimes appears as the Tet pillar, symbol of strength and stability in life and renewed power after death, and is then called Osiris Tet.

OSIRIS-AAH A composite god made up of Osiris, god of the dead, and Aah, a moon god. Osiris-Aah is portrayed with a crescent moon or full moon on his head.

OSIRIS-GEB A composite god made up of Osiris, god of the dead, and Geb, the earth god, who according to some ancient texts produced the cosmic egg.

OSIRIS-HORUS A composite god made up of Osiris, god of the dead, and his son Horus. Together they form a god of the rising sun.

OSIRIS-NEB-HEU A form of the god Osiris as Lord of Eternity, portrayed as a mummy with the head of the Benu bird.

quered death, and the Egyptians believed his followers would also conquer death. In every funeral inscription from the Pyramid Texts to the Roman Period, what happened to Osiris was also done for the deceased, since the deceased was identified with Osiris during the rites.

Originally the personification of the flooding of the Nile, Osiris absorbed the characteristics of so many gods that he became both the god of the

115

OSIRIS-NEPER A composite god of Osiris, god of the dead, and Neper, a grain god.

OSIRIS-ORION see Osiris-Sah.

OSIRIS-RA A composite god of Osiris, god of the dead, and Ra, the sun god. Together they represented the day and night suns. The night sun appeared when the sun went into the underworld, and darkness covered the earth.

OSIRIS-SAH A composite god who is the male counterpart of the composite goddess, Isis-Sept or Isis-Sothis. He is sometimes called Osiris-Orion.

OSIRIS'S BODY According to Egyptian texts the body of Osiris was cut up into fourteen or sixteen parts by his evil brother Set. The parts were then scattered throughout the various sections of Egypt. Isis discovered the remains (except for the penis which had been eaten by a fish) and built shrines for them throughout Egypt. Thus Abydos claimed to possess the head of Osiris, while Heliopolis said it had a relic of a bone from his back.

OSIRIS-TUA A title applied to Osiris, god of the dead, meaning "Osiris, the begetter."

"OTHERWORLD" see Tuat.

OXYRHYNCHUS The fish that ate the phallus of the god Osiris after he was hacked to pieces by the demonic god Set. The Oxyrhynchus was worshipped in the Egyptian city by the same name. In certain sections of Egypt, this fish was not eaten because of its sacrilegious connotation, although elsewhere the Oxyrhynchus was eaten for the very reason that it contained the phallus of the god.

OZYMANDIAS Greek form of the Egyptian name Rameses. At the Ramesseum near Thebes there is a gigantic statue of Rameses II. The Greek historian Diodorus Siculus translated the inscription at its foot: "My name is Ozymandias, king of kings: if any would know how great I am and where I lie, let him surpass me in any of my works." The English poet Shelley (1792–1822) based his poem "Ozymandias" on the inscription, which he changed to: "My name is Ozymandias, king of kings: Look on my works, ye Mighty, and despair!"

P

PAI   A guardian of the twelfth section of Tuat, the underworld.

PAKHETH   A lion-headed goddess whose statue was often placed on the doors of palaces and tombs to guard both the living and the dead from evil spirits.

PAN   Greek god of pastures and flocks identified by the Greeks with the Egyptian god Ba-neb-djet, who was often portrayed as a ram.

PAPYRUS   A plant which could be woven into a paper-like material or used for ropes, sandals, and baskets that once grew in the Delta of Egypt. The Egyptians called the Delta "the land of papyrus." The plant symbolized all that was life-giving and was portrayed on an amulet, the Uadj, as well as on the scepters of the goddesses. Bouquets of papyrus were offered to the gods and to the dead.

The columns of Egyptian temples often resembled stylized papyrus plants, for the temple was believed to represent the Island of Creation, where all life had begun. The Latin word papyrus as well as the English word paper are derived from the Greek *papyros*.

PAPYRUS AMULET   see Uadj.

PAR   A form of the god Amen-Ra, called "Lord of the Phallus," "lofty of plumes," and "lord of transformations, whose skins [i.e., complexions] are manifold."

PEASANT AND THE WORKMAN, THE   Egyptian tale popular during the Middle Kingdom. The translation is by William Flinders Petrie in his *Egyptian Tales*. The tale is sometimes called "The Tale of the Eloquent Peasant."

There dwelt in the Sekhet Hemat—or Salt Country—a peasant called the Sekhti, with his wife and children, his asses and his dogs; and he trafficked in all good things of the Sekhet Hemat to Henenseten. Behold now he went with rushes, natron, and salt, with wood and pods, with stones and seeds, and all good products of the Sekhet Hemat. And this Sekhti journeyed to the south unto Henenseten; and when he came to the lands of the house of Fefa, north of Denat, he found a man there stand-

117

ing on the bank, a man called Hemti—the workman—son of a man called Asri, who was a serf of the high steward Meruitensa. Now said this Hemti, when he saw the asses of Sekhti, that were pleasing in his eyes, "Oh that some good god would grant me to steal away the goods of Sekhti from him!"

Now the Hemti's house was by the dike of the towpath, which was straightened, and not wide, as much as the width of a waistcloth: on the one side of it was the water, and on the other side of it grew his corn. Hemti said then to his servant, "Hasten! bring me a shawl from the house," and it was brought instantly. Then spread he out this shawl on the face of the dike, and it lay with its fastening on the water and its fringe on the corn.

Now Sekhti approached along the path used by all men. Said Hemti: "Have a care, Sekhti! you are not going to trample on my clothes!" Said Sekhti, "I will do as you like, I will pass carefully." Then went he up on the higher side. But Hemti said, "Go you over my corn, instead of the path?" Said Sekhti: "I am going carefully; this high field of corn is not my choice, but you have stopped your path with your clothes, and will you then not let us pass by the side of the path?" And one of the asses filled its mouth with a cluster of corn. Said Hemti: "Look you, I shall take away your ass, Sekhti, for eating my corn; behold it will have to pay according to the amount of the injury." Said Sekhti: "I am going carefully; the one way is stopped, therefore

took I my ass by the inclosed ground; and do you seize it for filling its mouth with a cluster of corn? Moreover, I know unto whom this domain belongs, even unto the lord steward Meruitensa. He it is who smites every robber in this whole land; and shall I then be robbed in his domain?"

Said Hemti, "This is the proverb which men speak: 'A poor man's name is only his own matter.' I am he of whom you spake, even the lord steward of whom you think." Thereon he took to him branches of green tamarisk and scourged all his limbs, took his asses, and drave them into the pasture. And Sekhti wept very greatly, by reason of the pain of what he had suffered. Said Hemti, "Lift not up your voice, Sekhti, or you shall go to the demon of silence." Sekhti answered: "You beat me, you steal my goods, and now would take away even my voice, O demon of silence! If you will restore my goods, then will I cease to cry out at your violence."

Sekhti stayed the whole day petitioning Hemti, but he would not give ear unto him. And Sekhti went his way to Khenensuten to complain to the lord steward Meruitensa. He found him coming out from the door of his house to embark on his boat, that he might go to the judgment hall. Sekhti said: "Ho! turn, that I may please thy heart with this discourse. Now at this time let one of thy followers, whom thou wilt, come to me that I may send him to thee concerning it." The lord steward Meruitensa made his follower, whom he chose, go straight unto

118

him, and Sekhti sent him back with an account of all these matters. Then the lord steward Meruitensa accused Hemti unto the nobles who sat with him; and they said unto him: "By your leave: As to this Sekhti of yours, let him bring a witness. Behold thou it is our custom with our Sekhtis; witnesses come with them; behold, that is our custom. Then it will be fitting to beat this Hemti for a trifle of natron and a trifle of salt; if he is commanded to pay for it, he will pay for it." But the high steward Meruitensa held his peace; for he would not reply unto these nobles, but would reply unto the Sekhti.

Now Sekhti came to appeal to the lord steward Meruitensa, and said, "O my lord steward, greatest of the great, guide of the needy:

When thou embarkest on the lake of truth—
Mayest thou sail upon it with a fair wind;
May thy mainsail not fly loose.
May there not be lamentation in thy cabin;
May not misfortune come after thee.
May not thy mainstays be snapped;
Mayest thou not run aground.
May not the wave seize thee;
Mayest thou not taste the impurities of the river;
Mayest thou not see the face of fear.

May the fish come to thee without escape;
Mayest thou reach unto plump water-fowl.
For thou are the orphan's father, the widow's husband,
The desolate woman's brother, the garment of the motherless.

Let me celebrate thy name in this land for every virtue.
A guide without greediness of heart;
A great one without any meanness.

Destroying deceit, encouraging justice;
Coming to the cry, and allowing utterance.

Let me speak, do thou hear and do justice;
O praised! whom the praised ones praise.

Abolish oppression, behold me, I am overladen,
Reckon with me, behold me defrauded."

Now the Sekhti made this speech in the time of the majesty of the King Neb-ka-n-ra, blessed. The lord steward Meruitensa went away straight to the King and said: "My lord, I have found one of these Sekhti, excellent of speech, in very truth; stolen are his goods, and he has come to complain to me of the matter."

His Majesty said: "As thou wishest that I may see health! lengthen out his complaint, without replying to any of his speeches. He who desireth him to continue speaking should be silent; behold, bring us his words in writing, that we may listen to them. But provide for his wife and his children, and let the Sekhti himself also have a living. Thou must cause one to give him his portion without letting him know that thou are he who is giving it to him."

There were given to him four loaves and two draughts of beer each day; which the lord steward Meruitensa provided for him, giving it to a friend

119

of his, who furnished it unto him. Then the lord steward Meruitensa sent the governor of the Sekhet Hemat to make provision for the wife of the Sekhti, three rations of corn each day.

Then came the Sekhti a second time, and even a third time, unto the lord steward Meruitensa; but he told two of his followers to go unto the Sekhti, and seize on him, and beat him with staves. But he came again unto him, even unto six times, and said:

"My Lord Steward—
Destroying deceit, and encouraging justice;
Raising up every good thing, and crushing every evil;
As plenty comes removing famine,
As clothing covers nakedness,
As clear sky after storm warms the shivering;
As fire cooks that which is raw,
As water quenches the thirst;
Look with thy face upon my lot; do not covet, but content me without fail; do the right and do not evil."

But yet Meruitensa would not hearken unto his complaint; and the Sekhti came yet, and yet again, even unto the ninth time. Then the lord steward told two of his followers to go unto the Sekhti; and the Sekhti feared that he should be beaten as at the third request. But the lord steward Meruitensa then said unto him: "Fear not, Sekhti, for what thou hast done. The Sekhti has made many speeches, delightful to the heart of his Majesty, and I take an oath—as I eat bread, and as I drink water—that thou shalt be remembered to eternity." Said the lord steward, "Moreover, thou shalt be satisfied when thou shalt hear of thy complaints." He caused to be written on a clean roll of papyrus each petition to the end, and the lord steward Meruitensa sent it to the majesty of the King Neb-ka-n-ra, blessed, and it was good to him more than anything that is in the whole land: but his Majesty said to Meruitensa: "Judge it thyself; I do not desire it."

The lord steward Meruitensa made two of his followers to go to the Sekhet Hemat, and bring a list of the household of the Sekhti; and its amount was six persons, beside his oxen and his goats, his wheat and his barley, his asses and his dogs; and moreover he gave all that which belonged unto the Hemti to the Sekhti, even all his property and his officers, and the Sekhti was beloved of the King more than all his overseers, and ate of all the good things of the King, with all his household.

PENNANT   see Netcher.

PERCH   Fish sacred to the goddess Neith.

PERFUMES   In ancient Egypt, both men and women employed perfumes for their personal use, as well as for cultic rites. Many Egyptian texts describe beautiful goddesses giving forth a perfume more lovely than any mortal woman. Perfumes were used in many temple rites and were manufactured in part of the temple complex. Nefertem was the god of perfumes.

PERFUMES, GOD OF see Nefertem.

PERIT One of twelve goddesses in the ninth section, or hour, of Tuat, the underworld, who, when greeted by the sun god Ra, begins to utter words of power causing the life and strength to arise in Osiris. The other goddesses are Shemat-khu, Nebt-shat, Nebt-shef-shefet, Aat-aatet, Nebt-setau, Hent-nut-s, Nebt-mat, Tesert-ant, Aat-khu, Sekhet-metu, and Neтert-en-khentet-Ra.

PERSEA TREE A sacred tree in ancient Egyptian belief that was often shown in temple scenes of the king's coronation. The king's name was inscribed by the gods on the persea tree. Opinions about which tree in the natural world the Persea represents vary.

PERSEPHONE Greek goddess of the underworld whom the Greeks identified with the Egyptian goddess Isis.

PER-UADJIT see Buto.

PESTHI A god who carries a bow in the tenth section, or hour, of Tuat, the underworld. Pesthi helps the sun god Ra as he travels toward the east, to slay his enemies.

PETESUCHOS Greek name for the sacred crocodile of the god Sebek, meaning, "the one whom Sebek has given." Suchos is the Greek name form of the Egyptian Sebek.

PETRA A god who has a disk on his head and appears in the eleventh section, or hour, of Tuat, the underworld. His arms would stretch in order to keep apart the wings of the serpent Tchet-s.

PETRIE, WILLIAM FLINDERS (1853–1942) Egyptologist who founded the Egyptian Research Account in 1894, and excavated various sites in Egypt, such as Abydos and Tell el-Amarna. He published many books, including translations of ancient Egyptian folktales.

PHALLUS GODDESS see Sekhmet-Bast-Ra.

PHALLUS, LORD OF see Par.

PHARAOH The King of Egypt. The name Pharaoh means "great house" and refers to the royal palace. The Pharaoh was the sole agent of the gods, and he alone was entitled to sacrifice to them, or to appoint priests to take his place in the temples of Egypt. He was commander-in-chief of the army, chief judge of the land, head of the administration and the treasury, and was considered a living god. During the Fifth Dynasty the Pharaoh came to be regarded as the son of Ra, the great sun god and this belief continued through all Dynasties. He was also believed to be an incarnation of Horus, the son of Osiris. When the Pharaoh died he became Osiris.

The Pharaoh was essential to the balance of life and the harmony of Egypt. His many roles were reflected

Pharaoh

PHILAE   A tiny island, "The Pearl of Egypt," with fourteen buildings, which was one of the main centers of worship for Isis. The island is now threatened with submersion by the Aswan dam, but its various structures have been moved to the neighboring island of Agilkia. The very last hieroglyphic inscription carved in Egypt is on Philae. Worship of Isis continued on the island into the sixth century of the Christian era.

PHOENIX   see Benu.

PHRA   see Ra.

PHYSICAL BODY OF A MAN   see Khat.

PIG   The pig was generally regarded as evil by the ancient Egyptians and was associated with the evil god Set. The *Book of the Dead* offers the myth explaining this view.

in his daily life as well as in his royal insignia. He carried a scepter with the head of the god Set, the brother of Osiris, and his headdress was the uraeus spitting out flames of death on his enemies. Attached to his belt was a bull's tail to indicate his power. His false beard was worshipped as a separate divinity. The Pharaoh usually celebrated a great festival, called Sed, on the 30th anniversary of his reign. The Sed was believed to renew his vital force and to make him his own successor. The Pharaoh had one chief wife, as well as a harem.

One day Ra said to Horus, "Let me see what is coming to pass in thine eye." Peering into Horus's eye Ra said, "Look at that black pig." Thereupon Horus looked, and instantly felt that a great injury had been done to his eye. He said to Ra, "Verily, my eye seemeth as if it were an eye upon which Suti had inflicted a blow." Suti was another name for the evil god Set who inflicted this wound upon his enemy Horus. As a result, Ra decreed that the pig was to be held as an abomination.

Herodotus in his *History* (Book 2) writes that if an Egyptian so much as

touched a pig with his garment he had
to go immediately to the Nile and
cleanse himself of the pollution. He also
notes that swineherds were the only
men not allowed to enter temples and
that the Egyptians sacrificed pigs to
the moon. Although the exact connection is not known, evidence suggests
that the pig was in some way associated with Osiris. The sow was sacred
to Nut who was sometimes portrayed
as a sow with her piglets painted on
her belly. It was thought that she ate
them each morning. The piglets were
believed to be the stars eaten by the
sky goddess.

PILLOW AMULET   see Weres.

PLANETS   The Egyptians assigned
gods to be protectors of the planets.
They were:

Saturn: Horus
Mars: Ra
Mercury: Set
Venus: Osiris
Jupiter: no god assigned.

PLINY THE ELDER   (A.D. 23–79)
Author of *Natural History* which includes descriptions of various Egyptian sites.

PLUTARCH   (c. A.D. 46–120) Greek
historian, biographer, and philo-
sopher noted for his *Parallel Lives,*
which contrasts the lives of famous
Greeks and Romans. Plutarch's *Isis
and Osiris,* an account of the myth of
Osiris and the cult practices that surrounded it, is the most famous of his

studies of religious practices. It is the
only comprehensive and continuous
narrative of the myth of Osiris that
has come down to us from the ancient
world.

P-NEB-TAUI   Son of Haroeris, or
Horus the Elder, worshipped with his
mother, Ta-sent-nefert.

PRAYERS   see Hymns and Prayers.

PRIAPUS   Greek god of fertility
identified by the Greeks with the
Egyptian god Ba-neb-djet who was
often portrayed as a ram.

PRIESTS   The titles for priests varied with their office and function in
ancient Egypt. The general term, Ueb
(Uab or Wab), meaning "pure," was
used for the priests who officiated at
the offering of drinks to the gods. Another order was charged with reciting
from the sacred books. The Hen-neter
or Hem-netcher, "servant of the god,"
was a prophet.

Priests as well as lay people were
employed to honor the god of the temple. The office of priest could be held on
a part-time basis, divided into four
shifts of one month, with each group of
priests serving for a total of three
months a year. Priests also functioned
as scribes, artists, or doctors.

The high priest was called Khorp
hemtiu, "chief of the artificers," at the
temple of Ptah, and was elsewhere
known as War-mau, or "great of
sight." The high priest was the dele-
gate of the Pharaoh, who alone had the

direct authority to offer sacrifice to the gods. These offices often passed from father to son.

In the Old Kingdom the priests appear to have worn the same garments as lay people, although a few, such as the high priest of Ptah, wore some chest covering. In an illustration from the Middle Kingdom the officiating priest wears a skirt in an earlier fashion than the others depicted, which indicates that the priesthood may have turned ordinary dress into ritual clothes when styles changed.

During the Middle Kingdom the priests did not adopt the mantle or double dress of the lay people, but wore instead the simple plain skirt of earlier fashions. The priests of the New Kingdom are shown in the narrow short skirt common at the beginning of the Fourth Dynasty, while others wore the long wide skirt of the Middle Kingdom. The priests wound a scarf around the upper part of the body, or put a wide cape that reached below the arms over the skirt, or wrapped their whole body in a great cloak. At funeral services the Sem priest and the high priest at Heliopolis wore a panther skin. The chief priest of Memphis under the Eighteenth and Nineteenth Dynasties wore a badge around his neck, in the same style as worn during the Fourth Dynasty.

While the cultic outfits of various orders differed, priests throughout the New Kingdom uniformly followed the custom of shaving their heads. Herodotus, in his *History* (Book 2), attributes this fashion to cleanliness.

Laymen shaved their heads often and wore wigs over their naked scalps; priests went without wigs.

PROSTITUTION   see Family.

PSCHENT   see Crowns.

PTAH   The craft god, protector of artisans and artists.

Ptah was the great worker in metals, and the chief smelter, caster, and sculptor of the gods. It is said that through his heart and tongue he rendered power to the gods.

According to one version of the Egyptian creation myths Ptah was the master craftsman who brought forth everything. He fashioned the gods, made the cities, founded the nomes, installed the gods in their shrines, established their offerings, equipped their holy places, and made likenesses of their bodies to the satisfaction of their hearts.

Ptah was worshipped at Memphis with his consort, Sekhmet, lioness goddess of war and battle, and their son, Nefertem, forming the Memphis Triad. The celebrated Apis bull, said to be a living incarnation of the god, was kept near his temple. Ptah was surpassed in importance in the Egyptian pantheon only by Amen, Ra, and Osiris. He was of such importance that his name was frequently joined to other gods, forming such composite gods as Ptah-Osiris, Ptah-Seker, Ptah-Seker-Osiris, Ptah-Seker-Tem, Ptah-Hap, Ptah-Nun, and Ptah-Tatenn.

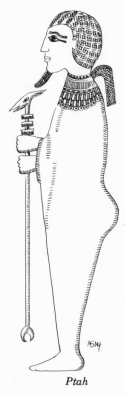

Ptah

In Egyptian art Ptah was portrayed as a bearded man with a tightly fitting cap and tightly fitting garment from which his hands extended. The Menat, a counterpoise of weight used to balance the necklace of the god, hung from the back of his neck.

The Greeks identified Ptah with their god Hephaestus, whereas the Romans equated him with Vulcan.

PTAH-HAP A composite god made up of Ptah, the craft god, and the Nile god Hap.

PTAH-NUN A composite god made up of the gods Ptah and Nun.

PTAH-OSIRIS A composite god made up of the craft god Ptah and the god of the dead, Osiris.

PTAH-SEKER A composite god made up of the craft god Ptah and the death god Seker.

PTAH-TATENN A composite god made up of Ptah, the craft god, and Tatenn, or Tenen, an ancient and obscure creation god. In one Egyptian hymn, written about B.C. 1200, Ptah-Tatenn is called the god who makes "the earth bring forth fruits so that gods and men may have abundance."

Ptah-Tatenn was portrayed as a mummy with a pair of horns and a disk and two plumes on his head.

PTOLEMIES Greek house that ruled in Egypt. When Alexander the Great died he left his four-year old son as his heir. The boy was promptly killed and his empire divided among his generals. In B.C. 305 Egypt came under the rule of Ptolemy, who was one of Alexander's generals. The reign of the Ptolemies lasted from B.C. 305 to 30 when Cleopatra, the last queen, killed herself, and Octavius, later Augustus, made Egypt part of the Roman Empire.

PYGMIES In Egypt pygmies, who are first mentioned during the Sixth Dynasty, were used as dancers who greeted the sun god with acrobatics each day.

PYLONS Two great towers that stood in front of the main entrance to Egyptian temples.

125

PYRAMID The Egyptians called this structure a *mer.* Our word pyramid is believed to come from the Greek *pyramis,* which may mean "a wheaten cake" or "mound of fire." Pyramids were originally constructed as tombs for the kings. The most famous are the great pyramids of Gizeh built during the Old Kingdom.

The largest pyramid is the great Pyramid of Khufu (Cheops) which covers 13 acres and was built to a height of 480 feet, constructed of over two million stones. The entire structure was covered with polished limestone. The buildings were put up by specialists, such as quarrymen, stonecutters, masons, carpenters, draughtsmen, engravers, decorators, and painters, who worked around the year. The unskilled labor force was taken from the army and laborers who may have been conscripted to do the work. There were not many prisoners of war during the time of the building of the pyramids; thus slave labor played a very small part in the building. A good part of slave labor consisted of prisoners of war in the later dynasties.

PYRAMID TEXTS Series of sacred texts found in the pyramid of King Unas of the Fifth Dynasty, as well as in four other pyramids of the Sixth Dynasty. The texts are engraved on the walls and corridors of the pyramids. They consist of prayers, magical formulas, and various rubrics to guarantee the deceased a safe journey to the other world.

Q

QEB   see Geb.

QEBHET   A personification of "cool water" who in some texts is said to be the daughter of Anubis. A variant spelling is Qebhut.

QEBHUT   see Qebhet.

QEBH-SENNUF   One of the four sons of Horus and Isis who guarded the intestines and was portrayed as hawk-headed. A variant spelling is Qebsnuf.

QEBSNUF   see Qebh-sennuf.

QEBUI   God of the north wind portrayed as a four-headed ram with four wings, or as a man with four ram heads.

QEMET   see Kemet.

QERHET   A serpent goddess, patron of the eight nomes of Lower Egypt.

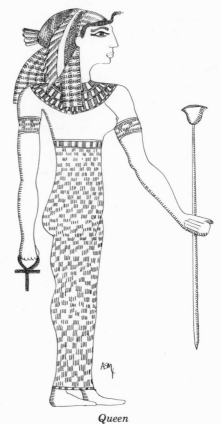

Queen

QUEEN   Although the Pharaoh could have many wives, he had only one queen. The Queen was called the "Great Wife," and her children generally supplied the sucession to the throne. In the Old Kingdom she was

127

called, "She who sees the gods Horus and Set" (that is, the possessor of Upper and Lower Egypt), "the most pleasant, the highly praised, the friend of Horus, the beloved of him who wears the two crowns." Under the New Kingdom she is called, "The Consort of the god, the mother of the god, the great consort of the King." The queen's name along with the king's was enclosed in a cartouche when it appeared to indicate their importance. The Queen, who is often believed to have been the sister-wife of the king, might in fact have come from a foreign country, or she might have been descended from the descendant of a fallen dynasty, or the daughter of the king by some other wife. After the death of the Pharaoh the Queen, as the Royal Mother, still maintained a function at court, with her own property held under special management.

QUEEN'S CROWN   see Crowns.

R

RA   A sun god described in many texts as the creator of everything. Although the original significance of this name is unknown, it is said that Ra once meant "creator" or "creative power," reflecting the god's position as the greatest of the deities and true father of the gods.

Ra's sun disk appeared above the waters of the Nun, or Chaos, as one of the first acts of creation, and thus signaled the beginning of time. The Egyptians believed that Ra made his journey over the waters in a boat since they thought that the sun was made of fire and could not have risen out of the waters of chaos on its own. The morning boat was called Matet, "becoming strong," and the evening boat Semktet, or "becoming weak." The course of Ra was said to have been mapped out by the goddess Maat, the personification of physical and moral law. In the evening after the sun had set in the west, Ra entered Tuat, the underworld, and was assisted by the gods who lived there. Two fishes, Abtu and Ant, swam before his boat as pilots. As he passed through so that he might appear in the sky the next morning, Ra gave air, light, and food to the unfortunate condemned to Tuat. Before leaving, he was drawn into battle by Apophis, a giant serpent and night demon whose attacks failed; Ra cast a spell that made him incapable of movement. The monster was then bound in chains, hacked to pieces by Ra's followers, and destroyed by the sun god's flames. This was symbolic of the sun destroying the vapors and dampness of the night.

In the *Books of the Overthrowing of Apophis,* a ritual is prescribed that was recited daily in the temple of Amen-Ra at Thebes (Amen-Ra being another form of the sun god). The recitation catalogued in great detail the destruction that was to befall Apophis and his monstrous helpers, Sebau and Nak.

The worship of the sun is very ancient and was practiced throughout Egypt. In dynastic times the center of the cult of Ra was at Heliopolis. Its site is marked by the present-day village of Matariyeh, about five miles northeast of Cairo. The early Christians placed great value on the oil made from the olive trees that grew there. According to Christian tradition, the Virgin Mary washed the garments of the

Christ Child in the "fountain of the sun," which was the lake or pool of that region where the ancient Egyptians claimed that Ra bathed each morning at sunrise.

All the kings of Egypt in the early Empire believed themselves to be the sons of Ra. It was said that whenever the divine blood of the kings needed replenishing, the god took the form of the reigning king of Egypt, visited the queen in her chamber, and impregnated her with his seed. The child born of this union was regarded as the god incarnate and in time was presented to the sun god in his temple. This scheme undoubtedly gave the priests of Ra great power in ancient Egypt.

Under the Fifth Dynasty the worship of the man god Osiris spread over the delta region from Busiris, the northern center of the cult, and the priests of the sun god fought to maintain Ra's authority from Abydos, the southern center throughout Upper Egypt. However, before the end of the Sixth Dynasty the cult of Osiris had won out and Ra was relegated to an inferior position, with the greatest of his attributes ascribed to Osiris. From the Twelfth Dynasty onward all the attributes of Ra were absorbed by Amen, who was the dominant god of Upper Egypt.

During the Nineteenth and Twentieth Dynasties, seventy-five forms of Ra were known, the names comprising part of a litany to Ra, which is believed to have been sung during services in the temples. The litany was painted on the walls of several tombs, such as those of Seti I and Rameses IV.

At a very early period Ra was associated with the hawk god Horus, who personified the height of heaven. In Egyptian art Ra is usually portrayed as a hawk-headed man or sometimes in the form of a hawk. He wears the disk of the sun encircled by a serpent on his head. When he appears in human form, he holds the Ankh, emblem of life, in his right hand and a scepter in his left.

Variants of his name are Re and Phra.

RABBIT-HEADED DEITIES see Wenenu and Wenenut.

RACES Ritual races were an important part of Egyptian cultic practices. The Pharaoh is sometimes portrayed on the walls of temples wearing a Shento (loin-cloth) and running a ritual race before the gods. These races were repeated at the Seb, the ceremony held after the Pharaoh had ruled for thirty years. It is believed that the races were to display the king's power as well as his willingness to serve the gods.

RA-HORAKHTY A composite god made up of the sun god Ra and Horus, called Horakhty, or "Horus who is on the horizon." The Greeks called him Harmachis. Ra-Horakhty was portrayed as a hawk-headed man wearing the solar disk and triple crown or the uraeus and the Atef crown.

RAIN, GOD OF see Min.

RAMESSEUM Name given to the mortuary site of Rameses II at Thebes, dedicated to the god Amen. The area contained a temple, a royal palace, a mortuary temple built by Sethos I and several storerooms. All the buildings were enclosed by a rectangular brick wall.

RAM-HEADED GOD see Khnemu.

RAM OF MENDES see Ba-neb-djet.

RA-STAU Name given to passages in tombs that were said to lead from this world to the "other world." Rastau originally indicated the cemetery of Sakkara, which was the domain of the death god Seker.

RAT Wife of the sun god Ra, who was called "mother of the gods," as Ra was called "father of the gods." However, Rat was a late development in the cult of Ra and amounts to little more than a feminization of Ra's name. The sun god was said to have sired the first divine couple without having had intercourse with a female. Rat was portrayed in Egyptian art as a woman wearing a headdress of a disk with horns and the uraeus and sometimes with two feathers on the disk.

RAU A god who carries a javelin in the tenth section, or hour, of Tuat, the underworld. He helps the sun god Ra slay his enemies, during his travels toward the east.

RE see Ra.

REASON AND INTELLIGENCE, GOD OF see Saa.

RED see Colors.

RED CROWN see Crowns.

RED LAND see Deshret.

REM A god believed in some Egyptian texts to be a personification of the sun god Ra's tears. His name means "to weep."

REMI A god mentioned in the *Book of the Dead,* identified by some scholars as a fish god, and by others as a variant form of Rem, the tears of the sun god Ra.

RENENET A title of the goddess Isis as goddess of the harvest.

RENNIU Four bearded gods found in the eleventh section of Tuat, the underworld.

RENPET Goddess of the year's duration. She was associated with springtime and youth in particular. Renpet was portrayed as a woman wearing a long palmshoot curving above her head at the end, which was the ideogram of her name.

REREK   A form of the monster serpent taken by the evil god Set to oppose the sun god Ra from appearing daily in the East. The monster was identified with Apophis, the great serpent.

RERT, RERTU   see Taurt.

RESHPU   A Syrian god worshipped in Egypt described as the "great god, the lord of eternity, the prince of everlastingness. . . ." He is often portrayed as a warrior holding a shield, spear, and a club. A variant spelling is Reshep.

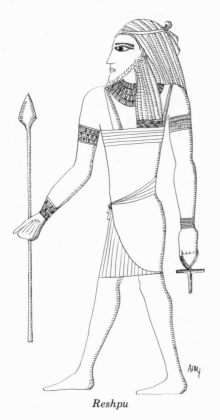

Reshpu

RESURRECTION, GOD OF   see Osiris.

RETA   see Fa.

RHAMPSINITUS   see Treasure of Rhampsinitus, The.

RITUAL   see Temples.

RITUAL GARMENTS OF PRIESTS   see Priests.

RITUAL RACES   see Races.

ROBERTS, DAVID   (1796–1864) Scottish painter who traveled to Egypt and the Holy Land, and produced a six-volume work, *The Holy Land,* containing numerous romantic views of Egyptian sites. His renderings did much to stir interest in ancient Egypt.

ROSETTA STONE   Name given to a slab of black basalt containing inscriptions in hieroglyphics, demotic, and Greek. It was found by a French artillery officer, Pierre François-Xavier Bouscard (1772–1832), among the ruins of Fort Saint Julien, near the Rosetta mouth of the Nile in 1799. The work was used by Jean François Champollion to decipher the meaning of the hieroglyphics.

The inscriptions on the Rosetta Stone are a version of a decree issued by the priesthood assembled at Memphis in honor of Ptolemy V, Epiphanes. The inscription tells that Ptolemy consecrated revenues of silver and wheat to the temples, that he suppressed certain taxes and reduced others, granted privileges to priests and soldiers, and that when, in the eighth year of his reign, the Nile rose and flooded all the plains, he undertook the task of damming the river. In return for these gracious acts, the priests at Memphis decreed that a statue of the king should be set up in a conspicuous place in all the temples in Egypt, and inscribed with the name and title of "Ptolemy, the savior of Egypt."

The Rosetta Stone came into the possession of the British Museum after the French were defeated by the British in 1801.

RUTY   Epitaph meaning "the pair of lions" which refers to the god Shu and his consort Tefnut.

S

SA Sign of "protection," actually a stylized life-preserver worn by river travelers and made of papyrus. It appears with the hippopotamus goddess Taurt, who rests her hand on it.

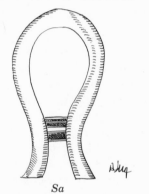

Sa

SAA see Sia.

SAA-SET A huge serpent that stands on his tail, found in the first section of Tuat, the underworld.

SACHARIS see Seker.

SACRED LAKE Each Egyptian temple had a sacred lake, in a rectangular or horseshoe shape as part of its design. The Sacred Lake was believed to be a reproduction of the primordial lake of creation where all life began. The priests of the temple would wash themselves in the Sacred Lake at dawn, before they began their rites. In some temples the mysteries associated with Osiris were acted out on the sides of the lake during the night.

SAIS, GODDESS OF THE CITY OF see Neith.

SAKHMIS see Sekhmet.

SAKKARA A necropolis located near Memphis which contains the Step Pyramid of Zoser I and various other monuments and tombs of the Old Kingdom. Variant spellings are Sakkareh and Saqqara.

SAKKAREH see Sakkara.

SANDALS White sandals were worn during various cultic rites. Most Egyptians, however, went about barefoot.

SANDYS, GEORGE (1578–1664) English traveler and translator who visited Egypt in 1610 and wrote *Relation of a Journey Begun A.D. 1610,* which tells of his visit to the Great Pyramid, and to Alexandria and Cairo. Sandys also made an allegorical translation of Ovid's *Metamorphoses* into heroic couplets.

SAQQARA   see Sakkara.

SARAPIS   see Serapis.

SARCOPHAGUS Protective container for coffins, made of various materials, such as stone or wood. During the first six Dynasties they are rectangular, and their cover is either flat as a plank, or vaulted. A projection about two inches deep runs around the edge of the inside of the cover and has been carefully chiselled to fit a corresponding hollow on the sarcophagus. When the cover was lowered, a layer of fine cement was inserted in between, hermetically sealing the container.

During the Eleventh and Twelfth Dynasties rectangular wooden coffins came into use. The Eighteenth Dynasty coffins are in the shape of a mummy and made of granite. In the Twentieth Dynasty granite was also used, but the deceased is now portrayed lying on the cover, wearing a thick, square beard, his hands freed from their bandages and holding the ankh, Tet, and Thet symbols.

The Sixteenth Dynasty coffins are usually rectangular and made of green and black basalt and variegated hard stone. After the Sixteenth Dynasty the sarcophagi are sometimes rounded at the head and the covers have human faces. They are decorated with rows of figures of the gods, the four children of Horus, and various spirits of the underworld.

Under the rule of the Ptolemies and Romans, wooden sarcophagi became very common. They consisted of two parts, the board upon which the mummy in his coffin was laid, and the rectangular vaulted cover, which was sometimes as high as eighteen inches. The mummies in these coffins were covered with a linen cloth on which was painted the god Osiris, with the features of the deceased, and the symbols associated with the god.

SATET   see Satis.

SATIS Goddess who spread the life-giving waters of the Nile over the land. Her name means "she who runs like an arrow" and indicates that Satis may originally have been a goddess of the hunt.

Satis is portrayed as a woman holding the ankh, emblem of life, in her hand and wearing the white crown of the south of Egypt. She is sometimes confused with the goddess Satet (Satet also being a variant spelling of Satis's name), who was a local form of the goddess Isis. She was sometimes called Isis-Satis or Isis-Sothis.

SATNI-KHAMOIS Hero of *The Adventures of Satni-Khamois with the Mummies,* an ancient Egyptian tale of unknown date. The story tells how Satni-Khamois, a "magician who had no equal in the land of Egypt," met a mummy, Nenoferkephtah, and visited his tomb, hoping to obtain some Hermetic books that contained secret

Scarab

lore. The mummies are members of Nenoferkephtah's family and have none of the demonic qualities of their depictions in films and horror stories.

SATURN The planet Saturn was under the protection of the god Horus.

SCARAB The scarab or beetle is one of the most common symbols in Egyptian mythology and religion. It was associated with the sun. One early text says: "This Unas flieth like a bird, and alighteth like a beetle; he flieth like a bird and he alighteth like a beetle upon the throne which is empty in thy boat, O Ra." In another text, the king is described as "like a scarab," while another claims that Pepi I is "the son of the scarab which is born in Hetepet. . . . "

The beetle was a symbol for the creator god Khepera, for the Egyptians associated the beetle with spontaneous creation and regeneration.

In *Isis and Osiris,* which deals with Egyptian religious beliefs, Plutarch writes: "As for the scarab-beetle, it is held that there are no females of this species; they are all males. They place their seed in a round pellet of material, which they roll along, pushing it with their hind legs, imitating by their action the course of the sun from east to west which seems to follow a direction to that which the sky follows."

The amulet of the scarab has been found in incalculable thousands throughout ancient Egypt. They are often made of green basalt, green granite, limestone, green marble, blue paste, blue glass, purple, blue, and green glazed porcelain. The "words of power" are usually cut in outline on the base. In rare instances, the scarab has a human face or head, and sometimes the backs are inscribed with figures of the boat of the sun god Ra, or the Benu bird, "the soul of Ra."

When the custom of buying scarabs with the bodies of the dead was established, the living began to wear them as protection. Scarabs passed into use in both the Greek and Roman world.

From one Greek papyrus on magic we learn that there was a "ceremony of the beetle" associated with the goddess Isis. The rather elaborate ceremony was supposed to have taken place on the seventh, ninth, tenth, twelfth, fourteenth, sixteenth, twenty-first, twenty-fourth, and twenty-fifth day from the beginning of the month. The spell that was recited began: "I am Thoth, the inventor and founder of medicines and letters; come to me, thou that art under the earth, rise up to me, thou great spirit."

Scepter

SCEPTERS   Various kinds of scepters are held by the gods and goddesses, as well as the Pharaoh. The most common form has on it the head of the god Set as a stylized animal that somewhat resembles a dog with long ears. The bottom of the scepter is forked. Goddesses often carry the Lotus Scepter or the Papyrus Scepter.

SCIENCE, GOD OF   see Thoth.

SCORPION   The scorpion was venerated in Egypt from earliest times, and was associated with the scorpion goddess Serqet as well as the goddess Isis. In one myth Seven Scorpions accompany Isis on her journey and aid the goddess, while in another part of the myth an evil scorpion finds its way to Horus and stings him. The Egyptians believed that scorpions respected Isis and would therefore not kill a woman, only men.

SCRIBES   The Egyptian word for scribe means "he who writes," and the profession was under the patronage of the god Thoth, the divine scribe of the gods. Aside from their various secular duties, the scribes produced the sacred texts for temples and for religious rites. One of the many advantages of this position was that the scribe did not have to pay taxes.

SEB   see Geb.

SEBEK   Crocodile god. In primitive times when the canals of Egypt had dried up, the crocodile was able to wander about the fields at will, to kill and eat whatever came into its path. The Egyptians came to regard this animal as a personification of the powers of evil and death, and they associated it with their demonic god Set.

In later times, according to Herodotus in his *History* (Book 2), crocodiles became sacred in parts of Egypt, such as at Shedet (called

138

Crocodilopolis by the Greeks) where a sacred crocodile was kept in a lake dug alongside Sebek's sanctuary. The sacred crocodile, which was adorned with crystal and gold earrings and bracelets on its forepaws, was said to be the god incarnate. Visitors brought offerings of food which the priests of Sebek were obliged to feed to it. The crocodile was embalmed and buried in a sacred vault when it died. In classical times the Greeks rendered the god's name Suchos and called the sacred crocodile Petesuchos, "the one whom Suchos has given."

The crocodile plays an important part in Egyptian mythology. He appears as both friend and enemy of the god Osiris. One myth tells that the crocodile god carried the dead body of Osiris upon its back safely to land, and another that Isis, the sister-wife of Osiris, made a little ark of papyrus plants to protect her son Horus from attack by the crocodile god. In later Egyptian mythology the crocodile was regarded as a symbol of the sun and was associated with the sun god Ra, forming the composite god, Sebek-Ra.

In Egyptian art Sebek is portrayed as a crocodile-headed man, wearing either a solar disk encircled with the uraeus or a pair of ram's horns surmounted by a disk and a pair of plumes. A small pair of horns is sometimes shown above the large horns. Often the god is depicted simply as a crocodile. Variants of the name are Sebeq, Suchos, and Sobek.

SEBEQ   see Sebek.

SEBI   A monster serpent who guards the entrance to the twelfth section of Tuat, the underworld, as the sun god Ra passes in his boat.

SECHMET   se Sekhmet.

SED   Royal festival held in honor of the Pharaoh after he ruled for thirty years. Every three years after the first celebration another festival was held. The Sed always took place at Mem-

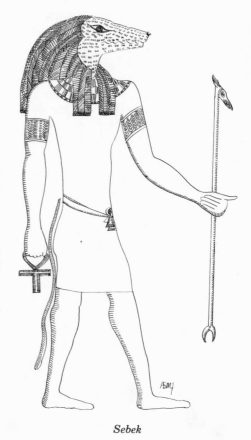

Sebek

139

phis. The king was crowned King of Upper and Lower Egypt, ran ritual races, and was carried in procession. This process was believed to renew his vital forces, thus making him his own successor. Sometimes it is called Heb-sed.

SEFER   Fantastic animal with the winged body of a lion and the head of an eagle.

SEFKHET-AABUT   Goddess of literature and the library. She was closely associated with Thoth, the god of wisdom. Her chief duties were connected with the writing of history. A king was considered very fortunate if his deeds were recorded by her.

In Egyptian art she was portrayed wearing a close-fitting, panther-skin garment and holding a scribe's palette and writing reed. In this form she was called "the great one, the lady of the house of books." Variants of her name are Sesheta and Seshat.

SEGER   see Seker.

SEKER   Death god of the necropolis at Memphis. His kingdom was described in the *Book of the Dead,* as a land of utter darkness. The dead of Memphis remained in sleep and were given light only when the sun god Ra passed through.

It is thought that Seker was originally a vegetation god. He was later combined with the god Osiris and worshipped under the composite name Seker-Osiris. As death gods, Seker

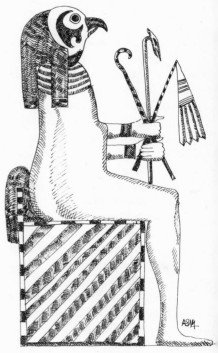

Seker

and Osiris shared many attributes, but Seker came to represent absolute death when Osiris triumphed over all other gods of death in Egypt. Osiris was then identified with the death that was only a temporary state through which the righteous must pass to obtain reward in the kingdom of Osiris. The union of Ptah with Seker and Osiris created the great funerary god of Memphis, Ptah-Seker-Osiris. Ptah provided new bodies for the souls of the righteous, and thus symbolized the addition of creative power (Ptah) to death (Seker and Osiris).

In Egyptian art Seker is portrayed as a hawk-headed man in mummified form. His hands extend from the front of his close-fitting garment and hold the emblems of sovereignty and dominion. He sometimes has the head of a man and holds a knife in each hand. Ptah-Seker-Osiris usually has the form of Osiris, but Egyptian artists also depicted the god as a squat pigmy with a large bald head and thick limbs, a beetle on top of his head, and a lock of hair to the right of it.

Variants of Seker's name are Sacharis, Seger, Sokar, Sokare, and Sokaris.

SEKER BOAT Magical boat used in religious ceremonies in ancient Egypt.

The Seker Boat did not look like an ordinary boat. One end of it was much higher than the other and was constructed in the shape of the head of a gazelle or oryx. The center of the boat was occupied by a closed coffer surmounted by a hawk with protective wings stretching over the top of it. The coffer was said to contain the body of the dead sun god and rested upon a framework or sleigh which was furnished with runners.

On the great day of the festival of the god Seker, the ceremony of placing the Seker Boat, or Hennu Boat (as it is called in the *Book of the Dead*), upon its sleigh shape was performed at sunrise under the direction of the high priest of Memphis. The priest lifted the Seker Boat upon its sleigh and marched at the head of the procession of priests who drew the sleigh around the sanctuary. The ceremony sym-

bolized the Egyptian belief in the revolution of the sun and other heavenly bodies. A variant spelling is Sokar Boat.

SEKHAIT, SEKHAUIT, SEKHAUTET, AND SEKHEM see Sekhmet.

SEKHEM The vital power associated with the Akh, the spirit. Its exact function is not known.

SEKHEM EM PET The name for the god Anubis as a son of Osiris.

SEKHEM TAUI The name for the god Anubis as a form of his father, Osiris.

SEKHENU see Fa and Hentio.

SEKHET-AARU A name originally given to the island of the Delta where the souls of the dead lived. The name literally means "field of the reeds."

It was said that luxuriant crops of wheat as high as five cubits and barley as high as seven grew on this island. The spirits of the blessed dead, who measured nine cubits high lived here. And in the middle of Sekhet-Aaru there was a door through which the sun god Ra appeared each day.

Egyptian texts are not in agreement as to the location of the island. Some place it in the Great Oasis, or Al Khrgah, and others in the Delta. The Pyramid Texts claim that it was situated far beyond a large expanse of water.

141

The Egyptians believed that Sekhet-Aaru could only be reached with the personal help of the gods, who would transport their faithful worshippers to it. The island corresponds in many ways to the Greek concept of the Elysian Fields.

SEKHMET   A lion goddess who personified the fierce, destructive heat of the sun. Her name literally means "the powerful one." She has been called the great and terrible lion goddess who belched fire. She was also honored as a goddess of war and battle who could be both punitive and death-dealing.

According to one Egyptian text she came into being as an aspect of the cow goddess Hathor, to wreak vengeance on the people of Set, and her fury was so devastating that the other gods had to intervene to save mankind from total destruction. In her friendly form she was sometimes identified with the cat goddess Bast.

Sekhmet was the consort of the god Ptah, and together with their son, Nefertem, formed the divine Memphis Triad. Later it was said that her son by Ptah was the ruling Pharaoh himself.

In Egyptian art Sekhmet was portrayed as a woman with the head of a lioness which was surmounted by the solar disk encircled by the uraeus. The disk was sometimes omitted and only the uraeus was shown.

Vairants of her name are Sechmet, Sekhait, Sekhauit, Sekhautet and Sekhem. The Greeks rendered it as Sakhmis.

SEKHMET-BAST-RA   Composite deity portrayed with a male head on the body of a woman with a phallus.

SELKET; SELQET; AND SELQUET   see Serqet.

SEM   A priest who officiated at funerary rituals wearing a leopard skin slung across his linen undergarment.

SEMA   Amulet representing the lungs and windpipe. The word means "to join."

SEM-AF   A mummified form of Osiris, meaning "the image of Af," who appears in the twelfth section, or hour, of Tuat, the underworld.

SEMI   A large winged uraeus standing on its tail, found in the tenth section, or hour, of Tuat, the underworld.

SEMKTET   The evening boat meaning "becoming weak," in which the sun god Ra traveled when the sun set at the end of the day.

SEMSEM   see Fa.

SENENAHEMTHET   A serpent demon mentioned in a magical formula of Unas, a king of the Fifth Dynasty.

SEPES   A deity who lived in the persea tree at Heliopolis.

SERAPIS   Composite god worshipped by the Egyptians and Greeks.

Serapis was a link between the Egyptian god of the dead, Osiris, and the sacred bull of Memphis, Apis. The association was first made by the priests of Memphis, who regarded Apis as a manifestation of Osiris on earth.

Serapis's cult was founded in Alexandria during the reign of Ptolemy I, a ruler who wanted to symbolize his dynasty with a god venerated by both Greeks and Egyptians at a common shrine. The worship of Serapis later spread to Greece. For a time during the Roman Empire, the worship of Serapis, along with that of the goddess Isis, rivaled that of all other Mediterranean deities.

Serapis was often portrayed as a bull-headed man wearing the solar disk and the uraeus between his horns and holding symbols that were associated with Osiris. Variants of his name are Asar-Hapi, Hapi-Asar, and Asar-Hap, all of which are combinations of Osiris and Apis.

SERAPEUM   Large complex at Memphis dedicated to the cult of the Apil bulls, which consisted of subterranean burial chambers for the bulls as well as two temples. The temples no longer exist but the underground chambers were discovered in 1851 by Auguste Mariette, the French archaeologist. There is also a Serapeum at Alexandria.

SERDAD   see Mastaba.

SERPENT   see Snakes.

SERPENT'S HEAD AMULET   An amulet in the form of a serpent's head which was placed on the mummy to protect it from being bitten by snakes in Tuat, the underworld, and in the tomb.

SERQET   Scorpion goddess associated with the dead, who was often seen on the walls of tombs with her winged arms outstretched in a protective gesture.

Serqet was believed to have special province over the entrails of the deceased. She was a companion of the goddess Isis in her wanderings, and it was said that those who worshipped Isis were never stung by a scorpion.

Serqet was portrayed either as a woman with a scorpion on her head or as a scorpion with the head of a woman. Variants of her name are Salkis, Selket, Selqet and Selquet.

SESHAT; SHESHETA   see Sefkhet-Aabut.

SET   God of evil and darkness, the brother of Osiris and Isis.

He was the son of the earth, Geb, and the sky, Nut, who had torn himself violently from his mother's womb. He was abominated by the people for his harsh and bloody ways, and regarded as the personification of drought, darkness, and perversity, and the natural opponent to all that was good and life-giving in the universe.

Set's worship was one of the oldest cults of Egypt. He was originally a beneficent god of Upper Egypt, who resided in the abode of the blessed dead, where he performed friendly offices for the deceased. When the followers of Horus (the Elder), the supreme god of Lower Egypt, conquered the followers of Set, Set's place in the Egyptian pantheon of gods fell into disrepute. The priests of Horus eventually declared him a god of the unclean, an enemy of all other gods, and ordered that his images be destroyed.

Set was the archenemy of the sun god Ra, and almost all allusions and myths pertaining to him refer to the battles he waged against the sun. In the earliest and most simple form of the myth, Set represented the cosmic opposition of darkness and light. In a later form, he is the antagonist of the sun god Ra, and takes the form of the monstrous serpent Apophis, to prevent the sun god from appearing in the east each day. The result was always the same. Apophis was annihilated by the burning heat of Ra, and Set, who could renew himself daily, collected his noxious cohorts and readied himself for the next night's battle against the sunrise.

In the most famous and complex version of the myth, Set is the murderer and dismemberer of his brother Osiris, who was sometimes called Set's twin. He pursued and persecuted Osiris's widow Isis, who was also his own sister, and their child Horus (the Younger). Later, Horus was called upon to avenge his father's death, and in a series of battles defeated Set and would have destroyed him if Isis had not taken pity on her brother Set and spared him.

The Egyptians saw the battle between Set and Horus as the ultimate victory of good over evil. According to some interpretations, in the sphere of the eternal where there is no duality, Set and Horus are one; that is, death and life, darkness and light, are one force. In Egyptian religion this has been called "the secret of the two partners," referring to the hidden understanding between the two combatant gods. Set who represents strife is perenially subdued but never destroyed by Horus who represents peace. There is reconciliation in the end.

The Pharaoh, sometimes known as the Two Lords, was identified with each of these gods as an inseparable pair. As the great antagonist of light, Set was frequently symbolized by the black boar, whose emblem was the primeval knife, the instrument of dismemberment and death. His female counterpart was his sister Nephthys, who was herself a goddess of darkness and decay. In Egyptian art Set is usually portrayed as a man with the head of a fantastic beast, with pointed muzzle and high square ears. This unidentifiable creature has commonly been called the Typhonian animal, because Typhon was the god with whom the Greeks identified Set. Set is sometimes portrayed with horns, which made him the ideal image for the devil in Egyptian Christianity. Other animals associated with him were the antelope, the crocodile, and the ass.

In some texts Set was described as having a mane of red hair, and

Plutarch, in his *Isis and Osiris,* writes that an ass was thrown down a precipice by the Coptites because the animal bore a resemblance to Set in its redness. People who had red complexions were often treated with great disdain.

Variants of Set's name are Seth, Sethi, Sit, Sut, and Sutekh.

SET AMENTET Common name for a cemetery which was generally located on the west bank of the river. The name means, "place of the West."

SETA-TA A mummified god who stands at the end of the corridor in the fourth section of Tuat, the underworld, as the sun god Ra passes in his boat.

SETCHA Fantastic animal having the body of a leopard and the head and neck of a serpent.

SETCHEH A serpent demon mentioned in a magical formula of Unas, a king of the Fifth Dynasty.

SETEM God of the sense of hearing. He is depicted in Egyptian art with an ear above his head, which is both his chief attribute and the symbol of his name.

SETH; SETHI see Set.

SETHENIU-TEP Four divine beings wearing white crowns found in the eleventh section of Tuat, the underworld.

SET-HRA A monster serpent who guards the entrance to the eighth sec-

Set

tion of Tuat, the underworld, as the sun god Ra passes in his boat.

SETHU A monster serpent who guards the entrance to the tenth section of Tuat, the underworld, as the sun god Ra passes in his boat.

SETNA AND THE MAGIC BOOK Literary folktale believed to have been written during the Nineteenth Dynasty. The translation is by William Flinders Petrie from his *Egyptian Tales.* Those sections enclosed with [ ] are what Petrie added to the text, which in many places is incomplete.

The mighty King User.maat.ra (Rameses the Great) had a son named Setna Kha.em.uast who was a great scribe, and very learned in all the ancient writings. And he heard that the magic book of Thoth, by which a man may enchant heaven and earth, and know the language of all birds and beasts, was buried in the cemetery of Memphis. And he went to search for it with his brother An.he.hor.eru; and when they found the tomb of the King's son, Na.nefer.ka.ptah, son of the King of Upper and Lower Egypt, Mer.neb.ptah, Setna opened it and went in.

Now in the tomb was Na.nefer. ka.ptah, and with him was the *ka* of his wife Ahura; for though she was buried at Koptos, her *ka* dwelt at Memphis with her husband, whom she loved. And Setna saw them seated before their offerings, and the book lay between them. And Na.nefer.ka.ptah said to Setna, "Who are you that break into my tomb in this way?" He said, "I am Setna, son of the great King User.maat.ra, living forever, and I come for that book which I see between you." And Na.nefer.ka.ptah said, "It cannot be given to you." Then said Setna, "But I will carry it away by force."

Then Ahura said to Setna, "Do not take this book; for it will bring trouble on you, as it has upon us. Listen to what we have suffered for it."

"We were the two children of the King Mer.neb.ptah, and he loved us very much, for he had no others; and Na.nefer.ka.ptah was in his palace as heir over all the land. And when we were grown, the King said to the Queen, 'I will marry Na.nefer.ka.ptah to the daughter of a general, and Ahura to the son of another general.' And the Queen said, 'No; he is the heir, let him marry his sister, like the heir of a king; none other is fit for him.' And the King said, 'That is not fair; they had better be married to the children of the general.'

"And the Queen said, 'It is you who are not dealing rightly with me.' And the King answered, 'If I have no more than these two children, is it right that they should marry one another? I will marry Na.nefer.ka.ptah to the daughter of an officer, and Ahura to the son of another officer. It has often been done so in our family.'

"And at a time when there was a great feast before the King, they came to fetch me to the feast. And I was very troubled, and did not behave as I used to do. And the King said to me, 'Ahura, have you sent someone to me about this sorry matter, saying, "Let me be married to my elder brother"?' I said to him, 'Well, let me marry the son of an officer, and he marry the daughter of another officer, as it often happens so in our family.' I laughed, and the King laughed. And the King told the steward of the palace, 'Let them take Ahura to the house of Na.nefer. ka.ptah to-night, and all kinds of

146

good things with her.' So they brought me as a wife to the house of Na.nefer. ka.ptah; and the King ordered them to give me presents of silver and gold, and things from the palace.

"And Na.nefer.ka.ptah passed a happy time with me, and received all the presents from the palace; and we loved one another. And when I expected a child, they told the King, and he was most heartily glad; and he sent me many things, and a present of the best silver and gold and linen. And when the time came, I bore this little child that is before you. And they gave him the name of Mer-ab, and registered him in the book of the 'House of life.'

"And when my brother Na.nefer.ka.ptah went to the cementary of Memphis, he did nothing on earth but read the writings that are in the catacombs of the kings, and the tablets of the 'House of life,' and the inscriptions that are seen on the monuments, and he worked hard on the writings. And there was a priest there called Nesi-ptah; and as Na.nefer.ka.ptah went into a temple to pray, it happened that he went behind this priest, and was reading the inscriptions that were on the chapels of the gods. And the priest mocked him and laughed. So Na.nefer.ka.ptah said to him, 'Why are you laughing at me?' And he replied, 'I was not laughing at you, or if I happened to do so, it was at your reading writings that are worthless. If you wish so much to read writings, come to me, and I will bring you to the place where the book is which Thoth himself wrote with his own

hand, and which will bring you to the gods. When you read but two pages in this you will enchant the heaven, the earth, the abyss, the mountains, and the sea; you shall know what the birds of the sky and the crawling things are saying; you shall see the fishes of the deep, for a divine power is there to bring them up out of the depth. And when you read the second page, if you are in the world of ghosts, you will become again in the shape you were in on earth. You will see the sun shining in the sky, with all the gods, and the full moon.'

"And Na.nefer.ka.ptah said: 'By the life of the King! Tell me of anything you want done and I'll do it for you, if you will only send me where this book is.' And the priest answered Na.nefer. ka.ptah, 'If you want to go to the place where the book is, you must give me 100 pieces of silver for my funeral, and provide that they shall bury me as a rich priest.' So Na.nefer.ka.ptah called his lad and told him to give the priest 100 pieces of silver; and he made them do as he wished, even everything that he asked for. Then the priest said to Na.nefer.ka.ptah: 'This book is in the middle of the river at Koptos, in an iron box; in the iron box is a bronze box; in the bronze box is a sycamore box; in the sycamore box is an ivory and ebony box; in the ivory and ebony box is a silver box; in the silver box is a golden box, and in that is the book. It is twisted all round with snakes and scorpions and all the other crawling things around the box in which the book is; and there is a deathless snake

147

by the box.' And when the priest told Na.nefer.ka.ptah, he did not know where on earth he was, he was so much delighted.

"And when he came from the temple he told me all that had happened to him. And he said: 'I shall go to Koptos, for I must fetch this book; I will not stay any longer in the north.' And I said, 'Let me dissuade you, for you prepare sorrow and you will bring me into trouble in the Thebaid.' And I laid my hand on Na.nefer.ka.ptah, to keep him from going to Koptos, but he would not listen to me; and he went to the King, and told the King all that the priest had said. The King asked him, 'What is it that you want?' and he replied, 'Let them give me the royal boat with its belongings, for I will go to the south with Ahura and her little boy Mer-ab, and fetch this book without delay.' So they gave him the royal boat with its belongings, and we went with him to the haven, and sailed from there up to Koptos.

"Then the priests of Isis of Koptos, and the high-priest of Isis, came down to us without waiting, to meet Na.nefer.ka.ptah, and their wives also came to me. We went into the temple of Isis and Harpokrates; and Na.nefer. ka.ptah brought an ox, a goose, and some wine, and made a burnt-offering and a drink-offering before Isis of Koptos and Harpokrates. They brought us to a very fine house, with all good things; and Na.nefer.ka.ptah spent four days there and feasted with the priests of Isis of Koptos, and the wives of the priests of Isis also made holiday with me.

"And the morning of the fifth day came; and Na.nefer.ka.ptah called a priest to him, and made a magic cabin that was full of men and tackle. He put the spell upon it, and put life in it, and gave them breath, and sank it in the water. He filled the royal boat with sand, and took leave of me, and sailed from the haven: and I sat by the river at Koptos that I might see what would become of him. And he said, 'Workmen, work for me, even at the place where the book is.' And they toiled by night and by day; and when they had reached it in three days, he threw the sand out, and made a shoal in the river. And then he found on it entwined serpents and scorpions and all kinds of crawling things around the box in which the book was; and by it he found a deathless snake around the box. And he laid the spell upon the entwined serpents and scorpions and all kinds of crawling things which were around the box, that they should not come out. And he went to the deathless snake, and fought with him, and killed him; but he came to life again, and took a new form. He then fought again with him a second time; but he came to life again, and took a third form. He then cut him in two parts, and put sand between the parts, that he should not appear again.

"Na.nefer.ka.ptah then went to the place where he found the box. He uncovered a box of iron, and opened it; he found then a box of bronze, and opened that; then he found a box of sycamore wood, and opened that; again, he found a box of ivory and ebony, and opened that; yet, he found a box of silver, and

148

opened that; and then he found a box of gold; he opened that, and found the book in it. He took the book from the golden box, and read a page of spells from it. He enchanted the heaven and the earth, the abyss, the mountains, and the sea; he knew what the birds of the sky, the fish of the deep, and the beasts of the hills all said. He read another page of the spells, and saw the sun shining in the sky, with all the gods, the full moon, and the stars in their shapes; he saw the fishes of the deep, for a divine power was present that brought them up from the water. He then read the spell upon the workmen that he had made, and taken from the haven, and said to them, 'Work for me, back to the place from which I came.' And they toiled night and day, and so he came back to the place where I sat by the river of Koptos; I had not drunk nor eaten anything, and had done nothing on earth, but sat like one who is gone to the grave.

"I then told Na.nefer.ka.ptah that I wished to see this book, for which we had taken so much trouble. He gave the book into my hands; and when I read a page of the spells in it I also enchanted heaven and earth, the abyss, the mountains, and the sea. I also knew what the birds of the sky, the fishes of the deep, and the beasts of the hills all said. I read another page of the spells, and I saw the sun shining in the sky with all the gods, the full moon, and the stars in their shapes; I saw the fishes of the deep, for a divine power was present that brought them up from the water. As I could not write, I asked Na.nefer.ka.ptah, who was a

good writer, and a very learned one; he called for a new piece of papyrus, and wrote on it all that was in the book before him. He dipped it in beer, and washed it off in the liquid; for he knew that if it were washed off, and he drank it, he would know all that there was in the writing.

"We returned back to Koptos the same day, and made a feast before Isis of Koptos and Harpokrates. We then went to the haven and sailed, and went northward of Koptos. And as we went on Thoth discovered all that Na.nefer.-ka.ptah had done with the book; and Thoth hastened to tell Ra, and said, 'Now know that my book and my revelation are with Na.nefer.ka.ptah, son of the King Mer.neb.ptah. He has forced himself into my place, and robbed it, and seized my box with the writings, and killed my guards who protected it.' And Ra replied to him, 'He is before you, take him and all his kin.' He sent a power from heaven with the command, 'Do not let Na.-nefer.ka.ptah return safe to Memphis with all his kin.' And after this hour, the little boy Mer-ab, going out from the river: he called on Ra, and everybody who was on the bank raised a cry. Na.nefer.ka.ptah went out of the cabin, and read the spell over him; he brought his body up because a divine power brought him to the surface. He read another spell over him, and made him tell of all what happened to him, and of what Thoth had said before Ra.

"We turned back with him to Koptos. We brought him to the Good House, we fetched the people to him, and made one embalm him; and we buried him in his coffin in the cemetery of Koptos like a great and noble person.

"And Na.nefer.ka.ptah, my brother, said: 'Let us go down, let us not delay, for the King has not yet heard of what has happened to him, and his heart will be sad about it.' So we went to the haven, we sailed, and did not stay to the north of Koptos. When we were come to the place where the little boy Mer-ab had fallen into the water, I went out from the awning of the royal boat, and I fell into the river. They called Na.nefer.ka.ptah, and he came out from the cabin of the royal boat; he read a spell over me, and brought my body up, because a divine power brought me to the surface. He drew me out, and read the spell over me, and made me tell him of all that had happened to me, and of what Thoth had said before Ra. Then he turned back with me to Koptos, he brought me to the Good House, he fetched the people to me, and made one embalm me, as great and noble people are buried, and laid me in the tomb where Mer-ab my young child was.

"He turned to the haven, and sailed down, and delayed not in the north of Koptos. When he was come to the place where we fell into the river, he said to his heart: 'Shall I not better turn back again to Koptos, that I may lie by them? For, if not, when I go down to Memphis, and the King asks after his children, what shall I say to him? Can I tell him, "I have taken your children to the Thebaid, and killed them, while I remained alive, and I have come to

Memphis still alive"?' Then he made them bring him a linen cloth of striped byssus; he made a band, and bound the book firmly, and tied it upon him. Na.nefer.ka.ptah then went out of the awning of the royal boat and fell into the river. He cried on Ra; and all those who were on the bank made an outcry, saying: 'Great woe! Sad woe! Is he lost, that good scribe and able man that has no equal?'

"The royal boat went on, without anyone on earth knowing where Na.nefer.ka.ptah was. It went on to Memphis, and they told all this to the King. Then the King went down to the royal boat in mourning, and all the soldiers and high-priests of Ptah were in mourning, and all the officials and courtiers. And when he saw Na.nefer. ka.ptah, who was in the inner cabin of the royal boat—from his rank of high scribe—he lifted him up. And they saw the book by him; and the King said, 'Let one hide this book that is with him.' And the officers of the King, the priests of Ptah, and the high-priest of Ptah, said to the King, 'Our Lord, may the King live as long as the sun! Na.nefer.ka.ptah was a good scribe, and a very skilful man.' And the King had him laid in his Good House to the sixteenth day, and then had him wrapped to the thirty-fifth day, and laid him out to the seventieth day, and then had him put in his grave in his resting-place.

"I have now told you the sorrow which has come upon us because of this book for which you ask, saying, 'Let it be given to me.' You have no claim to it; and, indeed, for the sake of it, we have given up our life on earth."

And Setna said to Ahura, "Give me the book which I see between you and Na.nefer.ka.ptah; for if you do not I will take it by force." Then Na.nefer. ka.ptah rose from his seat and said: "Are you Setna, to whom my wife has told of all these blows of fate, which you have not suffered? Can you take this book by your skill as a good scribe? If, indeed, you can play games with me, let us play a game, then, of 52 points." And Setna said, "I am ready," and the board and its pieces were put before him. And Na.nefer.ka.ptah won a game from Setna; and he put the spell upon him, and defended himself with the game board that was before him, and sunk him into the ground above his feet. He did the same at the second game, and won it from Setna, and sunk him into the ground to his waist. He did the same at the third game, and made him sink into the ground up to his ears. Then Setna struck Na.nefer.ka.ptah a great blow with his hand. And Setna called his brother An.he.hor.eru and said to him, "Make haste and go up upon earth, and tell the King all that has happened to me, and bring me the talisman of my father Ptah, and my magic books."

And he hurried up upon earth, and told the King all that had happened to Setna. The King said, "Bring him the talisman of his father Ptah, and his magic books." And An.he.hor.eru hurried down into the tomb; he laid the talisman on Setna, and he sprang up again immediately. And then Setna reached out his hand for the book, and took it. Then—as Setna went out from the tomb—there went a Light before him, and Darkness behind him. And Ahura wept at him, and she said: "Glory to the King of Darkness! Hail to the King of Light! all power is gone from the tomb." But Na.nefer.ka.ptah said to Ahura: "Do not let your heart be sad; I will make him bring back this book, with a forked stick in his hand, and a fire-pan on his head." And Setna went out from the tomb, and it closed behind him as it was before.

Then Setna went to the King, and told him everything that had happened to him with the book. And the King said to Setna, "Take back the book to the grave of Na.nefer.ka.ptah, like a prudent man, or else he will make you bring it with a forked stick in your hand, and a fire-pan on your head." But Setna would not listen to him; and when Setna had unrolled the book he did nothing on earth but read it to everybody.

[Here follows a story of how Setna, walking in the court of the temple of Ptah, met Tabubua, a fascinating girl, daughter of a priest of Bast, of Ankhtaui; how she repelled his advances, until she had beguiled him into giving up all his possessions, and slaying his children. At the last she gives a fearful cry and vanishes, leaving Setna bereft of even his clothes. This would seem to be merely a dream, by the disappearance of Tabubua, and by Setna finding his children alive after it all; but on the other hand he comes to his senses in an unknown place, and is so terrified as to be quite ready to make restitution to Na.nefer.ka.ptah. The episode, which is not creditable to Egyptian society, seems to be intended for one of the vivid dreams which the credulous readily accept as half realities.]

So Setna went to Memphis, and embraced his children for that they were alive. And the King said to him, "Were you not drunk to do so?" Then Setna told all things that had happened with Tabubua and Na.nefer.ka.ptah. And the King said, "Setna, I have already lifted up my hand against you before, and said, 'He will kill you if you do not take back the book to the place you took it from.' But you have never listened to me till this hour. Now, then, take the book to Na.nefer.ka.ptah, with a forked stick in your hand, and a fire-pan on your head."

So Setna went out from before the King, with a forked stick in his hand, and a fire-pan on his head. He went down to the tomb in which was Na.nefer.ka.ptah. And Ahura said to him, "It is Ptah, the great god, that has brought you back safe." Na.nefer. ka.ptah laughed, and he said, "This is the business that I told you before." And when Setna had praised Na.nefer. ka.ptah, he found it as the proverb says, "The sun was in the whole tomb." And Ahura and Na.nefer.ka.ptah besought Setna greatly. And Setna said, "Na.nefer.ka.ptah, is it aught disgraceful (that you lay on me to do)?"

And Na.nefer.ka.ptah said, "Setna, you know this, that Ahura and Merab, her child, behold! they are in Koptos; bring them here into this tomb, by the skill of a good scribe. Let it be impressed upon you to take pains, and to go to Koptos to bring them here." Setna then went out from the tomb to the King, and told the King all that Na.nefer.ka.ptah had told him.

The King said, "Setna, go to Koptos and bring back Ahura and Mer-ab." He answered the King, "Let one give me the royal boat and its belongings." And they gave him the royal boat and its belongings, and he left the haven, and sailed without stopping till he came to Koptos.

And they made this known to the priests of Isis at Koptos and to the high-priest of Isis; and behold they came down to him, and gave him their hand to the shore. He went up with them and entered into the temple of Isis of Koptos and of Harpokrates. He ordered one to offer for him an ox, a goose, and some wine, and he made a burnt-offering and a drink offering before Isis of Koptos and Harpokrates. He went to the cemetery of Koptos with the priests of Isis and the highs priest of Isis. They dug about for three days and three nights, for they searched even in all the catacombs which were in the cemetery of Koptos; they turned over the steles of the scribes of the "double house of life," and read the inscriptions that they found on them. But they could not find the resting-place of Ahura and Mer-ab.

Now Na.nefer.ka.ptah perceived that they could not find the resting-place of Ahura and her child Mer-ab. So he raised himself up as a venerable, very old, ancient, and came before Setna. And Setna saw him, and Setna said to the ancient. "You look like a very old man; do you know where is the resting-place of Ahura and her child Mer-ab?" The ancient said to Setna: "It was told by the father of the father of my father to the father of my father, and the father of my father has told it to my father; the resting-place of Ahura and of her child Mer-ab is in a mound south of the town of Pehemato(?)" And Setna said to the ancient, "Perhaps we may do damage to Pehemato, and you are ready to lead one to the town for the sake of that." The ancient replied to Setna: "If one listens to me, shall he therefore destroy the town of Pehemato! If they do not find Ahura and her child Mer-ab under the south corner of their town may I be disgraced." They attended to the ancient, and found the resting-place of Ahura and her child Mer-ab under the south corner of the town of Pehemato. Setna laid them in the royal boat to bring them as honored persons, and restored the town of Pehemato as it originally was. And Na.nefer.ka.ptah made Setna to know that it was he who had come to Koptos, to enable them to find out where the resting-place was of Ahura and her child Mer-ab.

So Setna left the haven in the royal boat, and sailed without stopping, and reached Memphis with all the soldiers who were with him. And when they told the King he came down to the royal boat. He took them as honored persons escorted to the catacombs, in which Na.nefer.ka.ptah was, and smoothed down the ground over them.

This is the completed writing of the tale of Setna Kha.em.uast, and Na.nefer.ka.ptah, and his wife Ahura, and their child Mer-ab. It was written in the 35th year, the month Tybi.

SET-QESU A demon whose name means "crusher of bones." He is mentioned in the Negative Confession recited by the dead in the Hall of Judgment.

SETU A god who carries a javelin in the tenth section, or hour, of Tuat, the underworld. He helps the sun god Ra slay his enemies, as he goes toward the east.

SEVEN HATHORS Seven spirits who preside over an individual's fate.

SHADOW OF A MAN see Khaibit.

SHAI AND RENENET Personifications of Fate and Fortune, which were often deified as goddesses. Both were said to be under the jurisdiction of the god Thoth, who represented the divine intelligence of the gods. Shai was the goddess who determined a person's fate and Renenet was the goddess who brought good fortune. In the *Book of the Dead,* Shai stands by herself near the pillar of balance where the dead are judged.

SHAT AM TUAT Ancient Egyptian book describing Tuat, the underworld. It contained all the views of the Heliopolitan priesthood about the life of man after death. The supremacy of the sun god Ra, called "king of the gods and lord of the thrones of the Two Lands," is emphasized, while Osiris is assigned a lesser role.

The *Shat Am Tuat* divides Tuat into twelve sections, corresponding to the twelve hours of the night, when the bark of the sun god Ra passes over.

SHAT EN SBAU see Book of Pylons.

SHEHBUI God of the south wind portrayed as a lion-headed man with four wings.

SHEMAT-KHU see Perit.

SHEMERTHI A god who carries a bow in the tenth section, or hour, of Tuat, the underworld. He helps the sun god Ra slay his enemies, as he travels toward the east.

SHEMSU HERU Lesser divine beings, "Followers of Horus," who aided the god, as well as the dead. They are frequently referred to in funeral literature.

SHEMTI A monster serpent with four heads at each end of his body. He was found in the ninth section of Tuat, the underworld.

SHEN Hieroglyphic of a circle or ring with a flat sidepiece used to indicate indefinite repetition, or "eternity." It is often found in the claws of hawks and vultures. A familiar depiction of the goddess Isis and Nephthys has them kneeling and resting their hands on the shen.

SHENTO Two-piece loin cloth originally worn by the Pharaoh. It consisted of a pleated fabric that was wrapped around the waist, fastened in front, and then overlaid by a frontal piece with horizontal stripes. The dress of the Pharaoh for specific rites, the Shento was in time worn by nobles, and eventually adopted by the other classes.

SHEPES A form of the god Thoth who appears in the seventh section, or hour, of Tuat, the underworld.

SHEPU see Fa.

SHESERA A god armed with arrows, with a solar disk for a head, who appears in the tenth section, or hour, of Tuat, the underworld, to accompany the sun god Ra as he travels toward the east. Shesera slays the enemies of Ra who live in darkness, such as the evil serpent Neha-hra.

SHETA-AB A guardian of the sixth section of Tuat, the underworld, whose name means "secret heart."

SHETU A serpent monster, the constellation of the Tortoise, who appears in human form when addressed by the sun god Ra in the eleventh section, or hour, of Tuat, the underworld. The monster disappears into its own body when Ra ceases to speak. Shetu's duty was to "emit life for Ra every day."

SHIPWRECKED SAILOR, THE Literary folktale written in the Eleventh or Twelfth Dynasty. The abrupt opening of this tale within a tale suggests that part of it may be missing. The translation is by William Flinders Petrie, from his *Egyptian Tales:*

The wise servant said: "Let thy heart be satisified, O my lord, for that we have come back to the country; after we have long been on board, and rowed much; the prow has at last touched land. All the people rejoice, and embrace us one after another. Moreover, we have come back in good health, and not a man is lacking; although we have been to the ends of Wawat, and gone through the land of Senmut, we have returned in peace, and our land—behold, we have come back to it. Hear me, my lord; I have no other refuge. Wash thee, and turn the water over thy fingers; then go and tell the tale to the Majesty."

His lord replied: "Thy heart continues still its wandering words! but although the mouth of a man may save him, his words may also cover his face

with confusion. Wilt thou do then as thy heart moves thee? This that thou wilt say, tell quietly."

The sailor then answered: "Now I shall tell that which has happened to me, to my very self. I was going to the mines of Pharaoh, and I went down on the sea on a ship of 150 cubits long and 40 cubits wide, with 150 sailors of the best of Egypt, who had seen heaven and earth, and whose hearts were stronger than lions. They had said that the wind would not be contrary, or that there would be none. But as we approached the land the wind arose, and threw up waves eight cubits high. As for me, I seized a piece of wood; but those who were in the vessel perished, without one remaining. A wave threw me on an island, after that I had been three days alone, without a companion beside my own heart. I laid me in a thicket, and the shadow covered me. Then stretched I my limbs to try to find something for my mouth. I found there figs and grapes, all manner of good herbs, berries and grain, melons of all kinds, fishes and birds. Nothing was lacking. And I satisfied myself; and left on the ground that which was over, of what my arms had been filled withal. I dug a pit, I lighted a fire, and I made a burnt offering unto the gods.

"Suddenly I heard a noise as of thunder, which I thought to be that of a wave of the sea. The trees shook, and the earth was moved. I uncovered my face, and I saw that a serpent drew near. He was 30 cubits long, and his beard greater than two cubits; his body was as overlaid with gold, and his color as that of true lazuli. He coiled himself before me.

"Then he opened his mouth, while that I lay on my face before him, and he said to me: 'What has brought thee, what has brought thee, little one, what has brought thee? If thou sayest not speedily what has brought thee to this isle, I will make thee know thyself; as a flame thou shalt vanish, if thou tellest me not something I had not heard, or which I knew not, before thee.'

"Then he took me in his mouth and carried me to his resting place, and laid me down without any hurt. I was whole and sound, and nothing was gone from me. Then he opened his mouth against me, while that I lay on my face before him, and he said, 'What has brought thee, what has brought thee, little one, what has brought thee to this isle which is in the sea, and of which the shores are in the midst of the waves?'

"Then I replied to him, and holding my arms low before him, I said to him: 'I was embarked for the mines by the order of the majesty, in a ship; 150 cubits was its length, and the width of it 40 cubits. It had 150 sailors of the best of Egypt, who had seen heaven and earth, and the hearts of whom were stronger than lions. They said that the wind would not be contrary, or that there would be none. Each of them exceeded his companion in the prudence of his heart and the strength of his arm, and I was not beneath any of them. A storm came upon us while we were on the sea. Hardly could we reach to the shore when the wind waxed yet greater, and the waves rose even eight cubits. As for me, I seized a piece of wood, while those who were in the boat perished without one being left with me for three days. Behold me now before thee, for I was brought to this isle by a wave of the sea.'

"Then said he to me: 'Fear not, fear not, little one, and make not thy face sad. If thou hast come to me, it is God who has let thee live. For it is he who has brought thee to this isle of the blest, where nothing is lacking, and which is filled with all good things. See now, thou shalt pass one month after another, until thou shalt be four months in this isle. Then a ship shall come from thy land with sailors, and thou shalt leave with them and go to thy country, and thou shalt die in thy town.

" 'Converse is pleasing, and he who tastes of it pases over his misery. I will therefore tell thee of that which is in this isle. I am here with my brethren and my children around me; we are 75 serpents, children, and kindred; without naming a young girl who was brought unto me by chance, and on whom the fire of heaven fell, and burnt her to ashes.

" 'As for thee if thou art strong, and if thy heart waits patiently, thou shalt press thy infants to thy bosom and embrace thy wife. Thou shalt return to thy house, which is full of all good things; thou shalt see thy land, where thou shalt dwell in the midst of thy kindred.'

"Then I bowed, in my obeisance, and

I touched the ground before him. 'Behold now that which I have told thee before. I shall tell of thy presence unto Pharaoh, I shall make him to know of thy greatness, and I will bring to thee of the sacred oils and perfumes, and of incense of the temples with which all gods are honored. I shall tell, moreover, of that which I do now see (thanks to him), and there shall be rendered to thee praises before the fulness of all the land. I shall slay asses for thee in sacrifice, I shall pluck for thee the birds, and I shall bring for thee ships full of all kinds of the treasures of Egypt, as is comely to do unto a god, a friend of men in a far country, of which men know not.'

"Then he smiled at my speech, because of that which was in his heart, for he said to me: 'Thou art not rich in perfumes, for all that thou hast is but common incense. As for me I am Prince of the land of Punt, and I have perfumes. Only the oil which thou sayest thou wouldst bring is not common in this isle. But, when thou shalt depart from this place, thou shalt never more see this isle; it shall be changed into waves.'

"And, behold, when the ship drew near, according to all that he had told me before, I got me up into an high tree, to strive to see those who were within it. Then I came and told to him this matter; but it was already known unto him before. Then he said to me: 'Farewell, farewell; go to thy house, little one, see again thy children, and let thy name be good in thy town; these are my wishes for thee.'

"Then I bowed myself before him, and held my arms low before him, and he, he gave me gifts of precious perfumes, of cassia, of sweet woods, of kohl, of cypress, an abundance of incense, of ivory tusks, of baboons, of apes, and all kinds of precious things. I embarked all in the ship which was come, and, bowing myself, I prayed God for him.

"Then he said to me, 'Behold thou shalt come to thy country in two months, thou shalt press to thy bosom thy children, and thou shalt rest in thy tomb.' After this I went down to the shore unto the ship, and I called to the sailors who were there. Then on the shore I rendered adoration to the master of this isle and to those who dwelt therein.

"When we shall come, in our return, to the house of Pharaoh, in the second month, according to all that the serpent has said, we shall approach unto the palace. And I shall go in before Pharaoh, I shall bring the gifts which I have brought from this isle into the country. Then he shall thank me before the fulness of all the land. Grant them unto me a follower, and lead me to the courtiers of the King. Cast thy eye upon me, after that I am come to land again, after that I have both seen and proved this. Hear my prayer, for it is good to listen to people. It was said unto me, 'Become a wise man, and thou shalt come to honor,' and behold I have become such."

This is finished from its beginning unto its end, even as it was found in a

157

writing. It is written by the scribe of cunning fingers Ameni-amen-aa; may he live in life, wealth, and health!

SHOULDERS The Egyptians believed that when the kings of Egypt arrived in heaven, they mounted the shoulders of the gods Ra and Osiris. Thus in one of the Pyramid Texts it is written that Pepi I "seated himself on his [Ra's] shoulders."

SHREW-MOUSE According to Herodotus in his *History* (Book 2), the shrew-mouse was sacred to the goddess Buto. Quite a few mummies of the animal have been found in her city. In one myth the goddess takes the form of a shrew-mouse to help Horus escape when the evil god Set is out to destroy him.

The Egyptians believed that the shrew-mouse was blind, and sometimes used it as a symbol of darkness. In many bronze figures the animal is shown with Horus Khenty, the Blind Horus.

SHU God of the air. Shu and his twin sister Tefnut were the first couple of the Ennead, the group of gods worshipped at Heliopolis. According to one myth, they were conceived by the sun god without benefit of a partner, and spewed forth from his mouth. In other myths Shu appears as the first son of the sun god Ra and the sky goddess Hathor. His name has been translated as "he who holds up."

It was said that Shu separated the sky (Nut) from the earth (Geb), at Ra's request, so that light and space were created as well as heaven above and earth below. Shu maintained the division with his upraised arms. The god is often compared to Atlas in Greek mythology, who supported the heavens with his head and hands.

Shu was almost always portrayed in human form, wearing a feather, or feathers, upon his head and holding a scepter in his hand. He is sometimes depicted with his arms upraised and the four pillars of heaven near his head.

SHUTI Amulet representing two plumes, symbolizing light and air, which is often seen on the heads of the gods Ra, Osiris, and Amen-Ra.

SIA God of the sense of touch, or feeling, and of knowledge and understanding. He was said to have been born from the drops of blood that flowed when the sun god Ra mutilated his penis. He was subsequently invoked as a protector of the genitals of the deceased. Sia appears in the *Book of the Dead* as one of the gods who watches the heart of the deceased being weighed during the great judgment scene.

He is portrayed as a man with a fringed headband. A variant spelling is Saa.

SILENCE, GOD OF The Greeks identified Harpokrates, or "the Infant Horus," as the god of silence since he is portrayed with either one finger

Shu

placed over his lips or sucking his thumb.

SINUHE, TALE OF Popular Egyptian tale found in various manuscripts. The story was used by scribes and students during the Twelfth and Thirteenth Dynasties, who copied it on ostraca (limestone flakes) as part of their study. The following translation is by William Flinders Petrie in his *Egyptian Tales*. Petrie gives Sinuhe's name as Sanehat. The *Tale of Sinuhe* influenced Mika Waltari's novel *The Egyptian* (1949).

The hereditary prince, royal seal-bearer, confidential friend, judge, keeper of the gate of the foreigners, true and beloved royal acquaintance, the royal follower Sanehat says:

I attended my lord as a follower of the King, of the house of the hereditary princess, the greatly favored, the royal wife, Ankhet-Usertesen, who shares the dwelling of the royal son Amenemhat in Kanefer.

In the thirtieth year, the month Paophi, the seventh day, the god

159

entered his horizon, the King Sehotepabra flew up to heaven and joined the sun's disk, the follower of the god met his maker. The palace was silenced, and in mourning, the great gates were closed, the courtiers crouching on the ground, the people in hushed mourning.

His Majesty had sent a great army with the nobles to the land of the Temehu (Lybia), his son and heir, the good god King Usertesen as their leader. Now he was returning, and had brought away living captives and all kinds of cattle without end. The councillors of the palace had sent to the West to let the King know the matter that had come to pass in the inner hall. The messenger was to meet him on the road, and reach him at the time of evening: the matter was urgent. "A hawk had soared with his followers." Thus said he, not to let the army know of it. Even if the royal sons who commanded in that army send a message, he was not to speak to a single one of them. But I was standing near, and heard his voice while he was speaking. I fled far away, my heart beating, my arms failing, trembling had fallen on all my limbs. I turned about in running to seek a place to hide me, and I threw myself between two bushes, to wait while they should pass by. Then I turned me toward the south, not from wishing to come into this place—for I knew not if war was declared—nor even thinking a wish to live after this sovereign, I turned my back to the sycamore, I reached Shi-Seneferu, and rested on the open field. In the morn-

ing I went on and overtook a man, who passed by the edge of the road. He asked of me mercy, for he feared me. By the evening I drew near to Kherahau (? old Cairo), and I crossed the river on a raft without a rudder. Carried over by the west wind, I passed over to the east to the quarries of Aku and the land of the goddess Herit, mistress of the red mountain (Gebel Ahmar). Then I fled on foot, northward, and reached the walls of the prince, built to repel the Sati. I crouched in a bush for fear of being seen by the guards, changed each day, who watch on the top of the fortress. I took my way by night, and at the lighting of the day I reached Peten, and turned me toward the valley of Kemur. Then thirst hasted me on; I dried up, and my throat narrowed, and I said, "This is the taste of death." When I lifted up my heart and gathered strength, I heard a voice and the lowing of cattle. I saw men of the Sati, and one of them—a friend unto Egypt—knew me. Behold he gave me water and boiled me milk, and I went with him to his camp; they did me good, and one tribe passed me on to another. I passed on to Sun, and reached the land of Adim (Edom).

When I had dwelt there half a year Amu-an-shi—who is the Prince of the Upper Tenu—sent for me and said: "Dwell thou with me that thou mayest hear the speech of Egypt." He said thus for that he knew of my excellence, and had heard tell of my worth, for men of Egypt who were there with him bore witness of me. Behold he said to me:

"For what cause hast thou come hither? Has a matter come to pass in the palace? Has the King of the two lands, Sehetepabra, gone to heaven? That which has happened about this is not known." But I answered with concealment, and said: "When I came from the land of the Tamahu, and my desires were there changed in me, if I fled away it was not by reason of remorse that I took the way of a fugitive; I have not failed in my duty, my mouth has not said any bitter words, I have not heard any evil counsel, my name has not come into the mouth of a magistrate. I know not by what I have been led into this land." And Amu-an-shi said: "This is by the will of the god (King of Egypt); for what is a land like if it know not that excellent god, of whom the dread is upon the lands of strangers, as they dread Sekhet in a year of pestilence?" I spake to him, and replied: "Forgive me; his son now enters the palace, and has received the heritage of his father. He is a god who has none like him, and there is none before him. He is a master of wisdom, prudent in his designs, excellent in his decrees, with goodwill to him who goes or who comes; he subdued the land of strangers while his father yet lived in his palace, and he rendered account of that which his father destined him to perform. He is a brave man, who verily strikes with his sword; a valiant one, who has not his equal; he springs upon the barbarians, and throws himself on the spoilers; he breaks the horns and weakens the hands, and those whom he smites cannot raise the buckler. He

is fearless, and dashes the heads, and none can stand before him. He is swift of foot, to destroy him who flies; and none who flees from him reaches his home. His heart is strong in his time; he is a lion who strikes with the claw, and never has he turned his back. His heart is closed to pity; and when he sees multitudes, he leaves none to live behind him. He is a valiant one who springs in front when he sees resistance; he is a warrior who rejoices when he flies on the barbarians. He seizes the buckler, he rushes forward, he never needs to strike again, he slays and none can turn his lance; and when he takes the bow the barbarians flee from his arms like dogs; for the great goddess has given to him to strike those who know her not; and if he reaches forth he spares none, and leaves naught behind. He is a friend of great sweetness, who knows how to gain love; his land loves him more than itself, and rejoices in him more than in its own god; men and women run to his call. A king, he has ruled from his birth; he, from his birth, has increased births, a sole being, a divine essence, by whom this land rejoices to be governed. He enlarges the borders of the South; but he covets not the lands of the North: he does not smite the Sati, nor crush the Nemau-shau. If he descends here, let him know thy name, by the homage which thou wilt pay to his majesty. For he refuses not to bless the land which obeys him."

And he replied to me: "Egypt is indeed happy and well settled; behold thou art far from it, but whilst thou art with me I will do good unto thee." And he placed me before his children, he married his eldest daughter to me, and gave me the choice of all his land, even among the best of that which he had on the border of the next land. It is a goodly land, Iaa is its name. There are figs and grapes; there is wine commoner than water; abundant is the honey, many are its olives; and all fruits are upon its trees: there are barley and wheat, and cattle of kinds without end. This was truly a great thing that he granted me, when the prince came to invest me, and establish me as prince of a tribe in the best of his land. I had my continual portion of bread and of wine each day, of cooked meat, of roasted fowl, as well as the wild game which I took, or which was brought to me, beside what my dogs captured. They made me much butter, and prepared milk of all kinds. I passed many years, the children that I had became great, each ruling his tribe. When a messenger went or came to the palace, he turned aside from the way to come to me; for I helped every man. I gave water to the thirsty, I set on his way him who went astray, and I rescued the robbed. The Sati who went far, to strike and turn back the princes of other lands, I ordained their goings; for the Prince of the Tenu for many years appointed me to be general of his soldiers. In every land which I attacked I played the champion, I took the cattle, I led away the vassals, I carried off the slaves, I slew the people, by my sword, my bow, my marches and my good devices. I was excellent to the heart of my prince; he loved me when he knew my power, and set me over his children when he saw the strength of my arms.

A champion of the Tenu came to defy me in my tent: a bold man without equal, for he had vanquished the whole country. He said, "Let Sanehat fight with me"; for he desired to overthrow me; he thought to take my cattle for his tribe. The prince counselled with me. I said: "I know him not. I certainly am not of his degree, I hold me far from his place. Have I ever opened his door, or leaped over his fence? It is some envious jealousy from seeing me; does he think that I am like some steer among the cows, whom the bull overthrows? If this is a wretch who thinks to enrich himself at my cost, not a Bedawi and a Bedawi fit for fight, then let us put the matter to judgment. Verily a true bull loves battle, but a vainglorious bull turns his back for fear of contest; if he has a heart for combat, let him speak what he pleases. Will God forget what he has ordained, and how shall that be known?" I lay down; and when I had rested I strung my bow, I made ready my arrows, I loosened my poniard, I furbished my arms. At dawn the land of the Tenu came together; it had gathered its tribes and called all the neighboring people, it spake of nothing but the fight. Each heart burnt for me, men and women crying out; for each heart was troubled for me, and they said: "Is there another strong one who would fight with him? Behold the adversary has a buckler, a battle-axe, and an armful of javelins." Then I drew him to the attack; I turned aside his arrows, and they struck the ground in vain. One drew near to the other, and he fell on me, and then I shot him. My arrow fastened in his neck, he cried out, and fell on his face: I drove his lance into him, and raised my shout of victory on his back. While all the men of the land rejoiced, I, and his vassals whom he had oppressed, gave thanks unto Mentu. This prince, Amu-an-shi, embraced me. Then I carried off his goods and took his cattle, that which he had wished to do to me, I did even so unto him; I seized that which was in his tent, I spoiled his dwelling. As time went on I increased the richness of my treasures and the number of my cattle.

"Now behold what the god has done for me who trusted in him. Having once fled away, yet now there is a witness of me in the palace. Once having fled away, as a fugitive—now all in the palace give unto me a good name. After that I had been dying of hunger, now I give bread to those around. I had left my land naked, and now I am clothed in fine linen. After having been a wanderer without followers, now I possess many serfs. My house is fine, my land wide, my memory is established in the temple of all the gods. And let this flight obtain thy forgiveness; that I may be appointed in the palace; that I may see the place where my heart dwells. How great a thing is it that my body should be embalmed in the land where I was born! To return there is happiness. I have made offer-ing to God to grant me this thing. His heart suffers who has run away unto a strange land. Let him hear the prayer of him who is afar off, that he may revisit the place of his birth, and the place from which he removed.

"May the King of Egypt be gracious to me that I may live of his favor. And I render my homage to the mistress of the land, who is in his palace; may I hear the news of her children. Thus will my limbs grow young again. Now old age comes, feebleness seizes me, my eyes are heavy, my arms are fee-ble, my legs will not move, my heart is slow. Death draws nigh to me, soon shall they lead me to the city of eter-nity. Let me follow the mistress of all (the queen, his former mistress); lo! let her tell me the excellencies of her chil-dren; may she bring eternity to me."

Then the majesty of King Kheper-ka-ra, the blessed, spake upon this my desire that I had made to him. His Majesty sent unto me with presents from the King, that he might enlarge the heart of his servant, like unto the province of any strange land; and the royal sons who are in the palace ad-dressed themselves unto me.

"The Horus, life of births, lord of the crowns, life of births, King of Upper and Lower Egypt, Kheper-ka-ra, son of the Sun, Amen-em-hat, ever living unto eternity. Order for the follower Sanehat. Behold this order of the King is sent to thee to instruct thee of his will.

"Now, although thou hast gone through strange lands from Adim to Tenu, and passed from one country to

163

another at the wish of thy heart—behold, what has thou done, or what has been done against thee, that is amiss? Moreover, thou reviledst not; but if thy word was denied, thou didst not speak again in the assembly of the nobles, even if thou wast desired. Now, therefore, that thou hast thought on this matter which has come to thy mind, let thy heart not change again; for this thy Heaven (queen), who is in the palace is fixed, she is flourishing, she is enjoying the best in the kingdom of the land, and her children are in the chambers of the palace.

"Leave all the riches that thou hast, and that are with thee, altogether. When thou shalt come into Egypt behold the palace, and when thou shalt enter the palace, bow thy face to the ground before the Great House; thou shalt be chief among the companions. And day by day behold thou growest old; thy vigor is lost, and thou thinkest on the day of burial. Thou shalt see thyself come to the blessed state, they shall give thee the bandages from the hand of Tait, the night of applying the oil of embalming. They shall follow thy funeral, and visit the tomb on the day of burial, which shall be in a gilded case, the head painted with blue, a canopy of cypress wood above thee, and oxen shall draw thee, the singers going before thee, and they shall dance the funeral dance. The weepers crouching at the door of thy tomb shall cry aloud the prayers for offerings: they shall slay victims for thee at the door of thy pit; and thy pyramid shall be carved in white stone, in the com-

pany of the royal children. Thus thou shalt not die in a strange land, nor be buried by the Amu; thou shalt not be laid in a sheepskin when thou art buried; all people shall beat the earth, and lament on thy body when thou goest to the tomb."

When this order came to me, I was in the midst of my tribe. When it was read unto me, I threw me on the dust, I threw dust in my hair; I went around my tent rejoicing and saying: "How may it be that such a thing is done to the servant, who with a rebellious heart has fled to strange lands? Now with an excellent deliverance, and mercy delivering me from death, thou shalt cause me to end my days in the palace."

"The follower Sanehat says: In excellent peace above everything consider of this flight that he made here in his ignorance; Thou, the Good God, Lord of both Lands, Loved of Ra, Favorite of Mentu, the Lord of Thebes, and of Amen, lord of thrones of the lands, of Sebek, Ra, Horus, Hathor, Atmu, and of his fellow gods, of Sopdu, Neferbiu, Samsetu, Horus, lord of the east, and of the royal uraeus which rules on thy head, of the chief gods of the waters, of Min, Horus of the desert, Urrit, mistress of Punt, Nut, Harnekht, Ra, all the gods of the land of Egypt, and of the isles of the sea. May they give life and peace to thy nostril, may they load thee with their gifts, may they give to thee eternity without end, everlastingness without bound. May the fear of thee be doubled in the lands of the deserts. Mayest thou subdue the circuit of the sun's disk. This is the prayer to his master of the humble servant who is saved from a foreign land.

"O wise King, the wise words which are pronounced in the wisdom of the majesty of the sovereign, thy humble servant fears to tell. It is a great thing to repeat. O great God, like unto Ra in fulfilling that to which he has set his hand, what am I that he should take thought for me? Am I among those whom he regards, and for whom he arranges? Thy majesty is as Horus, and the strength of thy arms extends to all lands.

"Then let his Majesty bring Maki of Adma, Kenti-au-ush of Khenti-keshu, and Tenus from the two lands of the Fenkhu; these are the princes who bear witness of me as to all that has passed, out of love for thyself. Does not Tenu believe that it belongs to thee like thy dogs? Behold this flight that I have made: I did not have it in my heart; it was like the leading of a dream, as a man of Adehi (Delta) sees himself in Abu (Elephantine), as a man of the plain of Egypt who sees himself in the deserts. There was no fear, there was no hastening after me, I did not listen to an evil plot, my name was not heard in the mouth of the magistrate; but my limbs went, my feet wandered, my heart drew me; my god commanded this flight, and drew me on; but I am not stiff-necked. Does a man fear when he sees his own land? Ra spread thy fear over the land, thy terrors in every strange land. Behold me now in the palace, behold me in

this place; and lo! thou art he who is over all the horizon; the sun rises at thy pleasure, the water in the rivers is drunk at thy will, the wind in heaven is breathed at thy saying.

"I who speak to thee shall leave my goods to the generations to follow in this land. And as to this messenger who is come even let thy majesty do as pleaseth him, for one lives by the breath that thou givest. O thou who art beloved of Ra, of Horus, and of Hathor; Mentu, lord of Thebes, desires that thy august nostril should live forever."

I made a feast in Iaa, to pass over my goods to my children. My eldest son was leading my tribe, all my goods passed to him, and I gave him my corn and all my cattle, my fruit, and all my pleasant trees. When I had taken my road to the south, and arrived at the roads of Horus, the officer who was over the garrison sent a messenger to the palace to give notice. His Majesty sent the good overseer of the peasants of the King's domains, and boats laden with presents from the King for the Sati who had come to conduct me to the roads of Horus. I spoke to each one by his name, and I gave the presents to each as was intended. I received and I returned the salutation, and I continued thus until I reached the city of Thetu.

When the land was brightened, and the new day began, four men came with a summons for me; and the four men went to lead me to the palace. I saluted with both my hands on the ground; the royal children stood at the

165

courtyard to conduct me: the courtiers who were to lead me to the hall brought me on the way to the royal chamber.

I found his Majesty on the great throne in the hall of pale gold. Then I threw myself on my belly; this god, in whose presence I was, knew me not. He questioned me graciously, but I was as one seized with blindness, my spirit fainted, my limbs failed, my heart was no longer in my bosom, and I knew the difference between life and death. His Majesty said to one of the companions, "Life him up, let him speak to me." And his Majesty said, "Behold thou hast come, thou hast trodden the deserts, thou hast played the wanderer. Decay falls on thee, old age has reached thee; it is no small thing that thy body should be embalmed, that the Pedtiu shall not bury thee. Do not, do not, be silent and speechless; tell thy name; is it fear that prevents thee?" I answered in reply, "I fear, what is it that my lord has said that I should answer it? I have not called on me the hand of God, but it is terror in my body, like that which brings sudden death. Now behold I am before thee; thou art life; let thy Majesty do what pleaseth him."

The royal children were brought in, and his Majesty said to the Queen, "Behold thou Sanehat has come as an Amu, whom the Sati have produced."

She cried aloud, and the royal children spake with one voice, saying, before his Majesty, "Verily it is not so. O King, my lord." Said his Majesty, "It is verily he." Then they brought their collars, and their wands, and their sistra in their lands, and displayed them before his Majesty; and they sang—

"May thy hands prosper, O King;
May the ornaments of the Lady of
   Heaven continue.
May the Goddess Nub give life to thy
   nostril;
May the mistress of the stars favor
   thee, when thou sailest south and
   north.
All wisdom is in the mouth of thy
   Majesty;
Thy uraeus is on thy forehead, thou
   drivest away the miserable.
Thou art pacified, O Ra, lord of the
   lands;
They call on thee as on the mistress of
   all.
   Strong is thy horn,
   Thou lettest fly thine arrow.
Grant the breath to him who is
   without it;
Grant good things to this traveller,
   Samehit the Pedti, born in the
   land of Egypt,
Who fled away from fear of thee,
And fled this land from thy terrors.
Does not the face grow pale, of him
   who beholds thy countenance;
Does not the eye fear, which looks
   upon thee."

Said his Majesty, "Let him not fear, let him be freed from terror. He shall be a Royal Friend amongst the nobles; he shall be put within the circle of the courtiers. Go ye to the chamber of praise to seek wealth for him."

When I went out from the palace, the royal children offered their hands to me; we walked afterward to the Great Gates. I was placed in a house of a king's son, in which were delicate things, a place of coolness, fruits of the granary, treasures of the White House, clothes of the King's guardrobe, frankincense, the finest perfumes of the King and the nobles whom he loves, in every chamber. All the servitors were in their several offices.

Years were removed from my limbs: I was shaved, and polled my locks of hair; the foulness was cast to the desert with the garments of the Nemausha. I clothed me in fine linen, and anointed myself with the fine oil of Egypt; I laid me on a bed. I gave up the sand to those who lie on it; the oil of wood to him who would anoint himself therewith. There was given to me the mansion of a lord of serfs, which had belonged to a royal friend. There were many excellent things in its buildings; all its wood was renewed. There were brought to me portions from the palace, thrice and four times each day; beside the gifts of the royal children, always without ceasing. There was built for me a pyramid of stone among the pyramids. The overseer of the architects measured its ground; the chief treasurer wrote it; the sacred masons cut the well; the chief of the laborers on the tombs brought the bricks; all things used to make a strong building were there used. There were given to me peasants; there were made for me a garden, and fields in it before my mansion, as is done for the chief royal friend. My statue was inlaid with gold, its girdle of pale gold; his majesty caused it to be made. Such is not done to a man of low degree.

May I be in the favor of the King until the day shall come of my death!

(This is finished from beginning to end, as was found in the writing.)

SISTRUM   Ancient Egyptian rattle often used in the worship of Isis, Hathor, and Min. A woman might be called a "sistrum player of Min," a god invoked for his ability to confer fertility. The sistrum is usually a handle, at the top of which is sometimes the head of Hathor with cow's ears, and a horseshoe-shaped metal frame with loose cross-bars that rattle when the sistrum is shaken. Often there were metal disks along the strings. The sound was used to frighten away demons.

SIT   see Set.

SITULA   A ritual bronze vase used for libations of life-giving water.

SKY GODDESS   see Hathor.

SLAVES   Slavery was common in Egypt and the entire Near East. An Egyptian slave could own property, inherit land, marry whom he wished, and have servants. The crown, temples, and free Egyptians had control over the slave-population, which in part consisted of prisoners of war, as well as native Egyptians. According to scholars, the pyramids of the Old Kingdom were not mainly built by slave labor, even though various movies produced by Hollywood would have it so.

SMAM-UR The soul of the god Geb, sometimes spelled Suti.

SMA-TAWI Term used for the motif depicting the union of Upper and Lower Egypt, symbolized by the lotus and the papyrus tied together so that the male and female flowers are in contact. Set, patron god of Upper Egypt, and Horus, patron god of Lower Egypt, are often shown on either side, although in some cases Set is replaced by Thoth. The scene frequently appears on the throne of the Pharaoh.

SMITH GOD, THE see Ptah.

SMY One of the names of the evil god Set.

SNAKES Various kinds of demonic as well as beneficent snakes appear in Egyptian mythology. The sun god Ra, who, defeated daily by the monster-serpent Apophis, is sometimes himself portrayed as a snake, as are such deities as Buto, the cobra goddess Merseger, the snake goddess of Thebes, and Isis and Nephthys. The crown of the Pharaoh displayed the divine cobra on its front, representing the goddess Buto, who was one of the protective deities of Egypt.

SOKAR; SOKARE; SOKARIS see Seker.

SONG OF THE HARPER An Egyptian poem known in different versions, which was sung by a harper entertaining guests at a funeral feast.

In the translation of Ludwig Stern the narration of the poem found in the tomb of Neferhetep of the Eighteenth Dynasty begins:

> The great one is truly at rest,
> the good charge is fulfilled.
> Men pass away since the time of Ra
> and youths come in their stead.
> Like as Ra reappears every morning,
> and . . . sets in the horizon,
> men are begetting,
> and women are conceiving.
> Every nostril inhaleth once the breezes
> of dawn,
> but all born of woman go down to their
> places. . . .

SOPDU One of the gods of the four quarters of the earth, along with Horus, Set, and Thoth. When the goddess Nut's legs began to shake as, in the form of a cow, she carried Ra-Tem on her back to his home in heaven, the gods were called to steady her. Sopdu, Horus, Set, and Thoth each took one of Nut's four legs, and the god Shu supported her belly, which became the heavenly ocean, or river, on which the solar boat sailed.

SOPED A hawk-headed god who protected the roadway that led out of Lower Egypt. The beginning of the tract was called the "House of Soped, Lord of the East," while the end of the roadway was called the "House of Hathor, Lady of Turquoise."

SOUL see Ba.

SOUTH WIND, GOD OF see Shehbui.

SOW   see Pig.

SPEECH, GOD OF   see Thoth.

SPHINX   Figure with the body of a lion and the head of a man, woman, hawk, or ram. The sphinx was a symbol of the sun in ancient Egypt. The most famous of these figures is the Great Sphinx which portrays Harmachis, or "Horus who is on the Horizon," a massive work, 140 feet long and more than 60 feet high, hewn out of solid rock. It was raised near the Great Pyramid of Cheops. A story relating that the image spoke in a dream to the future king Thuthmosis IV is recorded on a stela. One day while hunting, Thuthmosis, who, though a prince, was not heir to the throne, fell asleep in the shadow of the sphinx. He dreamed that the statue ordered him to remove the sand that covered it and promised in return to cover him with favors. "Oh my son Thuthmosis," it said in the dream, "It is I, thy father, Harmachis. . . . The throne will be thine . . . so that thou shalt do what my heart desires. . . . "

The Greek sphinx, in contrast to the Egyptian, has a body which is part dog, accompanied by the tail of a snake, the wings of a bird, the paws of a lion, and a female head and voice. The Greeks believed that the sphinx was evil and that it was ultimately destroyed when Oedipus answered her question: "What is it that walks on four legs in the morning, two legs at noon and three legs in the evening?" The answer: "Man. He crawls on all

fours as a baby, walks upright in the prime of life, and uses a staff in old age." When the sphinx heard the answer she killed herself.

SPIRIT, THE   see Akh.

SPIRIT SOUL   see Khu.

SPITTING   Many Egyptian texts refer to spitting, which was used for both blessings and curses. The Pyramid Texts allude to a myth in which the god Tem has sexual union with himself, and then spits. From his spittle comes the gods Shu and Tefnut. When Tem places his arms around them, his Ka, or double, enters into the two gods. In the *Book of the Dead* the god Thoth heals the eye of the sun god Ra by spitting upon it. (In the New Testament Jesus also uses spit for healing a blind man.)

A book of magic details the use of spitting as a curse. One chapter of the *Book of the Overthrowing of Apophis* is entitled: "Of spitting upon Apophis." When the priests of Ra cast the wax figure of Apophis into the fire it was spat upon, and the priest would say: ". . . Ra, verily I have destroyed thine enemy, I have trampled upon him, I have spit upon him."

STATUES   see Images.

STEFIU   Four beings in the tenth section of Tuat, the underworld, who hold the archserpent Apophis on a chain as their prisoner.

STELE A rectangular stone slab, the upper part of which is sometimes shaped in a semi-circle. Stele giving the name, titles, and epithets of the deceased, so that he might carry them into the next world were often placed in tomb chapels. Steles were also found in temples and were inscribed with official statements of the government.

"STEPS AMULET" see Khet.

STRABO (B.C. 64—A.D. 22) Greek author who visited Egypt. He describes the geography, history, and religious details in the seventeenth book of his work, *Geography.*

SUCHOS see Sebek.

SUKATI One of the minor gods found in Tuat, the underworld, whom the deceased had to overcome. A formula was to be said over the "god of the lifted hand," who was Amen in his form as god of fertility. If the deceased was able to recite the formula and kept it secret from Sukati, he was allowed to drink from the deepest and purest part of the celestial stream, and eventually to become "like one of the stars in the heavens."

SUN The sun played a central part in Egyptian belief, and many of the most important gods such as Ra and Horus were identified with it. The sun god Ra traveled across the heavens as the sun each day and set in the West, the land of the dead, only to be reborn the next day. The journey was fraught with hazards, with night demons and other creatures who attempted to destroy the sun god and his boat. The son was believed to be the eye of Ra and of Horus as well.

SUN DISK see Aten.

SUT see Set.

SUTEKH see Set.

SUTI see Smam-ur.

SWALLOW The Egyptians believed that the swallow was one of the birds in which the human soul might house itself. The *Book of the Dead* says of the deceased, "he shall come forth by day, and he shall not be turned back at any gate in the underworld, and that he shall make his transformations into a swallow regularly and continually." According to Plutarch in *Isis and Osiris,* the goddess Isis took the form of a swallow when she was lamenting the death of Osiris.

SYCAMORE The sycamore tree was sacred to Ra, Hathor, Isis, and Mut. In one work the goddess Mut is said to pour water from the sycamore tree over both the deceased and his Ba, or soul, which is portrayed as a human-headed bird. Ra appeared each morning from between two sycamore trees of turquoise.

SYNCRETISM The merging of religious and cultic beliefs and practices.

The term was used by the Greek writer Plutarch for the union of Greek, Roman, and Egyptian cultic deities and beliefs during his day. The cult of Isis, which spread beyond Egypt, the homeland of the goddess, into Greece and Rome as well, is one of the best examples of Egyptian syncretism. The composite gods, deities made up of the combined attributes of two or more gods such as Amen-Ra, were precursors of this phenomenon. Some scholars believe that syncretism eventually leads to monotheism.

T

TABOO see Tabu.

TABU In ancient Egypt, as in many other ancient societies, certain people, animals, objects, places, and names were set apart, because they were believed to be too sacred, or dangerous, or contained mysterious power. For example, no skin or wool or any other product of rams or sheep was to be worn where the ram-headed god Khnemu was worshipped, at the risk of offending him. Thus when some Aramaic-speaking Jews sacrificed rams to their god Yahweh, in Elephantine, the land sacred to the ram-headed god, the Egyptians were extremely upset. In some places pigs were tabu, in others not.

TA-DJESART Title for Tuat, the underworld, meaning, "the holy land." A variant spelling is Ta-tchesert.

TAILS In Egyptian art the Pharaohs and gods, including Thoth, who is ibis-headed, and Horus, who is hawk-headed, are frequently portrayed with tails. The tail gave the wearer protection and the characteristics of the beast to whom it belonged. The Pharaoh, one of whose royal titles was, "Strong Bull rising in Thebes," wears a bull's tail attached to the belt of his kilt to imbue him with the strength of that animal.

TAIT Goddess of linen weaving, associated with Isis and the swathing of Osiris's body for burial.

TAKING OF JOPPA, THE Literary folktale found in a manuscript of the Nineteenth Dynasty. The following translation is by William Flinders Petrie in his *Egyptian Tales.*

There was once in the time of King Men-kheper-ra a revolt of the servants of his Majesty who were in Joppa; and his Majesty said, "Let Tahutia go with his footmen and destroy this wicked Foe in Joppa." And he called one of his followers, and said moreover, "Hide thou my great cane, which works wonders, in the baggage of Tahutia that my power may go with him."

Now when Tahutia came near to Joppa, with all the footmen of Pharaoh, he sent unto the Foe in Joppa, and said, "Behold now his Majesty, King Men-kheper-ra, has sent all this great army against thee; but what is that if my heart is as thy heart? Do thou come, and let us talk in the field, and see each other face to face." So Tahutia came with certain of his men; and the Foe in Joppa came likewise, but his charioteer that was with him was true of heart unto the King of Egypt. And they spoke with one another in his great tent, which Tahutia had placed far off from the soldiers. But Tahutia had made ready 200 sacks, with cords and fetters, and had made a great sack of skins with bronze fetters, and many baskets: and they were in his tent, the sacks and the baskets, and he had placed them as the forage for the horses is put in baskets. For while the Foe in Joppa drank with Tahutia, the people who were with him drank with the footmen of Pharaoh, and made merry with them. And when their bout of drinking was past, Tahutia said to the Foe in Joppa, "If it please thee, while I remain with the women and children of thy own city, let one bring of my people with their horses, that they may give them provender, or let one of the Apuro run to fetch them." So they came, and hobbled their horses, and gave them provender, and one found the great cane of Men-kheper-ra (Tahutmes III), and came to tell of it to Tahutia. And thereupon the Foe in Joppa said to Tahutia: "My heart is set on examining the great cane of Men-kheper-ra, which is named ' . . . tautnefer.' By the *ka* of the King Men-kheper-ra it will be in thy hands today; now do thou well and bring thou it to me." And Tahutia did thus, and he brought the

cane of King Men-kheper-ra. And he laid hold on the Foe in Joppa by his garment, and he arose and stood up, and said, "Look on me, O Foe in Joppa; here is the great cane of King Men-kheper-ra, the terrible lion, the son of Sekhet, to whom Amen his father gives power and strength." And he raised his hand and struck the forehead of the Foe in Joppa, and he fell helpless before him. He put him in the sack of skins and he bound with gyves the hands of the Foe in Joppa, and put on his feet the fetters with four rings. And he made them bring the 200 sacks which he had cleaned, and made to enter into them 200 soldiers, and filled the hollows with cords and fetters of wood, he sealed them with a seal, and added to them their rope-nets and the poles to bear them. And he put every strong footman to bear them, in all 600 men, and said to them, "When you come into the town you shall open your burdens, you shall seize on all the inhabitants of the town, and you shall quickly put fetters upon them."

Then one went out and said unto the charioteer of the Foe in Joppa, "Thy master is fallen; go, say to thy mistress, 'A pleasant message! For Sutekh has given Tahutia to us, with his wife and his children; behold the beginning of their tribute,' that she may comprehend the two hundred sacks, which are full of men and cords and fetters." So he went before them to please the heart of his mistress, saying, "We have laid hands on Tahutia." Then the gates of the city were opened before the footmen: they entered the city, they opened their burdens, they laid hands on them of the city, both small and great, they put on them the cords and fetters quickly; the power of Pharaoh seized upon that city. After he had rested Tahutia sent a message to Egypt to the King Men-kheper-ra his lord, saying: "Be pleased, for Amen thy good father has given to thee the Foe in Joppa, together with all his people, likewise also his city. Send, therefore, people to take them as captives that thou mayest fill the house of thy father Amen Ra, king of the gods, with men-servants and maid-servants, and that they may be overthrown beneath thy feet for ever and ever."

TALES Egyptian literature contains many narrative works, or tales, which are often based on folkloric motifs. It includes such adventure stories as *The Shipwrecked Sailor* and *The Taking of Joppa*, where realism and fantasy are combined. *The Tale of Two Brothers* presents one of the most important folk-motifs in world literature, the seduction of a youth by an older woman, and *The Doomed Prince* concerns a man's attempt to escape his fate. *The Tale of Sinuhe* describes the great love for his country of a man who must flee Egypt. *The Peasant and the Workman* is both a story and a moral lesson, and *The Treasure of Rhampsinitus,* found in Herodotus's *History* (Book 2), is a comic Egyptian folktale. Other tales are *Tales of the Magicians* and *Setna and the Magic Book.* (Each of the above tales is offered complete in the present work.)

TALES OF THE MAGICIANS Literary folktales in a narrative framework believed to have been written during the Twelfth Dynasty. The translation is by William Flinders Petrie from his *Egyptian Tales.*

One day, when King Khufu reigned over all the land, he said to his chancellor, who stood before him, "Go call me my sons and my councillors, that I may ask of them a thing." And his sons and his councillors came and stood before him, and he said to them, "Know ye a man who can tell me tales of the deeds of the magicians?"

Then the royal son Khafra stood forth and said, "I will tell thy Majesty a tale of the days of thy forefather Nebka, the blessed; of what came to pass when he went into the temple of Ptah of Ankhtaui."

"His Majesty was walking unto the temple of Ptah, and went unto the house of the chief reciter Uba-aner, with his train. Now when the wife of Uba-aner saw a page, among those who stood behind the King, her heart longed after him; and she sent her servant unto him, with a present of a box full of garments.

"And he came then with the servant. Now there was a lodge in the garden of Uba-aner; and one day the page said to the wife of Uba-aner, 'In the garden of Uba-aner there is now a lodge; behold, let us therein take our pleasure.' So the wife of Uba-aner sent to the steward who had charge over the garden, saying, 'Let the lodge which is in the garden be made ready.' And she remained there, and rested and drank

175

with the page until the sun went down.

"And when the even was now come the page went forth to bathe. And the steward said, 'I must go and tell Uba-aner of this matter.' Now when this day was past, and another day came, then went the steward to Uba-aner, and told him of all these things.

"Then said Uba-aner, 'Bring me my casket of ebony and electrum.' And they brought it; and he fashioned a crocodile of wax, seven fingers long: and he enchanted it, and said, 'When the page comes and bathes in my lake, seize on him.' And he gave it to the steward, and said to him, 'When the page shall go down into the lake to bathe, as he is daily wont to do, then throw in this crocodile behind him.' And the steward went forth bearing the crocodile.

"And the wife of Uba-aner sent to the steward who had charge over the garden, saying, 'Let the lodge which is in the garden be made ready, for I come to tarry there.'

"And the lodge was prepared with all good things; and she came and made merry therein with the page. And when the even was now come, the page went forth to bathe as he was wont to do. And the steward cast in the wax crocodile after him into the water; and, behold! it became a great crocodile seven cubits in length, and it seized on the page.

"And Uba-aner abode yet seven days with the King of Upper and Lower Egypt, Nebka, the blessed, while the page was stifled in the

crocodile. And after the seven days were passed, the King of Upper and Lower Egypt, Nebka, the blessed, went forth, and Uba-aner went before him.

"And Uba-aner said unto his Majesty, 'Will your Majesty come and see this wonder that has come to pass in your days unto a page?' And the King went with Uba-aner. And Uba-aner called unto the crocodile and said, 'Bring forth the page.' And the crocodile came forth from the lake with the page. Uba-aner said unto the King, 'Behold, whatever I command this crocodile he will do it.' And his Majesty said, 'I pray you send back this crocodile.' And Uba-aner stooped and took up the crocodile, and it became in his hand a crocodile of wax. And then Uba-aner told the King that which has passed in his house with the page and his wife. And his Majesty said unto the crocodile, 'Take to thee thy prey.' And the crocodile plunged into the lake with his prey, and no man knew whither he went.

"And his Majesty the King of Upper and Lower Egypt, Nebka, the blessed, commanded, and they brought forth the wife of Uba-aner to the north side of the harem, and burned her with fire, and cast her ashes in the river.

"This is a wonder that came to pass in the days of thy forefather the King of Upper and Lower Egypt, Nebka, of the acts of the chief reciter Uba-aner."

His Majesty the King of Upper and Lower Egypt, Khufu, then said, "Let there be presented to the King Nebka, the blessed, 1,000 loaves, 100 draughts of beer, an ox, two jars of incense; and let there be presented a loaf, a jar of beer, a jar of incense and a piece of meat to the chief reciter Uba-aner; for I have seen the token of his learning." And they did all things as his Majesty commanded.

BAU-F-RA'S TALE

The royal son Bau-f-ra then stood and spake. He said, "I will tell thy Majesty of a wonder which came to pass in the days of thy father Seneferu, the blessed, of the deeds of the chief reciter Zazamankh. One day King Seneferu, being weary, went through-out his palace seeking for a pleasure to lighten his heart, but he found none. And he said, 'Haste, and bring before me the chief reciter and scribe of the rolls Zazamankh;' and they straight-way brought him. And the King said, 'I have sought in my palace for some de-light, but I have found none.' Then said Zazamankh to him, 'Let thy Majesty go upon the lake of the palace, and let there be made ready a boat, with all the fair maidens of the harem of thy palace; and the heart of thy Majesty shall be refreshed with the sight, in seeing their rowing up and down the water, and seeing the goodly pools of the birds upon the lake, and beholding its sweet fields and grassy shores; thus will thy heart be light-ened. And I also will go with thee. Bring me twenty oars of ebony inlaid with gold, with blades of light wood inlaid with electrum; and bring me twenty maidens, fair in their limbs, their bosoms, and their hair, all vir-

gins; and bring me twenty nets, and give these nets unto the maidens for their garments.' And they did accord-ing to all the commands of his Majesty.

"And they rowed down the stream and up the stream, and the heart of his Majesty was glad with the sight of their rowing. But one of them at the steering struck her hair, and her jewel of new malachite fell into the water. And she ceased her song, and rowed not; and her companions ceased, and rowed not. And his Majesty said, 'Row you not further?' And they replied, 'Our little steerer here stays and rows not.' His Majesty then said to her, 'Wherefore rowest thou not?' She re-plied, 'It is for my jewel of new malachite which is fallen in the wa-ter.' And he said to her, 'Row on, for behold I will replace it.' And she an-swered, 'But I want my own piece back in its setting.' And his Majesty said, 'Haste, bring me the chief reciter Zazamankh,' and they brought him. And his Majesty said, 'Zazamankh, my brother, I have done as thou sayedst, and the heart of his Majesty is re-freshed with the sight of their rowing. But now a jewel of new malachite of one of the little ones is fallen in the water, and she ceases and rows not, and she has spoiled the rowing of her side. And I said to her, 'Wherefore rowest thou not?' and she answered to me, 'It is for my jewel of new malachite which is fallen in the wa-ter.' I replied to her, 'Row on, for be-hold I will replace it'; and she an-swered to me, 'But I want my own piece again back in its setting.' Then

177

the chief reciter Zazamankh spake his magic speech. And he placed one part of the waters of the lake upon the other, and discovered the jewel lying upon a shard; and he took it up and gave it unto its mistress. And the water, which was twelve cubits deep in the middle, reached now to twenty-four cubits after he turned it. And he spake, and used his magic speech; and he brought again the water of the lake to its place. And his Majesty spent a joyful day with the whole of the royal house. Then rewarded he the chief reciter Zazamankh with all good things. Behold, this is a wonder that came to pass in the days of thy father, the King of Upper and Lower Egypt, Seneferu, of the deeds of the chief reciter, the scribe of the rolls, Zazamankh."

Then said the majesty of the King of Upper and Lower Egypt, Khufu, the blessed, "Let there be presented an offering of 1,000 cakes, 100 draughts of beer, an ox, and two jars of incense to the King of Upper and Lower Egypt, Seneferu, the blessed; and let there be given a loaf, a jar of beer, and a jar of incense to the chief reciter, the scribe of the rolls, Zazamankh; for I have seen the token of his learning." And they did all things as his Majesty commanded.

HORDEDEF'S TALE

The royal son Hordedef then stood forth and spake. He said: "Hitherto hast thou only heard tokens of those who have gone before, and of which no man knoweth their truth. But I will show thy Majesty a man of thine own

days." And his Majesty said, "Who is he, Hordedef?" And the royal son Hordedef answered, "It is a certain man named Dedi, who dwells at Dedsneferu. He is a man of 110 years old; and he eats 500 loaves of bread and a side of beef, and drinks 100 draughts of beer, unto this day. He knows how to restore the head that is smitten off; he knows how to cause the lion to follow him trailing his halter on the ground; he knows the designs of the dwelling of Tahuti. The majesty of the King of Upper and Lower Egypt, Khufu, the blessed, has long sought for the designs of the dwelling of Tahuti, that he may make the like of them in his pyramid."

And his Majesty said, "Thou, thyself, Hordedef, my son, bring him to me." Then were the ships made ready for the King's son Hordedef, and he went up the stream to Dedsneferu. And when the ships had moored at the haven, he landed, and sat him in a litter of ebony, the poles of which were of cedar wood overlaid with gold. Now when he drew near to Dedi, they set down the litter. And he arose to greet Dedi, and found him lying on a palmstick couch at the door of his house; one servant held his head and rubbed him, and another rubbed his feet.

And the King's son Hordedef said, "Thy state is that of one who lives to good old age; for old age is the end of our voyage, the time of embalming, the time of burial. Lie, then, in the sun, free of infirmities, without the babble of dotage: this is the salutation to worthy age. I come from far to call thee, with a message from my father Khufu, the blessed, for thou shalt eat of the best which the King gives, and of the food which those have who follow after him; that he may bring thee in good estate to thy fathers who are in the tomb."

And Dedi replied to him: "Peace to thee! Peace to thee! Hordedef, son of the King, beloved of his father. May thy father Khufu, the blessed, praise thee, may he advance thee among the elders, may thy *ka* prevail against the enemy, may thy soul know the right road to the gate of him who clothes the afflicted; this is the salutation to the King's son." Then the King's son, Hordedef, stretched forth his hands to him, and raised him up, and went with him to the haven, giving unto him his arm. Then said Dedi, "Let there be given me a boat, to bring me my youths and my books." And they made ready for him two boats with their rowers. And Dedi went down the river in the barge in which was the King's son, Hordedef. And when he had reached the palace, the King's son, Hordedef, entered in to give account unto his Majesty the King of Upper and Lower Egypt, Khufu, the blessed. Then said the King's son Hordedef, "O King, life, wealth, and health! My lord, I have brought Dedi." His Majesty replied, "Bring him to me speedily." And his Majesty went into the hall of columns of Pharaoh (life, wealth, and health), and Dedi was led before him. And his Majesty said, "Wherefore is it, Dedi, that I have not

yet seen thee?" And Dedi answered: "He who is called it is that comes; the King (life, wealth, and health) calls me, and behold I come." And his Majesty said, "Is it true, that which men say, that thou canst restore the head which is smitten off?" And Dedi replied, "Truly, I know that, O King (life, wealth, and health), my lord." And his Majesty said, "Let one bring me a prisoner who is in prison, that his punishment may be fulfilled." And Dedi said: "Let it not be a man, O King, my lord; behold we do not even thus to our cattle." And a duck was brought unto him, and its head was cut off. And the duck was laid on the west side of the hall, and its head on the east side of the hall. And Dedi spake his magic speech. And the duck fluttered along the ground, and its head came likewise; and when it had come part to part the duck stood and quacked. And they brought likewise a goose before him, and he did even so unto it. His Majesty caused an ox to be brought, and its head cast on the ground. And Dedi spake his magic speech. And the ox stood upright behind him, and followed him with his halter trailing on the ground.

And King Khufu said, "And is it true what is said, that thou knowest the number of the designs of the dwelling of Tahuti?" And Dedi replied, "Pardon me, I know not their number, O King (life, wealth, and health), but I know where they are." And his Majesty said, "Where is that?" And Dedi replied: "There is a chest of whetstone in a chamber named the planroom, in Heliopolis; they are in this chest." And Dedi said further unto him, "O King (life, wealth, and health), my lord, it is not I that is to bring them to thee." And his Majesty said, "Who, then, is it that shall bring them to me?" And Dedi answered to him, "It is the eldest of the three children who are in the body of Rud-didet who shall bring them to thee." And his Majesty said: "Would that it may be as thou sayest! And who is this Rud-didet?" And Dedi replied: "She is the wife of a priest of Ra, lord of Sakhebu. And she has conceived these three sons by Ra, lord of Sakhebu, and the god has promised her that they shall fulfil this noble office (of reigning) over all this land, and that the eldest of them shall be high-priest in Heliopolis." And his Majesty's heart became troubled for this; but Dedi spake unto him: "What is this that thou thinkest, O King (life, wealth, health), my lord? Is it because of these three children? I tell thee thy son shall reign, and thy son's son, and then one of them." His Majesty said, "And when shall Rud-didet bear these?" And he replied, "She shall bear them on the twenty-fifth of the month Tybi." And his Majesty said, "When the banks of the canal of Letopolis are cut, I will walk there that I may see the temple of Ra, lord of Sakhebu." And Dedi replied, "Then I will cause that there be four cubits of water by the banks of the canal of Letopolis." When his Majesty returned to his palace, his Majesty said: "Let them place Dedi in the house of the royal son Hordedef, that he may

dwell with him, and let them give him a daily portion of 1,000 loaves, 100 draughts of beer, an ox, and 100 bunches of onions." And they did everything as his Majesty commanded.

And one day it came to pass that Rud-didet felt the pains of birth. And the majesty of Ra, Lord of Sakhebu, said unto Isis, to Nebhat, to Meskhent, to Hakt, and to Khnumu: "Go ye, and deliver Rud-didet of these three children that she shall bear, who are to fulfil this noble office over all this land; that they may build up your temples, furnish your altars with offerings, supply your tables of libation, and increase your endowments." Then went these deities; their fashion they made as that of dancing-girls, and Khnumu was with them as a porter. They drew near unto the house of Ra-user, and found him standing, with his girdle fallen. And they played before him with their instruments of music. But he said unto them, "My ladies, behold, here is a woman who feels the pains of birth." They said to him, "Let us see her, for we know how to help her." And he replied, "Come, then." And they entered in straightway to Rud-didet, and they closed the door on her and on themselves. Then Isis stood before her, and Nebhat stood behind her, and Hakt helped her. And Isis said, "O child, by thy name of User-ref, do not do violence." And the child came upon her hands, as a child of a cubit; its bones were strong, the beauty of its limbs was like gold, and its hair was like true lapis-lazuli. They washed him, and prepared him, and placed

180

him on a carpet on the brickwork. Then Meskhent approached him and said, "This is a king who shall reign over all the land." And Khnumu gave strength to his limbs. Then Isis stood before her, and Nebhat stood behind her, and Hakt helped her. And Isis said, "O child, by thy name of Sah-ra, stay not in her." Then the child came upon her hands, a child of a cubit; its bones were strong, the beauty of its limbs was like gold, and its hair was like true lapis-lazuli. They washed him, and prepared him, and laid him on a carpet on the brickwork. Then Meskhent approached him and said, "This is a king who shall reign over all the land." And Khnumu gave strength to his limbs. Then Isis stood before her, and Nebhat stood behind her, and Hakt helped her. And Isis said, "O child, by thy name of Kaku, remain not in darkness in her." And the child came upon her hands, a child of a cubit; its bones were strong, the beauty of its limbs was like gold, and its hair was like true lapis-lazuli. And Meskhent approached him and said, "This is a king who shall reign over all the land." And Khnumu gave strength to his limbs. And they washed him, and prepared him, and laid him on a carpet on the brickwork.

And the deities went out, having delivered Rud-didet of the three children. And they said, "Rejoice! O Ra-user, for behold three children are born unto thee." And he said unto them, "My ladies, and what shall I give unto ye? Behold, give this bushel of barley here unto your porter, that ye may take it as your reward to the brew-house." And Khnumu loaded himself with the bushel of barley. And they went away toward the place from which they came. And Isis spake unto these goddesses, and said, "Wherefore have we come without doing a marvel for these children, that we may tell it to their father who has sent us?" Then made they the divine diadems of the King (life, wealth, and health), and laid them in the bushel of barley. And they caused the clouds to come with wind and rain; and they turned back again unto the house. And they said, "Let us put this barley in a closed chamber, sealed up, until we return northward, dancing." And they placed the barley in a closed chamber.

And Rud-didet purified herself, with a purification of fourteen days. And she said to her handmaid, "Is the house made ready?" And she replied, "All things are made ready, but the brewing barley is not yet brought." And Rud-didet said, "Wherefore is the brewing barley not yet brought?" And the servant answered, "It would all of it long since be ready if the barley had not been given to the dancing-girls, and lay in the chamber under their seal." Rud-didet said, "Go down, and bring of it, and Ra-user shall give them in its stead when he shall come." And the handmaid went, and opened the chamber. And she heard talking and singing, music and dancing, quavering, and all things which are performed for a king in his chamber. And she returned and told to Rud-didet all that she had heard. And she

181

went through the chamber, but she found not the place where the sound was. And she laid her temple to the sack, and found that the sounds were in it. She placed it in a chest, and put that in another locker, and tied it fast with leather, and laid it in the storeroom, where the things were, and sealed it. And Ra-user came returning from the field; and Rud-didet repeated unto him these things; and his heart was glad above all things; and they sat down and made a joyful day.

And after these days it came to pass that Rud-didet was wroth with her servant, and beat her with stripes. And the servant said unto those that were in the house: "Shall it be done thus unto me? She has borne three kings, and I will go and tell this to his Majesty King Khufu the blessed." And she went, and found the eldest brother of her mother, who was binding his flax on the floor. And he said to her, "Whither goest thou, my little maid?" And she told him of all these things. And her brother said to her: "Wherefore comest thou thus to me? Shall I agree to treachery?" And he took a bunch of the flax to her, and laid on her a violent blow. And the servant went to fetch a handful of water, and a crocodile carried her away.

Her uncle went therefore to tell of this to Rud-didet; and he found Rud-didet sitting, her head on her knees, and her heart beyond measure sad. And he said to her, "My lady, why makest thou thy heart thus?" And she answered, "It is because of this little wretch that was in the house; behold

she went out saying, 'I will go and tell it.' " And he bowed his head unto the ground and said, "My lady, she came and told me of these things, and made her complaint unto me; and I laid on her a violent blow. And she went forth to draw water, and a crocodile carried her away."

(The rest of the tale is lost.)

TANAITIC Mouth of the Nile, where Isis found the body of her husband Osiris in a chest. Some children directed her to it.

TANEN see Tatunen.

TANENET see Tenenet.

TANIS A large temple to Amen was located at this ancient Egyptian site. Tanis reached its height during the Twenty-first Dynasty and flourished until the Roman conquest of Egypt.

TA-SENT-NEFERT Wife of Haroeris, a form of Horus, who was worshipped along with their son, P-neb-taui.

TASTE, GOD OF see Hu.

TA-TCHESERT see Ta-djesart.

TATUNEN A god sometimes identified with Ptah, who had a human form and wore two ostrich feathers and two ram's horns on his head. His name also appears as Tetenen, Tanen, and Tenen.

Tatunen

although she appears in some other accounts as the female counterpart of the demonic god Set.

In Egyptian art she is depicted as a female hippopotamus with large udders who is standing upright on her legs. Her left paw rests on the Sa, a symbol of protection represented by the stylized life-preserver, made of papyrus, worn by river travelers. Variant spellings are Taueret, Rert, Rertu, Apet, Opet. In Greek she appears as Thoueris.

TAU CROSS   see Ankh.

TAUERET   see Taurt.

TAURT   Hippopotamus goddess, a patron of childbirth and maternity, who was often identified with the great goddess Hathor. The literal translation of her name is "the great [fat] one." In the *Book of the Dead* she is portrayed as a protector of the dead,

Taurt

TCHABU The god of drink.

TCHEFT A name for Isis as the goddess of food that was offered to the gods.

TCHESER-TEP A serpent demon mentioned in a magical formula of Unas, a king of the Fifth Dynasty.

TCHETBI A monster serpent who guards the entrance to the fourth section of Tuat, the underworld, as the sun god Ra passes in his boat.

TCHET-S A winged monster serpent in the eleventh section, or hour, of Tuat, the underworld.

TEACHINGS OF AMEN-EM-OPE see Wisdom Literature.

TEBA see Nehata.

TEBI A name given to one of the solar gods.

TECHU AND TECHUTI see Thoth.

TEFNUT Goddess, who, with her twin brother Shu formed the first couple of the Ennead.

In one myth, it is said that the primeval sun god self-created Tefnut and Shu by an act of masturbation or, in another account, that they were born of the spittle of his mouth. Tefnut and Shu then engendered the sky goddess Nut, and the earth god Geb by their relations and in turn they bore

the great gods Osiris, Isis, Nephthys, and Set, thus completing the great Ennead. The two deities helped to support the sky and each day received the new sun as it rose in the east. Tefnut sometimes represented the power of sunlight.

However, the goddess could also be ferocious. In her original home, which was said to be the Nubian deserts, she roamed drenched in the blood of her enemies. When Thoth, the god of wisdom, upbraided her for having abandoned Egypt and leaving the country desolate, she wept great tears, but her tears soon turned to wrath. She changed into a bloodthirsty lioness, and her mane smoked with fire as her face glowed like the sun.

She was portrayed as a woman with the head of a lioness surmounted by either a disk or the uraeus, or both.

TEHUTI Title for Thoth, the scribe of the gods, meaning "the measurer." In this capacity he had the power to grant life to the deceased for millions of years.

TEKA-HRA A monster serpent who guards the entrance to the fifth section of Tuat, the underworld, as the sun god Ra passes in his boat.

TEKHI A goddess portrayed in human form, patron of the first month of the year, shown wearing a pair of high feathers. In some cases she was considered the female counterpart of Thoth.

TELL EL-AMARNA Capital city of the ruler Akhenaten, about 300 miles north of Luxor, near ancient Thebes. Akhenaten and his court spent fifteen years in Tell el-Amarna, the city he built and dedicated to the worship of Aten after deciding to leave Thebes. At Akhenaten's death his successor, Tutankhamen, returned to Thebes and the worship of Amen.

The city consisted of palaces, temples, government offices, a residential area, a business area, a northern suburb, and several outlying palaces. After the city was deserted it fell into ruin and many of its buildings were pulled down to reuse the stone. In 1887 a woman found some baked clay tablets, later called the "Amarna Letters," which record the actions of the court in relationship to foreign governments.

TEM The oldest of the creation gods in Egyptian mythology, variously called "divine god," "self-created," "maker of the gods" and "maker of men."

According to the Pyramid Text of Pepi I, Tem existed when:

not was sky,
not was earth,
not were men,
not were born the gods,
not was death.

What form he existed in, however, is not stated in the text.

To make a home for himself Tem created the celestial waters, which the Egyptians called Nun, and for a time he lived in them alone. Next, in a series of "thoughts," he created the heavens, the celestial bodies, gods, men, animals, and plants. The "thoughts" of Tem were translated into words by the god Thoth, who was his mind or intelligence. When Thoth uttered the words, all creation came into being.

The priests of Anu, or Heliopolis, made Tem, whom they identified with a form of the sun god, the head of their company of gods. He appears in the *Book of the Dead* as the evening or setting sun, with Khepera as the morning sun and Ra the noonday sun. In the Theban Recension of the book Tem is identified with Osiris as being among the gods whose flesh never saw physical corruption, and, according to one myth, he was responsible for the primeval flood which covered the entire earth and destroyed all mankind, except for those in the boat of the god. Many of his attributes were absorbed by Khepera, who was also a creation god. In later times the Egyptians devised Temt or Temit, a female counterpart of Tem.

In Egyptian art Tem is portrayed as a man, or king, wearing the crowns of the South and North of Egypt. Like many other gods he carries in his hands the scepter and Ankh, emblem of life.

Variations of his name are Tum, Temu, Atem, Atum, and Atmu.

TEMAU A god armed with arrows, with a solar disk for his head, who appears in the tenth section, or hour, of Tuat, the underworld. Temau accompanies the sun god Ra as he travels toward the east, and slays the serpent Neha-hra and the other enemies of the sun god who live in darkness.

TEMHIT A foreign goddess, "the Libyan," worshipped in Egypt. Her cult is believed to have been centered at Heliopolis.

TEMPLES In ancient Egypt the temple was the "mansion of the god," and the center of the observances of his cult. It was not a place of worship that belonged to the lay people.

In predynastic times the image of the god of each Egyptian tribe was enclosed by a reed shelter, which was supposed to be the god's home. On either side of the reed hut were poles. By the Third Dynasty, Egyptians began to construct stone temples and tombs, maintaining the same design of the shelter for the god. This model, which continued into later Pharaonic and Ptolemaic times, consisted of a sanctuary, hypostyle halls, open forecourts, and an enclosing wall with the main entrance set into it.

The main entrance was flanked by two stone towers, or pylons, to which pennants were attached. Beyond the pylons was the great court, surrounded by a colonnade of massive pillars. In the further wall of the court was the entrance to the hypostyle hall, a gigantic hall supported by pillars, and lighted by small windows under the roof.

The festivals were celebrated in the columned court and the hypostyle hall, but these areas were not the house of the god. The god lived behind the hypostyle hall, with his divine bark or ship, where his image, perhaps of wood and covered with gold, was also kept. Two adjoining rooms usually belonged to his consort and his son. These three rooms were the most sacred parts of the temple.

The legend, "He who enters must purify four times," was written near the sacred doors. At Karnak and Luxor, the Holy of Holies had a second entrance at the back which served as access to the storerooms for temple provisions.

Apart from the main complex there were other buildings that belonged to the temple—the storehouses and houses for the priests. These structures were located in the so-called temple circuit; that is, inside the great walls, some of which can still be seen in many temple ruins that enclosed a wide circle around the temple. The buildings of this sacred section, which were usually constructed of brick, have for the most part succumbed to time.

Because it was the center of the cult of the god or goddess, the structure and decoration of the temple were given symbolic meaning by the Egyptians. The building was believed to have been established at the "First Time"; that is, at creation. Each temple was seen as a symbol of the first temple built in mythical times, and thought to represent the Sacred Island out of which life emerged from the primeval ocean. It was here that the god, in the form of a hawk, had alighted on a reed and thus founded his first shrine. The reed temple was then built around the god and the island became the center for his worship.

The scenes painted on the temple walls, which often depicted the Pharaoh observing religious duties, were believed to "come alive" by performance of the ceremony of the "Opening of the Mouth." The rites were performed when the temple was consecrated and repeated annually. When all the figures gained life, the building became sacred, and was believed to have magical force.

Each temple followed a daily ritual. The Pharaoh, or more often the high priest who represented the Pharaoh, opened the doors of the innermost shrine which contained the statue of the god. He removed the ointments and clothing of the previous day, then censed the statue of the god and dressed it in new garments and ointment. After he had presented the statue with the insignia of its kingship and provided it with food, the high priest left the holy room, closing the door behind him. At the same time, prayers and purificatory censing were offered by other priests.

This ceremony was intended to symbolize the rebirth of the sun and the resurrection of Osiris. It reestablished the order in the universe, and was performed in the morning, midday, and in the evening, when the god was again presented with food. The priests later consumed the food which

of course remained uneaten by the god.

In addition to the regular rites of the god of the temple were festivals in which the people took part. The gods visited each other's temples; their statues were carried from one holy place to another. The most popular of these events was the festival of Osiris held at Abydos, where his life, death, and resurrection were reenacted.

TEMTU   see Nehata.

TEMU   see Tem.

TENEN   see Tatunen.

TENENET   A goddess often identified with Isis, sometimes shown with the double crown of Upper and Lower Egypt. A variant spelling is Tanenet.

TEPAN   A monster serpent in the fifth section, or hour, of Tuat, the underworld. He carries offerings made by the living to the hawk-headed god Seker.

TEPI   A monster serpent with four human heads, four breasts, and four pairs of human arms and legs, found in the ninth section of Tuat, the underworld.

TEPUI   A two-headed god who appears in the eleventh section, or hour, of Tuat, the underworld.

TER   A two-headed monster serpent in the fifth section, or hour, of Tuat, the underworld. He guards the Night Chamber to prevent the entrance of anyone who threatened to disturb or destroy the germ of life.

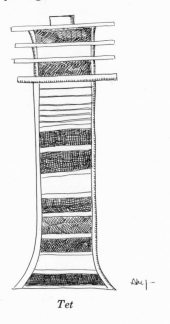

Tet

TESERT-ANT   see Perit.

TET   The symbol of Osiris, frequently found as an amulet, that represented "stability" or "durability." Like the Thet, the symbol of Isis, the wife and sister of Osiris, the Tet amulet had to be dipped in the water of ankham flowers. It was laid on the neck of the deceased to reconstitute the body and to make it a perfect spirit in the otherworld. On coffins the right hand of the deceased is often shown holding the Thet of Isis, while the left hand holds the Tet of Osiris. Variant spellings are Ded and Djed.

TETENEN   see Tatunen.

TETHYS   Greek Titaness identified by the Greeks with the Egyptian goddess Isis.

THAMOS, KING OF EGYPT Incidental music by W. A. Mozart to Von Gebler's play, written in 1779. The work contains a fine chorus to the sun: "The night, day's enemy, gives place to thee, O Sun!"

THAUT   see Thoth.

THEBES   Greek name for the Upper Egyptian city of Weset, called No in the Old Testament, located on the Nile about 330 miles south of Cairo. Thebes achieved its importance after the decline of Memphis, and was the capital of Egypt during the New Kingdom. In the *Iliad* Homer wrote: "Thebes, city where rich are the houses in treasure, a hundred has she of gates. . . . "

Two large temple precincts to the gods Amen, Karnak and Luxor were placed on the East side of Thebes while many royal funerary temples, as well as its famous necropolis were located on the West. The Prophet Jeremiah (46:25) spoke against the city:

The Lord of hosts, the God of Israel, saith;
Behold, I will punish the multitude of No,
and Pharaoh, and Egypt,
With their gods, and their kings;
Even Pharaoh, and all them that trust in him.

THENENET A title of Isis as goddess of Tuat, the underworld.

THES-HRAU A monster serpent with a head at each end of its body in the tenth section, or hour, of Tuat, the underworld. The serpent wears the white crown of Egypt on one head, and the red crown on the other. It has two pairs of human legs, one turned toward the right and the other toward the left.

THESU A god who carries a bow in the tenth section, or hour, of Tuat, the underworld. He helps the sun god Ra slay his enemies as he travels toward the east.

THET The buckle, girdle, or knot of Isis, which may have been a conventional representation of the uterus, with its ligatures, and the vagina. The Thet was often made of carnelian, red jasper, red glass, or some other red substance, perhaps to indicate blood. There are also Thet amulets of gold. The spell that accompanied it read:

"The blood of Isis, and the strength of Isis, and the words of power of Isis shall be mighty to act as powers to protect this great and divine being, and to guard him from him that would do unto him anything that he holdeth in abomination."

According to custom, the Thet, having first been dipped into water with ankham flowers, was attached to the

neck of the deceased. Variant spellings are Tjet or Djet.

Thet

THETHU A serpent demon mentioned in a magical formula of Unas, a king of the Fifth Dynasty.

THOTH Moon god, patron of the arts, speech, hieroglyphics, science, and wisdom. He was variously called the "heart of Ra," the "lord of divine words," and the "self-created, to whom none hath given birth, god one."

Thoth was one of the most important Egyptian gods and was believed to be the author of the *Book of the Dead,* in which he describes himself:

"I am Thoth, the excellent scribe, whose hands are pure; the lord of the two horns, who makes iniquity to be destroyed; the scribe of right and truth, who abominates wrongdoing. . . . I am Thoth, the lord of right and truth, who judges right and truth for the gods; the judge of words in their essence, whose words triumph over violence. I have scattered the darkness; I have driven away the whirlwind and the storm; and I have given the pleasant breeze of the north wind unto Osiris, the beautiful being, as he came forth from the body of her who gave him birth. . . . "

Thoth was regarded as both the heart and tongue of the great sun god Ra. He spoke for the wishes of Ra as when the heavens and earth were created or when Isis was given the words to revive the dead body of her son Horus, and the sun god's desires were fulfilled. In the judgment scene in the *Book of the Dead,* after weighing the words of the deceased, Thoth gives the gods the final verdict on whether a soul is to be blessed or punished.

Thoth was also called Tehuti, "the measurer." In this capacity he had the power to grant life to the deceased for millions of years. When the great battle between Horus and Set took place, Thoth acted as the judge, being called Wep-rehewy, the "Judge of the two opponent gods." During the struggle, he gave Isis a cow's head in place of her own, which had been severed in anger by Horus when Isis saved Set.

The Greeks identified Thoth with their god Hermes, and they credited him with inventing astronomy and astrology, the sciences of numbers and mathematics, geometry and land surveying, medicine, and botany. Also, they believed he was the first to organize religion and government, and to establish the rules concerning the worship of the gods. He was said to

have composed hymns, prayers, and liturgical works, and to have invented numbers, the alphabet, reading, writing, and oratory. In short, he was the author of every branch of knowledge, both human and divine.

In Egyptian art Thoth usually appears in human form with the head of an ibis, although he is sometimes depicted entirely as an ibis. The bird was sacred to him and was associated with the moon, as was Thoth as the measurer of time. He is occasionally portrayed as a seated baboon wearing the crescent moon upon his head, an image reflecting the belief that Thoth, as the moon god, took the place of Ra, the sun god, while Ra made his journey through the underworld. When shown in human form, Thoth holds a scepter and ankh, emblem of life, accessories common to all of the gods.

His headdress varies according to the form in which he is represented. As the reckoner of time and the seasons, Thoth wears the crescent moon and disk. At other times he appears in the Atef crown or in the united crowns of the South and North of Egypt. In the *Book of the Dead* he is called the "scribe of Maat," or justice, and holds a writing reed and palette. His close connection with the god Ra is indicated when he sometimes carries the utchat, which symbolized the strength of the eye of Ra.

Variants of his name are Techu, Techuti, Thaut, Thouth. Thouti, Dhouti, Zehuti, and Zhouti. Thoth is the form that the name Djehuti or Zehuti took in Greco-Roman times.

Thoth

THOUERIS see Taurt.

THOUTH AND THOUTI see Thoth.

THRONE Many Egyptian hymns to Osiris and to his son Horus emphasize that Horus inherited his father's throne. Thus in the *Book of the Dead* there is: "Thy throne hath descended to thy son Horus" and "Horus, his son, is seated upon the throne of the Dweller in the Lake of Fire as an heir. . . . Horus is established upon his

throne. . . . " The throne of Horus was the throne of Pharaoh, a living god.

The original throne may have contained relics of the body of Osiris, which protected Horus and gave him power. When the first king of Egypt sat upon it the spirit of Horus, as well as that of Osiris, protected and inspired him. No one could sit upon the throne of Horus as king without the god's permission.

In the *Book of the Dead* the beatified also possessed throne chambers with special seats.

191

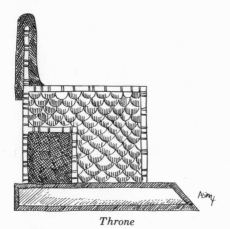

Throne

TJATY see Vizir.

TJET see Thet.

TOMBS The Egyptians called the tomb "the everlasting house," and believed that the Ka, or double of the deceased, lived in it as long as it contained the mummy of the perishable body. The Ka, which left and reentered the tomb to refresh itself with meat and drink, never failed to go back to the mummy. The Ba, or soul, however, did not live in the tomb.

The earliest burial sites were simple pits. The body, wrapped in a red mat, was placed in a fetal position in an oval or rectangular pit, and life provisions, such as tools, jars, food, and so on, were also placed in the grave. This form of burial for the poor continued throughout the ages in Egypt; the rich alone could afford elaborate tombs.

At the beginning of the Dynastic period, it became the custom to bury the Pharaoh and other nobility in a sand pit covered with a superstructure called a *mastaba*. According to some experts, this feature later developed into the pyramid, the most elaborate form of a tomb, and was set aside for the Pharaoh.

TOUCH, GOD OF see Sia.

TREASURE OF RHAMPSINITUS, THE Literary folktale told by Herodotus in his *History* (Book 2). Herodotus claimed that it was told to him by Egyptian priests. The following translation is by George Rawlinson.

King Rhampsinitus was possessed, they said, of great riches in silver—indeed to such an amount, that none of the princes, his successors, surpassed or even equalled his wealth. For the better custody of this money, he proposed to build a vast chamber of hewn stone, one side of which was to form a part of the outer wall of his palace. The builder, therefore, having designs upon the treasures, contrived, as he was making the building, to insert in this wall a stone, which could easily be removed from its place by two men, or even by one. So the chamber was finished, and the king's money stored away in it. Time passed, and the builder fell sick, when finding his end approaching, he called for his two sons, and related to them the contrivance he had made in the king's treasure chamber, telling them it was for their sakes he had done it, that so they might always live in affluence. Then he gave them clear directions concerning the mode of removing the stone, and communicated the measurements, bidding them carefully keep the secret, whereby they would be Comptrollers of the Royal Exchequer so long as they lived. Then the father died, and the sons were not slow in setting to work: they went by night to the palace, found the stone in the wall of the building, and having removed it with ease, plundered the treasury of a round sum.

When the king next paid a visit to the apartment, he was astonished to see that the money was sunk in some of the vessels wherein it was stored away. Whom to accuse, however, he knew not, as the seals were all perfect, and the fastenings of the room secure. Still each time that he repeated his visits, he found that more money was gone. The thieves in truth never stopped, but plundered the treasury ever more and more. At last the king determined to have some traps made, and set near the vessels which contained his wealth. This was done, and when the thieves came, as usual, to the treasure chamber, and one of them entering through the aperture, made straight for the jars, suddenly he found himself caught in one of the traps. Perceiving that he was lost, he instantly called his brother, and telling him what had happened, entreated him to enter as quickly as possible and cut off his head, that when his body should be discovered it might not be recognised, which would have the effect of bringing ruin upon both. The other thief thought the advice good, and was persuaded to follow it;—then, fitting the stone into its place, he went home, taking with him his brother's head.

When day dawned, the king came into the room, and marvelled greatly to see the body of the thief in the trap without a head, while the building was still whole, and neither entrance nor exit was to be seen anywhere. In this perplexity he commanded the body of the dead man to be hung up outside the palace wall, and set a guard to watch it, with orders that if any persons were seen weeping or lamenting near the place, they should be seized and brought before him. When the mother heard of this exposure of the corpse of her son, she took it sorely to heart, and spoke to her surviving child, bidding him devise some plan or other to get back the body, and threatening, that if he did not exert himself, she would go herself to the king, and denounce him as the robber.

The son said all he could to persuade her to let the matter rest, but in vain; she still continued to trouble him, until at last he yielded to her importunity, and contrived as follows: Filling some skins with wine, he loaded them on donkeys, which he drove before him till he came to the place where the guards were watching the dead body, when pulling two or three of the skins toward him, he untied some of the necks which dangled by the asses' sides. The wine poured freely out, whereupon he began to beat his head, and shout with all his might, seeming not to know which of the donkeys he should turn to first. When the guards saw the wine running, delighted to profit by the occasion, they rushed one and all into the road, each with some vessel or other, and caught the liquor as it was spilling. The driver pretended anger, and loaded them with abuse; whereon they did their best to pacify him, until at last he appeared to soften, and recover his good humor, drove his asses aside out of the road, and set to work to rearrange their burthens; meanwhile, as he talked and chatted with the guards, one of them began to rally him, and make him laugh, whereupon he gave them one of the skins as a gift. They now made up their minds to sit down and have a drinking bout where they were, so they begged him to remain and drink with them. Then the man let himself be persuaded, and stayed. As the drinking went on, they grew very friendly together, so presently he gave them another skin, upon which they drank so copiously that they were all overcome with the liquor, and growing drowsy lay down, and fell asleep on the spot. The thief waited till it was the dead of the night, and then took down the body of his brother; after which, in mockery, he shaved off the right side of all the soldiers' beards, and so left them. Laying his brother's body upon the asses, he carried it home to his mother, having thus accomplished the thing that she had required of him.

When it came to the king's ears that the thief's body was stolen away, he was sorely vexed. Wishing, therefore, whatever it might cost, to catch the man who had contrived the trick, he had recourse (the priests said) to an expedient, which I can scarcely credit. He sent his own daughter to the common stews, with orders to admit all comers, but to require every man to tell her what was the cleverest and wickedest thing he had done in the whole course of his life. If any one in reply told her the story of the thief, she was to lay hold of him and not allow him to get away. The daughter did as her father willed, whereon the thief, who was well aware of the king's motive, felt a desire to outdo him in craft and cunning. Accordingly he contrived the following plan: He procured the corpse of a man lately dead, and cutting off one of the arms at the shoulder, put it under his dress, and so went to the king's daughter. When she put the question to him as she had done to all the rest, he replied, that the wickedest thing he had ever done was cutting off the head of his brother when he was caught in a trap in the king's treasury, and the cleverest was making the guards drunk and carrying off the body. As he spoke, the princess caught at him, but the thief took advantage of the darkness to hold out to her the hand of the corpse. Imagining it to be his hand, she seized and held it fast; while the thief, leaving it in her grasp, made his escape by the door.

The king, when word was brought him of this fresh success, amazed at the sagacity and boldness of the man, sent messengers to all the towns in his dominions to proclaim a free pardon for the thief, and to promise him a rich reward, if he came and made himself known. The thief took the king at his word, and came boldly into his presence; whereupon Rhampsinitus, greatly admiring him, and looking on him as the most knowing of men, gave him his daughter in marriage. "The Egyptians," he said, "excelled all the rest of the world in wisdom, and this man excelled all other Egyptians."

TREES The Egyptians believed that some deities lived in trees, thus making those trees sacred. The persea tree, for example, was sacred to Ra, who, as Mau, in the form of the cat, defeated the archserpent of darkness Apophis at its base. An olive tree at Heliopolis was sacred to Horus, while the sycamore was sacred to Ra, Hathor, Isis, and Mut.

TRIAD Some Egyptian cities worshipped groups of three gods, often consisting of the father, mother, and son. Thus a triad of Osiris, Isis, and Horus might be holy to some areas, and replaced by Set, Nephthys, and Anubis in others. The members of the many triads varied at different times and locations. These variations were mainly due to the local gods' and goddesses' assimilation of the characteristics of the major deities of Egypt, such as Osiris or Isis.

TUAMUTEF One of the four sons of Horus and Isis, who guarded the stomach. He was portrayed as a jackal-headed god. A variant spelling is Duamutef.

TUAT The underworld, or "otherworld." Tuat was originally merely the place through which the sun god

Ra passed each evening after his setting, or death, on his journey to that portion of the sky where he would appear the next morning. Although generally called "the underworld," Tuat was not believed to be situated under the earth but rather away from the earth, in a part of the sky where the gods resided. Tuat was the realm of the great god Ósiris, who reigned over all the gods of the dead as well as the dead themselves. It was separated from the world by a range of mountains that surrounded it and formed a great valley. On one side the mountains divided the valley from the earth, and on the other side, the valley from the heavens. In Hebrew mythology, the blessed are separated from the damned by a wall. And in the New Testament (Luke 16:26), Lazarus is separated from Dives in hell by a "great gulf."

Through Tuat ran a river that was the counterpart of the Nile in Egypt and of the celestial Nile in heaven, and on each bank of this river lived a vast number of beasts and devils who were hostile to any being that invaded the valley. Tuat was further divided into 12 sections or nomes, each of which corresponded to one of the hours of the night.

According to one Egyptian text, *The Book of Pylons*, Tuat is a long, narrow valley, with sandy slopes, divided into two equal parts by a river on which the boat of the sun sails. Each of the 12 sections or nomes, of the valley has its own demons, or ordeals, that the deceased has to pass in order to be worthy of life with Osiris. This concept is used in Mozart's opera, *The Magic Flute* (1791), in which the hero, Tamino, undergoes a series of ordeals instigated by the high priest Sarastro, to be worthy to praise Isis and Osiris.

Tuat is sometimes called Ta-djesant or Ta-tchesert, "the holy land." Another common name for the abode of the dead in Egypt was Neter-khertet, or Khert Neter, or "divine subterranean place." A variant spelling is Duat.

TUM see Tem.

TUTANKHAMEN (c. B.C. 1361–1352). Pharaoh, successor of Akhenaten, who was his son-in-law (and also possibly his son, brother, or close relative), who reigned for nine years. He died at the age of 19. His name was originally Tutankhaten, or "Gracious of Life is Aten," indicating that he followed the beliefs of Akhenaten in his worship of Aten, the sun disk. However, he changed his name to Tutankhamen, or "the Living image of Amen," after he came to rule, and under the direction of the Theban priests restored the worship of the old god Amen-Ra.

Tutankhamen left the capital of Akhenaten and returned his court to Thebes, the city of Amen. An inscription ascribed to him reads: "I found the temples fallen into ruin, with their holy places overthrown, and their courts overgrown with weeds. I reconstructed their sanctuaries, I reendowed the temples, and made them gifts of all precious things. I cast statues of the gods in gold and elec-

trum, decorated with lapis lazuli and all fine stones."

The wife of the king, Ankhensenpaaten, a daughter of Akhenaten, changed her name to Ankhesenamen after the move to Thebes, indicating her allegiance to Amen-Ra. The king, who may have been murdered, was succeeded by a minister, Ay. The young king was buried and his tomb forgotten.

However, in 1922 Howard Carter and Lord Carnarvon discovered the tomb of Tutankhamen in the Valley of the Kings. The tomb had been untouched for thousands of years. Carter wrote:

It would be difficult to describe our emotions when for the first time the light of our powerful electric lamps flooded the Burial Chamber, illuminating the walls on which were painted representatives of Amentit, the catafalque drawn on a sled by the chief nobles of the land, King Ay before the Osiride Tutankhamen and lighting up the immense shrine overlaid with gold. . . .

The story of the discovery of "King Tut's tomb," as it became known, was published by Carter between 1923 and 1933. The entrance to the tomb had been concealed under the remains of ancient workmen's huts near the tomb of Ramesses VI. Fifteen steps led down to a plastered door with traces of the seals of kings, including that of Tutankhamen. The broken seals indicated that the tomb had been entered earlier. Behind the door was a passage that led to a second door which opened on a treasure room in some disarray. The thieves had obviously come this far. A final door between the antechamber and the burial chamber revealed the large shrine of gilded wood, and was as far as the thieves had penetrated. Carter and Carnarvon found three more gilded shrines, one within the other. They were carefully opened. The last door revealed the red sandstone sarcophagus of the king, untouched since the time the tomb had been sealed.

TWELVE DIVINE ROWERS Twelve gods who assist the sun god Ra in the ninth section, or hour, of Tuat, the underworld, as the god passes in his boat. As they row Ra's boat, they splash the spirits who stand on each bank of the river with water from their paddles. The rowers then lead Ra's soul to the place where he will reanimate the sun disk.

TWINS Many ancient societies looked upon twins as a curse and destroyed them. The ancient Egyptians, however, had no such hostility; the gods Osiris and Set were believed to be twins, as were the goddesses Isis and Nephthys. One text of the Eighteenth Dynasty tells that Horus and Set "came forth from the belly" at the same time. These gods were believed to watch over twins.

TWO BROTHERS, THE TALE OF Literary folktale, believed to have been written about B.C. 1225.

Sometimes called *Anpu and Bata,* the names of the two brothers, this story is modelled around the motif of the attempted seduction of a virtuous youth by an older married woman. Other famous examples of this genre are the stories of Joseph and Potiphar's wife in Genesis (39:7-20) and of Hippolytus and Phaedra in Greek mythology.

Some scholars regard *The Tale of Two Brothers* as a popular retelling of the myth of Anpu (who is more often called Anubis) and Bata, a pastoral god, whose cult image was a mummified ram or bull. There is little consensus about its interpretation, although most experts agree that it was intended for entertainment rather than for religious or moral edification.

The translation is by William Flinders Petrie in his *Egyptian Tales.*

Once there were two brethren, of one mother and one father; Anpu was the name of the elder, and Bata was the name of the younger. Now, as for Anpu he had a house, and he had a wife. But his little brother was to him as it were a son; he it was who made for him his clothes; he it was who followed behind his oxen to the fields; he it was who did the ploughing; he it was who harvested the corn; he it was who did for him all the matters that were in the field. Behold, his younger brother grew to be an excellent worker, there was not his equal in the whole land; behold, the spirit of a god was in him.

Now after this the younger brother

197

followed his oxen in his daily manner; and every evening he turned again to the house, laden with all the herbs of the field, with milk and with wood, and with all things of the field. And he put them down before his elder brother, who was sitting with his wife; and he drank and ate, and he lay down in his stable with the cattle. And at the dawn of day he took bread which he had baked, and laid it before his elder brother; and he took with him his bread to the field, and he drave his cattle to pasture in the fields. And as he walked behind his cattle, they said to him, "Good is the herbage which is in that place"; and he listened to all that they said, and he took them to the good place which they desired. And the cattle which were before him became exceeding excellent, and they multiplied greatly.

Now at the time of ploughing his elder brother said unto him: "Let us make ready for ourselves a goodly yoke of oxen for ploughing, for the land has come out from the water, it is fit for ploughing. Moreover, do thou come to the field with corn, for we will begin the ploughing in the morrow morning." Thus said he to him; and his younger brother did all things as his elder brother had spoken unto him to do them.

And when the morn was come, they went to the fields with their things; and their hearts were pleased exceedingly with their task in the beginning of their work. And it came to pass after this that as they were in the field they stopped for corn, and he sent his younger brother, saying, "Haste thou, bring to us corn from the farm." And the younger brother found the wife of his elder brother, as she was sitting tying her hair. He said to her: "Get up, and give to me corn, that I may run to the field, for my elder brother hastened me; do not delay." She said to him: "Go, open the bin, and thou shalt take to thyself according to thy will, that I may not drop my locks of hair while I dress them."

The youth went into the stable; he took a large measure, for he desired to take much corn; he loaded it with wheat and barley; and he went out carrying it. She said to him, "How much of the corn that is wanted, is that which is on thy shoulder?" He said to her: "Three bushels of barley, and two of wheat, in all five; these are what are upon my shoulder." Thus said he to her. And she conversed with him, saying, "There is great strength in thee, for I see thy might every day." And her heart knew him with the knowledge of youth. And she arose and came to him, and conversed with him, saying, "Come, stay with me, and it shall be well for thee, and I will make for thee beautiful garments." Then the youth became like a panther of the south with fury at the evil speech which she had made to him; and she feared greatly. And he spake unto her, saying: "Behold thou art to me as a mother, thy husband is to me as a father, for he who is elder than I has brought me up. What is this wickedness that thou hast said to me? Say it not to me again. For I will not tell it to any man, for I will not let it be uttered by the mouth of any man." He lifted up his burden, and he went to the field and came to his elder brother; and they took up their work, to labor at their task.

Now afterward, at eventime, his elder brother was returning to his house; and the younger brother was following after his oxen, and he loaded himself with all the things of the field; and he brought his oxen before him, to make them lie down in their stable which was in the farm. And behold the wife of the elder brother was afraid for the words which she had said. She took a parcel of fat, she became like one who is evilly beaten, desiring to say to her husband, "It is thy younger brother who has done this wrong." Her husband returned in the even, as was his wont of every day; he came unto his house; he found his wife ill of violence; she did not give him water upon his hands as he used to have, she did not make a light before him, his house was in darkness, and she was lying very sick. Her husband said to her, "Who has spoken with thee?" Behold she said: "No one has spoken with me except thy younger brother. When he came to take for thee corn he found me sitting alone; he said to me, 'Come, let us stay together, tie up thy hair.' Thus spake he to me. I did not listen to him, but thus spake I to him: 'Behold, am I not thy mother, is not thy elder brother to thee as a father?' And he feared, and he beat me to stop me from making report to thee, and if thou lettest him live I shall die. Now behold he

is coming in the evening; and I complain of these wicked words, for he would have done this even in daylight."

And the elder brother became as a panther of the south; he sharpened his knife; he took it in his hand; he stood behind the door of his stable to slay his younger brother as he came in the evening to bring his cattle into the stable.

Now the sun went down, and he loaded himself with herbs in his daily manner. He came, and his foremost cow entered the stable, and she said to her keeper, "Behold thou thy elder brother standing before thee with his knife to slay thee; flee from before him." He heard what his first cow had said; and the next entering, she also said likewise. He looked beneath the door of the stable; he saw the feet of his elder brother; he was standing behind the door, and his knife was in his hand. He cast down his load to the ground, and betook himself to flee swiftly; and his elder brother pursued after him with his knife. Then the younger brother cried out unto Ra Harakhti, saying, "My good Lord! Thou art he who divides the evil from the good." And Ra stood and heard all his cry; and Ra made a wide water between him and his elder brother, and it was full of crocodiles; and the one brother was on one bank, and the other on the other bank; and the elder brother smote twice on his hands at not slaying him. Thus did he. And the younger brother called to the elder on the bank, saying: "Stand still until the dawn of day; and when Ra ariseth, I shall judge with thee before him, and he discerneth between the good and the evil. For I shall not be with thee any more forever; I shall not be in the place in which thou art; I shall go to the valley of the acacia."

Now when the land was lightened, and the next day appeared, Ra Harakhti arose, and one looked unto the other. And the youth spake with his elder brother, saying: "Wherefore camest thou after me to slay me in craftiness, when thou didst not hear the words of my mouth? For I am thy brother in truth, and thou art to me as a father, and thy wife even as a mother: is it not so? Verily, when I was sent to bring for us corn, thy wife said to me, 'Come, stay with me'; for behold this has been turned over unto thee into another wise." And he caused him to understand of all that happened with him and his wife. And he swore an oath by Ra Harakhti, saying, "Thy coming to slay me by deceit with thy knife was an abomination." Then the youth took a knife, and cut off of his flesh, and cast it into the water, and the fish swallowed it. He failed; he became faint; and his elder brother cursed his own heart greatly; he stood weeping for him afar off; he knew not how to pass over to where his younger brother was, because of the crocodiles. And the younger brother called unto him, saying: "Whereas thou hast devised an evil thing, wilt thou not also devise a good thing, even like that which I would do unto thee? When thou goest to thy house thou must look

to thy cattle, for I shall not stay in the place where thou art; I am going to the valley of the acacia. And now as to what thou shalt do for me; it is even that thou shalt come to seek after me, if thou perceivest a matter, namely, that there are things happening unto me. And this is what shall come to pass, that I shall draw out my soul, and I shall put it upon the top of the flowers of the acacia, and when the acacia is cut down, and it falls to the ground, and thou comest to seek for it, if thou searchest for it seven years do not let thy heart be wearied. For thou wilt find it, and thou must put it in a cup of cold water, and expect that I shall live again, that I may make answer to what has been done wrong. And thou shalt know of this, that is to say, that things are happening to me, when one shall give to thee a cup of beer in thy hand, and it shall be troubled; stay not then, for verily it shall come to pass with thee."

And the youth went to the valley of the acacia; and his elder brother went unto his house; his hand was laid on his head, and he cast dust on his head; he came to his house, and he slew his wife, he cast her to the dogs, and he sat in mourning for his younger brother.

Now many days after these things, the younger brother was in the valley of the acacia; there was none with him; he spent his time in hunting the beasts of the desert, and he came back in the even to lie down under the acacia, which bore his soul upon the topmost flower. And after this he built himself a tower with his own hands, in the valley of the acacia; it was full of all good things, that he might provide for himself a home.

And he went out from his tower, and he met the Nine Gods, who were walking forth to look upon the whole land. The Nine Gods talked one with another, and they said unto him: "Ho! Bata, bull of the Nine Gods, art thou remaining alone? Thou hast left thy village for the wife of Anpu, thy elder brother. Behold his wife is slain. Thou hast given him an answer to all that was transgressed against thee." And their hearts were vexed for him exceedingly. And Ra Harakhti said to Khnumu, "Behold, frame thou a woman for Bata, that he may not remain alive alone." And Khnumu made for him a mate to dwell with him. She was more beautiful in her limbs than any woman who is in the whole land. The essence of every god was in her. The seven Hathors came to see her: they said with one mouth, "She will die a sharp death."

And Bata loved her very exceedingly, and she dwelt in his house; he passed his time in hunting the beasts of the desert, and brought and laid them before her. He said: "Go not outside, lest the sea seize thee; for I cannot rescue thee from it, for I am a woman like thee; my soul is placed on the head of the flower of the acacia; and if another find it, I must fight with him." And he opened unto her his heart in all its nature.

Now after these things Bata went to hunt in his daily manner. And the young girl went to walk under the acacia which was by the side of her house. Then the sea saw her, and cast its waves up after her. She betook herself to flee from before it. She entered her house. And the sea called unto the acacia, saying, "Oh, would that I could seize her!" And the acacia brought a lock from her hair, and the sea carried it to Egypt, and dropped it in the place of the fullers of Pharaoh's linen. The smell of the lock of hair entered into the clothes of Pharaoh; and they were wroth with the fullers of Pharaoh, saying, "The smell of ointment is in the clothes of Pharaoh." And the people were rebuked every day, they knew not what they should do. And the chief fuller of Pharaoh walked by the bank, and his heart was very evil within him after the daily quarrel with him. He stood still, he stood upon the sand opposite to the lock of hair, which was in the water, and he made one enter into the water and bring it to him; and there was found in it a smell, exceeding sweet. He took it to Pharaoh; and they brought the scribes and the wise men, and they said unto Pharaoh: "This lock of hair belongs to a daughter of Ra Harakhti: the essence of every god is in her, and it is a tribute to thee from another land. Let messengers go to every strange land to seek her: and as for the messenger who shall go to the valley of the acacia, let many men go with him to bring her." Then said his Majesty, "Excellent exceedingly is what has been said to us"; and they sent them. And many days after these things the people who were sent to strange lands came to give report unto the King: but there came not those who went to the valley of the acacia, for Bata had slain them, but let one of them return to give a report to the King. His Majesty sent many men and soldiers, as well as horsemen, to bring her back. And there was a woman among them, and to her had been given in her hand beautiful ornaments of a woman. And the girl came back with her, and they rejoiced over her in the whole land.

And his Majesty loved her exceedingly, and raised her to high estate; and he spake unto her that she should tell him concerning her husband. And she said, "Let the acacia be cut down, and let one chop it up." And they sent men and soldiers with their weapons to cut down the acacia; and they came to the acacia, and they cut the flower upon which was the soul of Bata, and he fell dead suddenly.

And when the next day came, and the earth was lightened, the acacia was cut down. And Anpu, the elder brother of Bata, entered his house, and washed his hands; and one gave him a cup of beer, and it became troubled; and one gave him another of wine, and the smell of it was evil. Then he took his staff, and his sandals, and likewise his clothes, with his weapons of war; and he betook himself forth to the valley of the acacia. He entered the tower of his younger brother, and he found him lying upon his mat; he was dead. And he wept when he saw his younger brother verily lying dead. And he went out to seek the soul of his younger brother under the acacia tree, under

which his younger brother lay in the evening. He spent three years in seeking for it, but found it not. And when he began the fourth year, he desired in his heart to return into Egypt; he said, "I will go tomorrow morn." Thus spake he in his heart.

Now when the land lightened, and the next day appeared, he was walking under the acacia; he was spending his time in seeking it. And he returned in the evening, and labored at seeking it again. He found a seed. He returned with it. Behold this was the soul of his younger brother. He brought a cup of cold water, and he cast the seed into it: and he sat down, as he was wont. Now when the night came his soul sucked up the water; Bata shuddered in all his limbs, and he looked on his elder brother; his soul was in the cup. Then Anpu took the cup of cold water, in which the soul of his younger brother was; Bata drank it, his soul stood again in its place, and he became as he had been. They embraced each other, and they conversed together.

And Bata said to his elder brother: "Behold I am to become as a great bull, which bears every good mark; no one knoweth its history, and thou must sit upon my back. When the sun arises I shall be in the place where my wife is, that I may return answer to her; and thou must take me to the place where the King is. For all good things shall be done for thee; for one shall lade thee with silver and gold, because thou bringest me to Pharaoh, for I become a great marvel, and they shall rejoice for me in all the land. And thou shalt go to thy village."

And when the land was lightened, and the next day appeared, Bata became in the form which he had told to his elder brother. And Anpu sat upon his back until the dawn. He came to the place where the King was, and they made his Majesty to know of him; he saw him, and he was exceeding joyful with him. He made for him great offerings, saying, "This is a great wonder which has come to pass." There were rejoicings over him in the whole land. They presented unto him silver and gold for his elder brother, who went and stayed in his village. They gave to the bull many men and many things, and Pharaoh loved him exceedingly above all that is in this land.

And after many days after these things, the bull entered the purified place; he stood in the place where the princess was; he began to speak with her, saying, "Behold, I am alive indeed." And she said to him, "And, pray, who art thou?" He said to her, "I am Bata. I perceived when thou causedst that they should destroy the acacia of Pharaoh, which was my abode, that I might not be suffered to live. Behold, I am alive indeed, I am as an ox." Then the princess feared exceedingly for the words that her husband had spoken to her. And he went out from the purified place.

And his Majesty was sitting, making a good day with her: she was at the table of his Majesty, and the King was exceeding pleased with her. And she said to his Majesty, "Swear to me by God, saying, 'What thou shalt say, I will obey it for thy sake.'" He hearkened unto all that she said, even this. "Let me eat of the liver of the ox, because he is fit for naught." Thus spake she to him. And the King was exceeding sad at her words, the heart of Pharaoh grieved him greatly. And after the land was lightened, and the next day appeared, they proclaimed a great feast with offerings to the ox. And the King sent one of the chief butchers of his Majesty, to cause the ox to be sacrificed. And when he was sacrificed, as he was upon the shoulders of the people, he shook his neck, and he threw two drops of blood over against the two doors of his Majesty. The one fell upon the one side, on the great door of Pharaoh, and the other upon the other door. They grew as two great Persea trees, and each of them was excellent.

And one went to tell unto his Majesty, "Two great Persea trees have grown, as a great marvel of his Majesty, in the night by the side of the great gate of his Majesty." And there was rejoicing for them in all the land, and there were offerings made to them.

And when the days were multiplied after these things, his Majesty was adorned with the blue crown, with garlands of flowers on his neck, and he was upon the chariot of pale gold, and he went out from the palace to behold the Persea trees: the princess also was going out with horses behind his Majesty. And his Majesty sat beneath one of the Persea trees, and it spake thus with his wife: "Oh thou deceitful one, I am Bata, I am alive, though I have been evilly entreated. I knew who caused the acacia to be cut down by Pharaoh at my dwelling. I then became an ox, and thou causedst that I should be killed."

And many days after these things the princess stood at the table of Pharaoh, and the King was pleased with her. And she said to his Majesty, "Swear to me by God, saying, 'That which the princess shall say to me I will obey it for her.'" And he hearkened unto all she said. And he commanded, "Let these two Persea trees be cut down, and let them be made into goodly planks." And he hearkened unto all she said. And after this his Majesty sent skilful craftsmen, and they cut down the Persea trees of Pharaoh; and the princess, the royal wife, was standing looking on, and they did all that was in her heart unto the trees. But a chip flew up, and it entered into the mouth of the princess; she swallowed it, and after many days she bore a son. And one went to tell his Majesty, "There is born to thee a son." And they brought him, and gave to him a nurse and servants; and there were rejoicings in the whole land. And the King sat making a merry day, as they were about the naming of him, and his Majesty loved him exceedingly

at that moment, and the King raised him to be the royal son of Kush.

Now after the days had multiplied after these things, his Majesty made him heir of all the land. And many days after that, when he had fulfilled many years as heir, his Majesty flew up to heaven. And the heir said, "Let my great nobles of his Majesty be brought before me, that I may make them to know all that has happened to me." And they brought also before him his wife, and he judged with her before him, and they agreed with him. They brought to him his elder brother; he made him hereditary prince in all his land. He was thirty years King of Egypt, and he died, and his elder brother stood in his place on the day of burial.

Excellently finished in peace, for the Ka of the scribe of the treasury Kagabu, of the treasury of Pharaoh, and for the scribe Hora, and the scribe Meremapt. Written by the scribe Anena, the owner of this roll. He who speaks against this roll, may Tahuti smite him.

TYPHON Greek monster giant identified by the Greeks with the evil Egyptian god Set. In *Isis and Osiris* Plutarch calls the god Typhon rather than Set.

U

UAB see Priests.

UADJ Amulet in the form of a budding papyrus shoot. The Uadj was placed on the neck of the mummy to confer renewed youth and virility—qualities the papyrus plant was thought to possess—on the deceased. The papyrus was the symbol of Lower Egypt. A variant spelling is Wadjet.

UATCHET see Buto.

UATCH-URA see Buto.

UDJAT see Utchat.

UEB see Priests.

UENNOFRE see Unnefer.

UFA A serpent demon mentioned in a magical formula of Unas, a king of the Fifth Dynasty.

UKHUKH God worshipped near the site of the modern Meir. His symbol was a staff decorated with two feathers and two serpents.

UNAS Deified Egyptian king of the Fifth Dynasty said to be the son of the god Tem. Unas became great by eating the flesh of both his enemies and the gods. He ate the largest and finest of the gods at daybreak, the smaller-sized gods at sunset, and the smallest at night. Those gods who were old and worn out (Egyptian gods aged and died) were used as fuel for Unas's furnace. After eating the gods, and absorbing their power and spirits, he journeyed through the day and night sky and became the star Sahu, or Orion. Variant spellings are Unus, Unis, and Onnos.

UNDERWORLD, THE see Tuat.

UNG A god who appears in some texts as a "son of the solar deity," or as a messenger of the gods. He is also identified with Shu, or with Osiris.

UNIS see Unas.

UNNEFER A title applied to Osiris, meaning "he who is continually happy," in his role as god of resurrection. Other spellings are Wenenefer, Wenen-nefer, Unnofre, and Onnophris.

Ur-Uatchti

UNNET   see Wenut.

UNUS   see Unas.

UPPER EGYPT   Term used for the southern part of Egypt, once a separate state. It was often called the White Land or the South. Its crown was a white conical shape, its flower the lotus, its protective god Set, and its protective goddess Nekhebet, the vulture goddess. The ancient capital was Nekheb.

UPSET   A goddess often identified with Isis and other goddesses worshipped at Philae.

UPUAUT   see Wepwawet.

UPWAUT   see Wepwawet.

URAEUS   The divine snake, a cobra, identified with the goddess Buto of Lower Egypt. It appears on the white crown of Lower Egypt. (The vulture appears on the red crown of Upper Egypt, which is dedicated to the goddess Nekhebet.) The Uraeus and the vulture were represented on the double crown of the United Egypt. The Uraeus appears with many sun gods since it spits fire to protect the wearer from his enemies. It is often repeated on the long friezes on tombs and tem-ples as a warning to anyone who would enter.

UR-HEKA   A god portrayed either as a man or a serpent, whose name means, "great in magic."

UR-MER   see Apis.

URS   see Weres.

URSHU   Egyptian word that means "the watchers," and may have been used for a group of well-known gods who "watched over" and protected cities. Some scholars believe Urshu refers to lesser beings, messengers of the gods, instead of the gods themselves.

URT   One of the four earthly forms of Osiris in the sixth section, or hour, of Tuat, the underworld.

UR-UATCHTI   A winged sun disk with two uraei—the goddess Nekhebet on the right, and Buto on the left. According to one myth the disk was made when the god Horus wished to protect himself from the evil god Set. Horus assumed the form of the winged sun disk and overcame Set. After the victory the god Thoth decreed that the Ur-uatchti should deck every temple as a protection against evil.

USEKH-T   Collar amulet tied to the neck of the mummy to give it freedom from all possible restraints about the neck. A variant spelling is Wesekh.

USERT   A name for the goddess Isis as the earth goddess.

USHABTI   Small statuettes used in burial rites by the ancient Egyptians. The name means "the answerer," and the figures often are inscribed with texts, such as instructions to move sand from East to West. They were not to serve at the beck and call of the owners. The Ushabti came into use from the Middle Kingdom and were often made of wood or faience.

UTCHAT   The eye of Ra. The concept of the Utchat, or the eye of Ra, varies from text to text. In the Pyramid Texts it is identified with the uraeus viper which spat venom and fire against the enemies of the sun god. In later mythology it is identified with Tefnut, the goddess of moisture and of the power of sunlight, who was sometimes said to be the daughter of Ra. The Utchat was also identified with

Maat, who was the personification of physical and moral law.

According to one myth, the eye of Ra (Tefnut in this version) was separated from her father Ra and went to live in the Nubian desert as a bloodthirsty lion. Ra wanted her back and sent the god Thoth to persuade her to return. On her death, she became the goddess Hathor, the great deity who represented the sky. (In Egyptian mythology the gods often change from one form to another.) In a variant of the myth, Tefnut was a cat, a form of the goddess Bast, who became a lion when she was angry. When the eye of Ra was removed from the god (the symbol was also given to other sun gods), it was said that a disturbance occurred in the natural order of the universe, and when it was returned, the natural order would be restored. A variant spelling is Udjat.

UTENNU BABOONS   The baboons who praised the evening sun.

UTET   A god, believed to have been worshipped in the form of a heron.

Utchat

Vulture

V

VALLEY OF THE KINGS Burial site of many pharaohs of the New Kingdom located near Thebes. This necropolis, called in Arabic *Biban el-Moluk* or The Gates of the Kings, is where the tomb of Tutankhamen was found.

VALLEY OF THE NOBLES A necropolis located near the Valley of the Kings on the west bank of the Nile. The nobility of the New Kingdom were buried here.

VALLEY OF THE QUEENS A necropolis situated on the west bank of the Nile, opposite modern Luxor, called in Arabic *Biban el-Harim,* or The Gates of the Women. The bodies of the queens, wives, and daughters of the Pharaoh lie here. The most famous tomb in the area is that of Rameses II's wife, Nefertari.

VASES Egyptian temples used various vessels for their rituals, such as ewers, censers, and small bowls for libations of wine or water. These vases were made of precious metals, though copies made of less costly material, such as the bronze *situla,* were placed in tombs, to be used for libations of life-giving water.

VENUS The planet Venus was under the protection of the god Osiris.

VIZIR Term used for the Egyptian word *tjaty,* the chief minister of Egypt, subordinate only to the Pharaoh.

VULCAN Roman smith or craft god, which the Romans equated with the Egyptian god, Ptah.

VULTURE The Egyptian cult of the vulture is believed by some scholars to date from pre-dynastic times since one of the early titles of the Pharaoh was, Nekhebet, or "Lord of the City of the Vulture." The vulture is associated with Nekhebet, Mut, Neith, and other deities identified with Nekhebet. Vultures were thought to follow men into battle, hover over warriors who were to be killed, and later to eat their flesh. All vultures were believed to be females who became impregnated by turning their back to the south, or southeast wind, while flying, and brought forth their young in three years. The vulture amulet was called Ner-t.

W

WAB   see Priests.

WADJET   see Buto.

WARBURTON, BISHOP WILLIAM
(1698-1779) Bishop of Gloucester
(1773) whose work, *The Divine
Legation of Moses,* was one of the
first to state that the Egyptian hieroglyphs were not mystical pictures,
but a form of writing. Warburton was
a friend of Alexander Pope and
defended the poet's *Essay on Man.*

WAR GOD   see Onuris.

WAR-MAU   Title of chief priest
which means "great of sight," but
some scholars suggest that it refers to
his privilege, translating as "the
greatest (priest) who is permitted to
see (the god)." Egyptian gods did not
reveal themselves to everybody, but
only to a select few.

WATER GODDESS   see Anqet.

WATERS, PRIMORDIAL   see Nun.

WEAVING, GODDESS OF   see
Tait.

WEIGHING OF THE HEART   In
one of the most important ceremonies
in the *Book of the Dead* the heart of the
deceased is weighed against Maat, the
goddess of justice and truth. The deceased is led by Anubis into the Judgment Hall in which Osiris, Isis,
Nephthys, and sometimes Ra, preside
along with forty-two judges. He then
recites the Negative Confession, in
which he says he has not committed
any faults, and in a second confession
to the forty-two judges again says he
has committed no crime. If the balance
is not in the deceased's favor, he is
immediately destroyed by a monster,
Amam, who waits at the foot of the
scale.

WENEN-NEFER   see Unnefer.

WENENUT   Hare- or rabbit-headed
goddess, who usually holds a knife in
each hand, though she is sometimes
shown with the ankh, symbol of life,
and a scepter. Her male counterpart
was the hare-headed god Wenenu.

WENENU   Hare- or rabbit-headed
god, identified in some texts as a form
of Osiris. His female counterpart is
Wenenut.

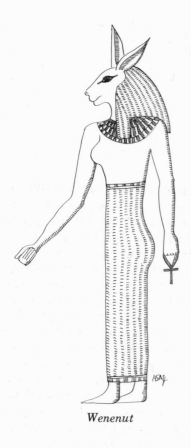

Wenenut

his warlike image appeared on one of the four sacred standards of Pharaoh, which preceded the king on his march to the palace chapel. In later times Wepwawet was often confused with Anubis and considered a god of the dead. According to one myth he shared the function of bringing the dead through the underworld to the kingdom of Osiris with the jackal-headed Anubis. Wepwawet was sometimes depicted piloting the sun's boat during its night voyage. Variant spellings of his name are Ap-uat, Upuaut, Upwaut, and Ophois Wepwawet.

WERET HEKAU The goddess of magic, whose name means "great of magic."

WERES Headrest or pillow amulet placed under the neck of the mummy to prevent its decapitation in Tuat, the underworld. The text on the amulet reads: "Their enemies shall have no power to cut off the heads of the deceased, but the deceased shall cut off the heads of their enemies." A variant spelling is Urs.

WENUT Goddess of the hours, depicted as a woman with a star upon her head. A variant spelling is Unnet.

WER-MER see Mnevis.

WEP-REHEWY A name for the god Thoth meaning "Judge of the two opponent gods." It refers to Thoth's role as judge in the strife between the gods Horus and Set for control of Egypt.

WESET Egyptian name for the city in Upper Egypt which the Greeks called Thebes, and which is called No in the Old Testament.

WEST, LAND OF see Amentet.

WEPWAWET A wolf god whose name means "the opener of the ways." He guided his followers into battle and

WEST WIND, GOD OF see Hutch-aiui.

212

WHITE see Colors.

WHITE CROWN see Crowns.

WIGS Ceremonial wigs, made of human hair and vegetable fiber, were often used by the ancient Egyptians. Their importance in daily Egyptian life is reflected by the fact that among the many artifacts placed in tombs, there are numerous boxes containing wigs.

WINDS, GODS OF The gods of the four winds were Qebui, the north wind, Shehbui, the south wind, Henkhisesui, the east wind, and Hutchaiui, the west wind.

WINE According to Egyptian mythology wine came from the divine eyes of the god Horus. Wine was used as part of the daily diet, and also in ritual, since men, as well as the gods and the departed, needed wine. Both Set and Hathor were worshipped in the areas of Egypt that produced the best wines and were thus regarded as its deities.

WINGED SUN DISK SYMBOL see Ur-uatchti.

WINGS Wings often appear in Egyptian art as a symbol of protection. Isis, in the shrine of Tutankhamen, is portrayed with massive wings, to indicate that she is the Great Enchantress. One myth claims that she gives breath to the dead with her wings. The goddess is frequently shown surrounding the Pharaoh with her wings, again a sign of protection. At times other goddesses are also depicted with wings.

WISDOM, GOD OF see Thoth.

WISDOM LITERATURE Name given to "wise sayings" and proverbs in Near Eastern literature, such as the Book of Proverbs in the Old Testament. They were valued by the Egyptians, like the Hebrews, and gathered into many collections. In I Kings (4:30) it is written: "And Solomon's wisdom excelled the wisdom of all the children of the east country, and all the wisdom of Egypt." This verse indicates that ancient Egyptian wisdom literature was highly regarded and respected in the ancient world.

It is not known for certain whether ancient Egypt had any direct effect on the Hebrew Bible, though there are striking similarities between the Hebrew Book of Proverbs and *The Teachings of Amen-em-ope*. Proverbs (22:17) says:

> Bow down thine ear, and hear the words of the wise,
> And apply thine heart unto my knowledge.

The Teachings of Amen-em-ope says:

> Give thine ear, and hear what I say,
> And apply thine heart to apprehend.

Proverbs (23:4-5) says:

> Labor not to be rich:
> Cease from thine own wisdom.
> Wilt thou set thine eyes upon that which is not?

213

For riches certainly make themselves
wings;
They fly away as an eagle toward
heaven.

The Teachings of Amen-em-ope says:

Toil not after riches;
If stolen goods are brought to thee,
For wealth maketh to itself wings,
Like an eagle that flieth heavenwards.

These are but two similar proverbs,
though both works show many examples of the same thoughts.

WOLF The wolf was often confused
with the jackal and the dog in ancient
Egypt. One city, Lycopolis, or Wolf
City, has a shrine to the gods Horus
and Set, who were believed to have
taken the form of wolves to fight one
another, as well as a shrine to the
god Wepwawet.

WTENNU Title meaning "The
Spirits of Heaven" and found in several Egyptian texts. In one, of Pepi II,
it says that Pepi gives "orders to the
Wtennu."

Y Z

YEAR, GODDESS OF THE see Renpet.

YOUNG, THOMAS (1773-1829) British doctor who discovered that the cartouches in hieroglyphic inscriptions contained the names of the Egyptian rulers. The results of his study were published in the article on Egypt which he wrote for the 1819 edition of the *Encylopaedia Britannica*. However, Young mistakenly believed that the names of rulers were the only hieroglyphs to possess phonetic values. His work set the stage for the discoveries of Jean François Champollion.

ZAUBERFLÖTE, DIE German opera by Wolfgang Amadeus Mozart, with a libretto by Johann Emanual Schikaneder, known in English as *The Magic Flute*. The work was first performed in 1791 and takes place in ancient Egypt. It uses both mythological and Masonic symbolism. Act II contains the great bass aria, "O Isis und Osiris" in honor of two of Egypt's most famous gods.

ZEHUTI see Thoth.

ZEUS Greek sky god, king of the gods, identified by the Greeks with the Egyptian god Amen-Ra.

ZHOUTI see Thoth.

ZOOLATRY The worship of animals as gods. Both the Greeks and the Romans believed that the Egyptian worship of animals was central to their religion. This concept is found in Juvenal's fifteenth satire, *On the Atrocities of Egypt,* in which he attacks the Egyptians for avoiding animal flesh because of sacred beliefs but not applying this principle to the eating of human flesh.

ZOSER A king of the Third Dynasty who had the Step Pyramid at Sakkara built by his minister, Imhotep. The oldest of the pyramids, it is surrounded by a complex of buildings, as well as a stone wall. This is believed to be the first complex in which dressed stone was used. Zoser is also spelled Djeser.

ANNOTATED
BIBLIOGRAPHY

ANNOTATED BIBLIOGRAPHY

Many books cited in the Annotated Bibliography are available in different editions, especially the earlier books on Egyptian mythology. When a reprint edition has been used it is so cited.

Those books marked with an * are recommended.

*Aldred, Cyril. *The Development of Ancient Egyptian Art.* London: Alec Tiranti, 1952. A study of Egyptian art from B.C. 3200–1315. Numerous illustrations with descriptive notes. No index.

*_____. *Akhenaten: Pharaoh of Egypt —A New Study.* New York: McGraw-Hill, 1968. An illustrated study of a complex figure which deromanticizes the general nineteenth-century opinion of Akhenaten as a religious revolutionary and places him as part of his times. Some of the results of the study are quite interesting and of great value to offset the standard approach. It is one of the few books to mention Akhenaten's homosexuality. Chronology. Notes. Select bibliography. List of illustrations. Index.

*_____. *Jewels of the Pharaohs.* New York: Praeger, 1971. A study of Egyptian jewelry of the Dynastic period. Illustrated. Bibliography. Index.

*Baker, Hollis S. *Furniture in the Ancient World.* New York: Macmillan, 1966. A fully illustrated book covering ancient furniture and Egyptian art works. Valuable for the background on Egyptian life. Scale drawings of some of the furniture are contained in the notes. Index.

Barocas, Claudio. *Monuments of Civilization: Egypt.* New York: Grosset & Dunlap (Madison Square Press), 1972. Colorful book covering various periods of Egyptian art. Index.

*Bell, H. Idris. *Cults and Creeds in Graeco-Roman Egypt.* Chicago: Argonaut, 1953. The relationship between Egyptian religion and early Christianity is explored in this work. Contains select bibliography. Index.

*Boylan, Patrick. *Thoth: The Hermes of Egypt*. London: Oxford University Press, 1922. A full study of the god Thoth and his various roles. No index.

Bradford, Ernle. *Cleopatra*. New York: Harcourt Brace Jovanovich, 1972. Beautifully written and illustrated life of Cleopatra. Select bibliography. Index.

Brandon, S. G. F. *Religion in Ancient History*. New York: Scribner's, 1969. A collection of essays, two of which, "Osiris, the Royal Mortuary God of Egypt," and "Akhenaten, the Heretic King of Egypt," deal with Egypt. Illustrated. Annotated bibliography. Index.

*Breasted, James Henry. *Ancient Records of Egypt: The Historical Documents*. Chicago: University of Chicago Press, 1905. A massive four-volume work covering the First through Sixteenth Dynasties.

_____. *Development of Religion and Thought in Ancient Egypt*. New York: Scribner's, 1912. Early study covering various aspects of Egyptian belief. Index.

_____. *A History of Egypt*. New York: Scribner's, 1905. Classic study of ancient Egypt with numerous illustrations. Dated, but still excellent reading in parts. Index.

Brodrick, M., and Morton, A. Anderson. *A Concise Dictionary of Egyptian Archaeology*. New York: Dutton, 1902. A handbook for students and travelers covering different aspects of ancient Egypt. Bibliography.

Bromage, Bernard. *The Occult Arts of Ancient Egypt*. London: Aquarian Press, 1960. A study of the magical side of Egyptian beliefs. No index.

Bryan, Cyril P. (trans.). *Ancient Egyptian Medicine: The Papyrus Ebers*. Chicago: Ares, 1930. An important work dealing with medicine and magic, translated from the German edition of the Egyptian text, with an introduction by G. Elliot Smith. Illustrated. No index.

Budge, E. A. Wallis. *Legends of the Gods*. London: Kegan Paul, Trench, Trubner, 1912. A translation, along with original Egyptian texts, of myths of ancient Egypt in translation. Illustrated. No index.

_____. *Amulets and Talismans*. New York: University Books, 1961. A retitled edition of Budge's work, *Amulets and Superstitions*. An extensive chapter is devoted to Egyptian amulets, but it must be read with caution, since it is inaccurate in many details. Index.

_____. *Egyptian Magic.* New York: University Books, (n.d.). Reprint of a work published in London in 1900 which deals with various aspects of Egyptian belief with emphasis on magic, amulets, and ceremonies. Illustrated. No index.

_____. *From Fetish to God in Ancient Egypt.* London: Oxford University Press, 1934. A full study with translations from various texts. Illustrated. Index.

_____. *Egyptian Religion.* New York: Bell, (n.d.). Reprint of a work published in London in 1900 that deals with various aspects of Egyptian belief with emphasis on life after death. The present volume contains more illustrations than the original edition as well as a new introduction. No index.

_____. *Book of the Dead: The Hieroglyphic Transcript of the Papyrus of Ani.* New York: University Books, 1960. A reissue of the Medici Society edition of 1913 which takes into account Budge's 1890, 1894, and 1913 editions of the work. The work is a major source book but difficult to read, since it is not a narrative, but a list of rubrics and formulas which allude to myths. Budge often contradicts his writing in *The Gods of the Egyptians* (1904). In addition transliteration of the Egyptian names varies in both books, making it difficult for the reader to sort out the various deities. Index.

_____. *The Gods of the Egyptians, or Studies in Egyptian Mythology.* New York: Dover, 1969. A two-volume (reprint of the original 1904 edition) study of Egypt's deities by the one-time Keeper of Egyptian and Assyrian Antiquities in the British Museum. The work contains many translations of texts, but is in many cases outdated. It is very poorly arranged and often contradicts itself from one section to another. Budge's transliteration of Egyptian names differs in many cases from the system used in his edition of the *Book of the Dead,* making any comparison difficult. Index.

_____. *Tutankhamen: Amenism, Atenism and Egyptian Monotheism.* New York: Bell, (n.d.). Reprint of a work originally published in London in 1923 just after the discovery of Tutankhamen's tomb. It deals with the king and the cults of Amen and Aten. It contains many translations of hymn texts as well as illustrations. Index.

Carter, Howard. *The Tomb of Tutankhamen.* New York: Dutton (Excalibur Books), 1972. The original edition of this book appeared in three volumes: Volume 1 was written by Carter and A. C. Mace, and published in 1923; Volume 2 came out in 1927 and Volume 3 in 1933. The present edition omits prefaces to each of the three volumes as well as the biographical sketch of Lord

Bibliography

Carnarvon by Lady Burghclere, his daughter. Illustrated. Short index.

*Cerny, Jaroslav. *Ancient Egyptian Religion*. London: Hutchinson, 1952. Short study covering many aspects of ancient Egyptian belief. Bibliography. Index.

Clark, R. T. Rundle. *Myth and Symbol in Ancient Egypt*. London: Thames and Hudson, 1959. Mythological symbols such as the eye, the lotus, and so forth are discussed. Illustrated. Notes. Index.

Cottrell, Leonard. *Egypt*. London: Nicholas Vane, 1966. A short study of Egypt with many full-color illustrations. Short index.

———. *The Mountains of Pharaoh*. New York: Holt, Rinehart and Winston, 1956. A study of the pyramids with a short chapter on Egyptian religion. Short bibliography. No index.

David, A. Rosalie. *The Egyptian Kingdoms*. New York: Dutton (Elsevier Phaidon), 1975. A fully illustrated study of various aspects of Egyptian civilization. Glossary. Index.

*De Cenival, Jean-Louis. *Living Architecture: Egyptian*. New York: Grosset & Dunlap, 1964. An excellent guide with brilliant illustrations of the architecture of ancient Egypt. Preface by Marcel Breuer. Bibliography. Index.

Elgood, P. G. *The Ptolemies of Egypt*. Bristol: Arrowsmith, 1938. A book for the general reader covering an important part of Egyptian history. Index.

*Erman, Adolf. *A Handbook of Egyptian Religion*. London: Constable, 1907. A cool, critical approach to the subject, which served as a guide to the Egyptian collection in the Berlin Museum. Contains many line drawings. The work was translated from the German by A. S. Griffith. Short index.

*———. *Life in Ancient Egypt*. New York: Dover, 1971. One of the classic studies done in 1894 of ancient Egyptian society by the great German scholar and translated by H. M. Tirard. The work covers every aspect of Egyptian life with numerous illustrations. It suffers, however, from Erman's extremely cool approach, and he often dismisses those concepts which go against his rationalistic thought. This is a reprint of the 1894 edition and contains a new introduction by Jon Manchip White. Index is quite useful.

*Fagan, Brian M. *The Rape of the Nile: Tomb Robbers, Tourists, and Archaeologists in Egypt*. New York; Scribner's, 1975. A fascinating book covering one of the most interesting facets of Egypt. The work is fully illustrated, well written, and enjoyable. Contains a chronology of ancient Egypt. Index.

Fairman, H. W. (trans.). *The Triumph of Horus*. London: Batsford, 1974. A play based on the texts found at the Temple of Horus at Edfu. It tells of the battle between Horus and Set. Notes. Bibliography. Glossary. No index.

Faulkner, R. O. (trans.). *The Ancient Egyptian Coffin Texts*. Warminster: Aris & Phillips, 1973. Important texts dating from the Middle Kingdom which were inscribed inside the large rectangular wooden coffins used for interring the wealthy. No index.

————. *The Ancient Egyptian Pyramid Texts*. Oxford: Clarendon Press, 1969. A translation with various indexes on divinities and localities.

*Frankfort, Henri. *Ancient Egyptian Religion*. New York: Harper Torchbooks, 1961. A short interesting work originally published in 1948 that attempts to see the unity between Egyptian mythology and religion. The author often has a good line of reasoning, but often stretches a point and ignores those facts that would weaken his arguments. The reproductions of art works in this edition are quite poor. Index.

Gardiner, Alan H. *Egypt of the Pharaohs: An Introduction*. Oxford: Clarendon Press, 1961. Although called an introduction the work is over 400 pages. It contains a chronology of Egyptian history. Illustrated. Index.

————and Sethe, Kurt. *Egyptian Letters to the Dead*. London: Egypt Exploration Society, 1928. The original text with translation into English and commentary.

———— (trans.). *The Admonitions of an Egyptian Sage*. Hildesheim: George Olms Verlag, 1969. Reprint of the 1909 edition of a translation of a Hieratic Papyrus in Leiden. Contains original text, translation, and commentary.

————. *Egyptian Grammar*. Oxford: Clarendon Press, 1927. An introduction to the study of hieroglyphs. Egyptian-English vocabulary. Index.

Garstang, John. *The Burial Customs of Ancient Egypt*. London: Constable, 1907. An illustrated study of tombs from the Middle Kingdom. Index.

*Ghalioungui, Paul. *Magic and Medical Science in Ancient Egypt*. London: Hodder and Stoughton, 1963. A study of magic and medicine as practiced in ancient Egypt. Index.

Glanville, S. R. K. (ed.). *The Legacy of Egypt*. Oxford: Clarendon Press, 1942. A collection of essays by various writers treating different aspects of Egyptian life such as art, science, and medicine. A chapter deals with Egypt and Israel but there is nothing on ancient Egyptian religion or mythology. Index.

Bibliography

*Godolphin, Francis R. B. (ed.). *The Greek Historians*. New York: Random House, 1942. A two-volume work that contains the complete text of Herodotus as translated by George Rawlinson. Notes. Index.

Grinsell, Leslie V. *Barrow, Pyramid and Tomb*. London: Thames and Hudson, 1975. A study of ancient burial customs in Egypt, the Mediterranean, and the British Isles with 150 illustrations. Index.

Guirand, Felix (ed.). *New Larousse Encyclopedia of Mythology*. London: Prometheus, 1968. Contains a fully illustrated section on ancient Egypt by J. Viaud. Index.

Hawkes, Jacquetta. *Pharaohs of Egypt*. New York: American Heritage and Harper & Row, 1965. A popular study, with numerous illustrations, some in color, of various aspects of Egyptian civilization. Short reading list. Index.

Herodotus. *The Famous History of Herodotus*. New York: Knopf, 1924. An edition of the translation by "B.R." originally published in 1584. It is part of the Tudor Translations series and has an introduction by Leonard Whibley. This edition contains only the first two books of the *History*, but the second covers Egypt. No index.

*———. *The History of Herodotus*. New York: Dutton (Everyman's Library),

1910. A two-volume edition of the classic translation by George Rawlinson done in the nineteenth century. Notes.

*Hogarth, James (trans.). *Nagel's Encylopedia-Guide: Egypt*. Geneva: Nagel, 1972. The most complete guide to present-day Egypt with coverage of all the ancient sites. Index.

Ions, Veronica. *Egyptian Mythology*. London: Hamlyn, 1965. A fully-illustrated study of the deities and beliefs of ancient Egypt. Index.

*James, T. G. H. *Myths and Legends of Ancient Egypt*. New York: Grosset & Dunlap, 1971. Popular retelling of various myths with contemporary illustrations in color. Index.

Juvenal and Persius. *Juvenal and Persius*. London: Loeb Classical Library, 1918. An edition of the satires of Juvenal and Persius in the original Latin with an English prose translation by G. G. Ramsay. The fifteenth satire, called in this translation "An Egyptian Atrocity," deals with Egyptian beliefs and religion. Introduction. Notes. Index.

Juvenal. *The Satires of Juvenal*. Bloomington: Indiana University Press, 1958. A very lively translation of all the satires by Rolfe Humphries. The fifteenth satire, entitled "On the Atrocities of

Egypt," presents the Roman view of Egyptian religion.

*Kaster, Joseph. *Wings of the Falcon: Life and Thought in Ancient Egypt.* New York: Holt, Rinehart and Winston, 1968. A lively introduction to Egypt with modern translations of various texts as well as commentaries. No index.

Knight, Alfred E. *Amentet.* London: Longmans, 1915. An alphabetized study covering gods, sacred animals, amulets, and scarabs. Index.

Kramer, Samuel Noah (ed.). *Mythologies of the Ancient World.* New York: Doubleday (Anchor Books), 1961. A study of many different mythologies with a chapter, "Mythology of Ancient Egypt," by Rudolf Anthes. Index.

Lane, E. W. *Manners and Customs of the Modern Egyptians.* London: Dent (Everyman's Library), 1908. An edition of the 1836 book which has become a classic study of Egyptian life. It covers nearly every aspect including chapters on superstitions and magic. Some of the beliefs and customs of nineteenth-century Egyptians can be traced back to ancient Egypt. Illustrated. Index.

*Lange, Kurt, and Hirmer, Max. *Egypt: Architecture. Sculpture. Painting in Three Thousand Years.* New York: Phaidon, 1956. A large and beautiful volume covering the art of Egypt with over 300 illustrations, some in color, as well as a long essay, "Gods and Temples," by Eberhard Otto. Extensive notes on the plates. Short bibliography. Index.

*Lichtheim, Miriam (ed.). *Ancient Egyptian Literature: A Book of Readings.* Berkeley: University of California Press, 1972. A two-volume work covering the Old, Middle, and New Kingdoms. Indexes.

Lindsay, Jack. *Men and Gods on the Roman Nile.* New York: Barnes & Noble, 1968. A study of the religious beliefs of the late period in Egyptian history. Illustrated. Notes. Index.

_____. *Daily Life in Roman Egypt.* London: Muller, 1963. All aspects of life are covered in this important part of Egyptian history. Illustrated. Notes. Index.

Mackenzie, Donald A. *Egyptian Myth and Legend.* London: Gresham, (n.d.). Popular retellings of the myths, legends, and history of ancient Egypt. Index.

*MacQuitty, William. *Island of Isis: Philae, Temple of the Nile.* New York: Scribner's, 1976. A beautifully illustrated book describing one of the important places of Egyptian worship in the ancient world. Philae, which was to be flooded when the Aswan dam was completed, contained one of the main centers of the worship of Isis. The Egyptian government with the aid of UNESCO sponsored the rescue of the temples, moving them to the neighboring island of Agilkia. The work has a foreword by T. G. H. James, Keeper of Egyptian Antiquities at the British Museum. Chronological table. List of principal gods and goddesses. Further reading. Index.

Manetho. *Manetho with an English Translation*. London: Loeb Classical Library, 1940. A translation of the remaining fragments of Manetho's *History of Egypt* as preserved in the works of such writers as Josephus. Contains original texts, translations, and an introduction. Index.

Maspero, Gaston. *Popular Stories of Ancient Egypt*. New York: University Books, 1967. A translation from the French 1882 edition by A. S. Johns. The present edition was originally published in English in 1915. The volume contains seventeen complete stories and six fragments.

_____.*Life in Ancient Egypt and Assyria*. New York: Ungar, 1971. A short overview of life in ancient Egypt that is a republication of the 1892 English edition of *Lectures historiques: Egypte, Assyrie*. Many parts of this work are dated. No index.

May, Herbert G., and Metzger, Bruce M. (eds.). *The Oxford Annotated*

Bible with the Apocrypha. New York: Oxford University Press, 1965. An excellent edition of the Revised Standard Version with notes, charts, and tables. The various references to Egypt can be explored in the text and notes.

Mendelssohn, Kurt. *The Riddle of the Pyramids*. New York: Praeger, 1974. A discussion of the pyramids of Egypt as well as those of Mexico. Bibliography. Index.

Mercatante, Anthony S. *Good and Evil: Mythology and Folklore*. New York: Harper & Row, 1978. A study of good and evil in various mythologies with the first chapter devoted to ancient Egypt. Illustrated. Annotated bibliography. Index.

_____. *The Magic Garden*. New York: Harper & Row, 1976. Covers the myths and folklore of flowers, plants, trees, and herbs, with various entries on Egyptian plant life. Illustrated. Annotated bibliography. Index.

_____. *Zoo of the Gods: Animals in Myth, Legend and Fable*. New York: Harper & Row, 1974. A study of real and imaginary animals in world mythology and folklore with a fair amount devoted to ancient Egypt. Illustrated. Annotated bibliography. Index.

Mercer, Samuel A. B. *Horus: Royal God of Egypt*. Society of Oriental

Research, Mass. (n.d.). A full study of the god Horus and the various roles he plays in Egyptian belief. Index.

———(trans.). *The Pyramid Texts.* New York: Longmans, 1952. A four-volume work of a basic ancient Egyptian text. Glossary. Indexes in the last volume.

———. *The Religion of Ancient Egypt.* London: Luzac, 1949. A full study covering varying aspects of Egyptian belief. Index.

Meyerowitz, Eva L. R. *The Divine Kingship in Ghana and Ancient Egypt.* London: Faber & Faber, 1960. Complex study of the subject and its relation to ancient Egypt. Illustrated. Index.

Montet, Pierre. *Eternal Egypt.* New York: New American Library, 1964. A translation from the French by Doreen Weightman of a book that deals with the history and art of ancient Egypt. Maps. Bibliography. Index.

Müller, W. Max. *Egyptian Mythology.* New York: Cooper Square, 1964. Reprint of part of the thirteen-volume *The Mythology of All Races,* originally published in 1918. There are many line drawings. This edition has extensive notes, but lacks an index. Bibliography.

Murray, Margaret A. (ed.). *Egyptian Religious Poetry.* London: John Murray, 1949. Collection of texts with a long introduction. Index of first lines.

Patrick, Richard. *All Color Book of Egyptian Mythology.* London: Octopus, 1972. A very short, full-color book of Egyptian mythology covering creator gods, centers of religious thought, principal gods, the Lord of the Two Lands, the afterlife, and sacred animals. The text is mostly a series of long captions to the illustrations. There is an introduction by Margaret Drower which is quite readable. No index.

Peet, T. Eric. *Egypt and the Old Testament.* Liverpool: University Press, 1972. A study of Egypt and its relationship to the Old Testament. Bibliography. Index.

Petrie, W. M. Flinders. *Religion and Conscience in Ancient Egypt.* London: Methuen, 1898. A collection of lectures delivered at University College, London. No index.

———. *Religious Life in Ancient Egypt.* London: Constable, 1924. Short study with a chapter on folk beliefs. Index.

———. *Amulets.* Warminster: Aris & Phillips, 1972. Reprint of a work first published in 1914 with a new introduction by G. T. Martin. It contains hundreds of illustrations of various amulets, which are described and catalogued in the text. Index.

227

———. *Egyptian Tales.* New York: Benjamin Blom, 1971. A two-volume collection of the translation of original Egyptian texts published in 1899. It contains the well-known tales as well as extensive notes on the tales. Illustrated by Tristram Ellis. Index in each volume.

———. *The Religion of Ancient Egypt.* Chicago: Open Court, (n.d.). A very short study of various aspects of belief. Index.

Piankoff, Alexandre (trans.). *The Litany of Re.* Bollingen Series XL.4 New York: Pantheon Books, 1964. A translation of original texts and complete photographic copy of the reconstructed text of the Litany. Indexes.

———(trans.). *Mythological Papyri.* Bolingen Series XL.3 New York: Pantheon Books, 1957. A two-volume work with texts and illustrations. A chapter on the symbolism of the papyri by N. Rambova is included.

———(trans.). *The Shrines of Tut-Ankh-Amon.* Bollingen Series XL.2 New York: Pantheon Books, 1955. Includes translation and reconstructed texts inscribed on the interior and exterior panels of the shrines, together with the diagrams of important representations. The work was edited by N. Rambova. Illustrated. No index.

*Plutarch. *Plutarchs De Iside Et Osiride.* University of Wales Press, 1970. Greek text of Plutarch's classic Greek study of Egyptian beliefs with English translation, notes, and commentary by J. Gwyn Griffiths. General index.

———. *Plutarch's Morals.* London: Loeb Classical Library, 1935. Volume five of the sixteen-volume set contains the Greek text and English translation by F. C. Babbitt of *Isis and Osiris, The E at Delphi, The Oracles at Delphi No Longer Given in Verse,* and *The Obsolescence of Oracles.* Index.

———. *Plutarch's Moralia.* London: Bell, 1882. Translation by C. W. King of Plutarch's essay *On Isis and Osiris* and other essays related to religion and mythology. Index.

*Pritchard, James B. (ed.). *Ancient Near Eastern Texts Relating to the Old Testament.* Princeton: Princeton University Press, 1955. Standard work dealing with mythological texts of the Near East and containing many Egyptian works. Translations are very stiff and designed for scholars. Numerous notes. Index of biblical references. Index of names.

De Rachewiltz, Boris. *An Introduction to Egyptian Art.* London: Spring Books, 1960. General study with black-and-white illustrations, translated from the French by R. H. Boothroyd. Bibliography. Index.

Rawlinson, George. *Ancient Egypt.* New York: Putnam, 1887. Study of Egyptian history and life, including mythology and religion. Illustrated with line drawings. Maps. Index.

Read, F. W. *Egyptian Religion and Ethics.* London: Watts, 1925. A study basically covering religion and some mythology. No index.

Reisner, George Andrew. *The Egyptian Conception of Immortality.* London: Constable, 1912. A very short study once given as an Ingersoll Lecture in 1911. No index.

Reymond, E. A. E. *The Mythical Origin of the Egyptian Temple.* New York: Barnes & Noble, 1969. A full study of the subject with illustrations. Contains indexes of gods, sacred places, Edfu sacred books, and texts. Index.

Rugoff, Milton (ed.). *A Harvest of World Folk Tales.* New York: Viking, 1949. A collection of folktales from around the world including a selection from ancient Egypt. Index of sources, editors, and translators.

*Saunerson, Serge. *The Priests of Ancient Egypt.* New York: Grove Press, 1960. Short illustrated study, translated by Ann Morrissett from the French. Chronological table. No index.

Sayce, A. H. *The Religion of Ancient Egypt.* Edinburgh: Clark, 1913. Covers major aspects of Egyptian belief with chapters on animal worship and the gods. Index.

Schäfer, Heinrich. *Principles of Egyptian Art.* Oxford: Clarendon, 1974. A translation from the German, edited by John Baines, of a study of the principles of Egyptian art. Bibliography. Indexes.

Shorter, Alan W. *Everyday Life in Ancient Egypt.* London: Sampson, Low, Marston, (n.d.). A study in which the various aspects of daily life are dealt with from Pharaoh to commoner. Index.

———. *The Egyptian Gods: A Handbook.* London: Kegan Paul, Trench, Trubner, 1937. A short study including a list of the principal gods. No index.

———. *An Introduction to Egyptian Religion.* New York: Macmillan, 1932. Deals with religion in ancient Egypt during the Eighteenth Dynasty. Illustrations. Index.

Silverberg, Robert. *Akhnaten: The Rebel Pharaoh.* Philadelphia: Chilton, 1964. A popular study of the ruler. Illustrated. Index.

*Simpson, William Kelly. *The Literature of Ancient Egypt: An Anthology of Stories, Instructions and Poetry.*

New Haven: Yale University Press, 1972. An excellent anthology of various texts, many related to Egyptian mythology. The translations vary in merit. Notes. Selected bibliography. No index.

Smith, G. Elliot. *Tutankhamen and the Discovery of His Tomb by the Late Earl of Carnarvon and Mr. Howard Carter.* New York: Routledge, 1923. A study of the event with illustrations. No index.

*———and Warren R. Dawson. *Egyptian Mummies.* London: Allen & Unwin, 1924. An illustrated study with an appendix covering the tomb of Tutankhamen and the robberies at the royal tombs. Index.

Tompkins, Peter. *Secrets of the Great Pyramid.* New York: Harper & Row, 1971. An illustrated study of the Great Pyramid, with many of the theories of the past and the present. "Notes on the Relation of Ancient Measures to the Great Pyramid" by Livio Catullo Stecchini appears in the appendix. Glossary of names and terms. Bibliography. Index.

Vandenberg, Philipp. *The Curse of the Pharaohs.* Philadelphia: Lippincott, 1975. A popular recounting of the modern legend of the "Curse of the Pharaoh's tomb," translated from the German by Thomas Weyr. Illustrated, and with a bibliography made up almost entirely of German works. Index.

Waley-e-dine Sameh. *Daily Life in Ancient Egypt.* New York: McGraw-Hill, 1964. A short study with numerous illustrations, some in color, in translation from the German by Michael Bullock. Chronological table. Bibliography. No index.

Waltari, Mika. *The Egyptian.* New York: Putnam, 1949. A novel set in ancient Egypt, translated by Naomi Walford, which tells the life of Sinuhe. The work was inspired by the ancient Egyptian tale and was subsequently made into a motion picture.

White, Jon Manchip. *Everyday Life in Ancient Egypt.* New York: Putnam, 1963. A short study with drawings by Helen Nixon Fairfield of ancient Egyptian life covering the home, professions, and private life. Index.

*Wilkinson, J. Gardner. *The Manners and Customs of the Ancient Egyptians.* London: John Murray, 1878. A three-volume edition of the classic study published in 1837, with numerous illustrations, covering every aspect of life in ancient Egypt.

Wilson, Epiphanius (ed.). *Egyptian Literature.* London: Colonial Press, 1901. Egyptian tales, hymns, litanies, invocations, *The Book of the Dead,* and other works. The merits of the translations vary.

Wilson, John A. *The Burden of Egypt.* Chicago: University of Chicago Press, 1951. Called "an interpretion of Ancient Egyptian culture," the work discusses various aspects of ancient Egypt. Illustrated. Index.

Wiseman, D. J. (ed.). *Peoples of Old Testament Times.* Oxford: Clarendon Press, 1973. A collection of essays by various writers, one on the Hebrews by H. Cazelles and one on the Egyptians by R. J. Williams. Chronological chart. Index of biblical references. General index.

Woldering, Irmgard. *The Art of Egypt.* New York: Crown, 1963. A study of all periods of Egyptian art, translated from the German by Ann E. Keep. Glossary. Index.

Wortham, John David. *The Genesis of British Egyptology 1549–1906.* Oklahoma City: University of Oklahoma Press, 1971. A study from the sixteenth century to the end of the nineteenth century. Illustrated. Notes. Bibliography. Index.

*Yoyotte, Jean. *Treasures of the Pharaohs.* New York: Skira, World, 1968. A large, full-color study of art covering the Early Period, the New Kingdom, and the Late Period. No index.

Ziock, Hermann. *Guide to Egypt.* Cairo: Lehnert & Landrock, 1965. A guidebook for visitors to Egypt with a good deal of information on the ancient sites. In many places, however, the book is now somewhat outdated. Index.